March 1930

# HUMANISM
# AND
# AMERICA

# HUMANISM AND AMERICA

### ESSAYS
### ON THE OUTLOOK
### OF MODERN CIVILISATION

*Edited by*
NORMAN FOERSTER

FARRAR AND RINEHART
INCORPORATED
PUBLISHERS                    NEW YORK

# Preface

"Life's a long headache in a noisy street," sang the poet Masefield in *The Widow in the Bye Street* seventeen years ago. Since then, we have all come to live in Main rather than Bye Street, and our headache has grown apace despite the best efforts of the physicians of the age. The noise and whirl increase, the disillusion and depression deepen, the nightmare of Futility stalks before us in the inevitable intervals when activity flags. Heroically or mock-heroically we distrust or reject such stimulants and anodynes as religion, moral conventions, the dignity of manners, the passion for beauty, and even our recent faith in democracy, in liberalism, in progress, in science, in efficiency, in machinery. At length revolt and scepticism themselves have ceased to be interesting. The modern temper has produced a terrible headache.

In vain does our Chief Executive assure us that "we have reached a higher degree of comfort and security than ever existed before in the history of the world." Like Mr. Punch when it was announced that the government would soon be broadcasting intelligence by radio, we wonder "Where will the government get it?" All governments, all nations, are to-day in this predicament.

The alleged Americanisation of Europe appears to signify, at bottom, that tendencies native to Europe are being worked out most thoroughly in the United States and are therefore making the United States the model of twentieth-century Europe. At the same time Europe knows that the model is, to speak very gently, inadequate. For a good many years our own writers have deplored the condition of civilisation

v

in the United States, with exaggeration but essential truth. But they have generally made of revolt and scepticism ends rather than beginnings of wisdom. For materialistic complacency they have substituted a smart superiority resting on the most dubious foundations. Their feebleness in constructive power is very patent. They are part of the disease —symptoms not remedies.

Our "intellectual atmosphere," however, is now rapidly changing, is becoming charged with new interests. More and more persons, oppressed with the stale scepticism of the post-war period, are beginning to grow sceptical of that scepticism, and are looking for a new set of controlling ideas capable of restoring value to human existence. Certain forces are making for order and for new objectives. They are not strong forces, they can scarcely be called movements, but they are receiving a hearing and they contain the promise of growth.

One of these forces is known as "humanism," which is rapidly becoming a word to conjure with. In its broadest signification, it denotes a belief that the proper study of mankind is man, and that this study should enable mankind to perceive and realise its humanity. But the study of mankind is capable of yielding all manner of results, so that, for a long time to come, we may expect the word denoting this study to carry a large variety of meanings. Since man may be conceived as living on three planes, the natural, the human, and the religious, the content of the middle term will frequently tend to be invaded by that of the extremes. Thus, many persons who call themselves humanists, in this naturistic era from which we have not yet emerged, are unwittingly naturists yearning stoically for adaptation to the universe or mystically for a fusion of the human and the natural. Such persons might call themselves, paradoxically, humanistic naturists. In the interest of clearness, as it seems

vi

to me, the word humanism should be confined to a working philosophy seeking to make a resolute distinction between man and nature and between man and the divine.

The most fruitful approximation to such a distinction, in the twentieth century, has been the work of two American scholar-critics, Irving Babbitt and Paul Elmer More. The characteristic thought of Irving Babbitt was already adumbrated in 1895 in an address at the University of Wisconsin on "The Rational Study of the Classics," published two years later in the *Atlantic Monthly* and in 1908 included in his book on *Literature and the American College*. This book contains in essence, one may almost say, everything in the series of volumes in which he has since applied his humanistic standards to various aspects of modern life and thought. With a tenacity of purpose unexampled in an age shifting aimlessly from one enthusiasm and disillusionment to another, with an effect growing more massive as he has worked out his ideas in such fields as æsthetics, literary criticism, ethics, psychology, education, and politics, with a remarkable power of relating his sense of permanent values to an historical sense (so that his books are in one view works of history, and in another, doctrinal inductions from facts), with a vast accumulation of learning that has been thoroughly assimilated, and with a mode of expression notable for weighty vigour, earnestness, brilliant ridicule, and an instinct for ruinous quotation, Professor Babbitt has done more than any one else to formulate the concept of humanism and gain for it an ever-widening hearing. A great teacher as well as writer, lecturing to students at Harvard for some thirty-five years, he has done much to shape the minds and purposes of a whole generation of young men, and thus to render possible the continuance of his task in the future.

Paul Elmer More, after a brief experience as teacher of

Sanskrit and Classical literature, entered criticism through the avenue of journalism, becoming literary editor of the *Independent* and the New York *Evening Post* and editor of the *Nation*. Through his relation with contributors to the *Nation*, in particular, he exerted a powerful influence upon the higher critical activity of the country, an influence extended more widely through his long series of *Shelburne Essays*, beginning in 1904, in which he united in fine balance a profound and far-ranging scholarship, unusual psychological insight, an humanistic point of view, and a gift of firm, luminous, urbane but penetrating writing. Undervalued because of their hostility to the popular tendencies of the epoch, these essays will one day be generally recognised, I believe, as the highest accomplishment in literary criticism in the whole of American literature. The fundamental unity in the work of our two leading humanistic thinkers may be seen by comparing, say, the conclusion of Mr. Babbitt's *Masters of Modern French Criticism* and the "Definitions of Dualism" at the close of the eighth series of *Shelburne Essays*, or the introduction to *Democracy and Leadership* and the first essay in the *New Shelburne Essays*, Volume I. The main difference, perhaps, lies in emphasis; while Mr. Babbitt has been first and last concerned with building up a sound conception of individualism, Mr. More has been progressively absorbed in the study of the duality of human nature. His strong religious bent in this study led, in the years following his retirement from journalism, to the writing of *The Greek Tradition*, in five volumes, on the relation of Platonic and Hellenistic to Christian thought—a monumental work, the full significance of which can scarcely be estimated in its own time.

In a book recently crowned by the French Academy, *Le Mouvement humaniste aux Etats-Unis*, Louis J. A. Mercier, professor of French at Harvard, restricts his account to Irving Babbitt, Paul Elmer More, and W. C. Brownell. In a broad view of the "movement" the late Mr. Brownell doubtless merits a conspicuous place. Entering criticism, like Mr. More, by way of journalism, Brownell performed valuable service through his acute non-provincial book on *French Traits* as far back as 1888, and through his perennial insistence on high standards in literature and the fine arts. Never a humanist in the strict doctrinal sense, before his death he inclined to respond to the humanitarian optimism of America. The tendency toward humanitarianism, emotional sympathy with divine or undivine average humanity, appeared more strikingly in the post-war writings of Stuart P. Sherman. A student under Professor Babbitt, a contributor to the *Nation* under Mr. More, Sherman became the author of two books written in a vigorous and accomplished style and permeated with humanistic principles, one on Matthew Arnold conceived as a Victorian humanist, and one *On Contemporary Literature* conceived as a chaos of naturalism. Then, carried away by admiration of Wilsonian idealism and hatred of "Prussian autocracy," and by an uncritical devotion to Emerson, he drifted from his humanistic position into an ever vaguer faith in the common man, and at length, as a literary journalist in New York, into a rather indulgent impressionism. In the field of the fine arts, the most humanistic writer has been Frank Jewett Mather, Jr., of Princeton. Among others who published significant books in various fields, prior to 1928, are P. H. Frye, Sherlock Bronson Gass, Robert Shafer, Percy H. Houston, and W. F. Giese. By 1928 something like a movement could indeed be discerned: books began to multiply, and periodicals were printing series of articles—the *Forum* and the *Bookman* in America, the *Criterion* (edited by T. S. Eliot) and the *Nineteenth Century and After* in England. Whether the movement will continue to develop, whether it will succumb to disunion and vagueness, or be submerged by a narrow conventionalism of one sort or other, it would be idle to predict.

Though we have in America the semblance of a new movement, humanism itself is not new. It was new, I conceive, when human wisdom was new. It was comparatively new in ancient Greece, Judea, India, and China. It was rather old by the time of the Renaissance, when the word humanist came into currency. In one way or another, its doctrine and discipline have been clarified by persons as various as Homer, Phideas, Plato, Aristotle, Confucius, Buddha, Jesus, Paul, Virgil, Horace, Dante, Shakspere, Milton, Goethe; more recently, by Matthew Arnold in England and Emerson and Lowell in America: a strange assortment of names, no doubt, but also an indication of the inner diversity as well as the central unity of the humanist ideal. For into the aim of human perfection enter many elements, no less than that central order which is the fruit of discipline.

Yet, if humanism is never new, it must constantly confront new problems in time and place. In the Renaissance, its great foe was mediæval otherworldliness; to-day its great foe is thisworldliness, obsession with physical things and the instincts that bind us to the animal order—in a word, the many forms of naturism that have all but destroyed humane insight, discipline, and elevation. In a given age, humanism may have the task of urging the claims of beauty; in another age the claims of science, or of conduct. It may have one problem in France, and another across the Channel. So long as America tends to set the pattern for the twentieth century, so long will the greatest problem of humanism lie here in the United States.

This relativity of humanistic needs will perhaps go far toward explaining the special traits of the movement in America and the corresponding special lines of attack by its

x

naturistic opponents. Romantics, realists, and sceptics are daily attacking on four fronts: humanists, it is held, are academic, un-American, reactionary, and Puritanic.

Humanists are said to be academic. If this means that they are all university teachers, it is obviously not true. If it means that they are not interested in the present, it is obviously not true. If it means that they are interested in theory and not in practical affairs, it is not true, for what specially concerns them is the relation of theory and practice. They can scarcely be convicted of displaying what Stuart P. Sherman, who knew American academic life from the inside, termed "the professorial vices of pedantry, indolence, timidity, and intellectual quietism, which is a euphemism for the sluggish tolerance of men without philosophic conviction or intellectual purpose." If it means that our humanists have been more interested than the workaday journalist critics in concrete knowledge and in general ideas, then indeed they may be termed academic. They perceive that when a new movement of thought and life is to be got under way, the first stage is naturally one of acquiring and organising knowledge—particularly neglected knowledge. This was clear to Emerson, Longfellow, and Lowell in our little New England renaissance; it was clear to Lessing, Herder, and the Schlegel brothers in Germany; it was clear to the humanists of the Renaissance throughout Europe. Let us remember that the first of all universities was Plato's "Academy," the object of which was to attain a wisdom deeper than that of the market-place. Let us remember that "mere" theories are often high explosives, destructive of the prevailing practical life of the market-place, as witness Locke and Rousseau and the German thinkers from Kant to Hegel and Nietzsche.

Humanists are said to be un-American. According to those who cultivate the nationalist conception, a valid new criticism, new literature, new culture must spring from our American experience, not from imported ideas. They forget the lesson of the past that cultural movements have two sexes, so to speak, one native and one foreign, and that the native expresses itself in the main unconsciously under the incitement of the foreign. The native for the most part takes care of itself, the foreign must be sedulously cultivated. In the Renaissance a humanism imported from Italy fructified the native genius of most of Europe. Later, England, for example, drew upon France and then Germany; Germany upon France and England; France upon Spain and England; the United States upon England and Germany. Unlike some of his followers our Walt Whitman himself finally perceived the need of America's assimilation of foreign culture—even from "all former lands" beginning with ancient India and Greece. It is doubtful whether a *real* American culture could ever spring from our own experience; it is certain that it could be *caused* to spring from our own experience by a happy use of foreign culture.

Humanists are supposed to be reactionary. According to those who pride themselves on living in the present if not in the future, humanists want "to return to Buddha and the Bho Tree, to Socrates and the ilex." Being, in the main, historically educated men, however, humanists are well aware that a return to the past is impossible. On the other hand, they are also aware that, as cultural movements must draw upon foreign supplies, so they must also draw upon past culture. If a present age appears to be bad, it can be changed only by the introduction of forces not vitally existing in that age, and since the future is always a blank, these forces can be found only through a reinterpretation of the past. Thus, to a large extent the Renaissance was rendered possible through the "revival of learning" by the humanists, and the romantic movement of the late eighteenth century

xii

was in part a "return" to the Middle Ages and the national
past. Even the typical modernist, in his efforts to escape
being a Victorian or a Puritan, is plainly bent on "returning"
to the primitive.

This brings us to the last and most frequent charge: that
humanists are Puritans in disguise. It is hard to answer.
Nobody knows what a Puritan is, and when he is disguised
such a person is not easy to deal with. Even Professor Percy
Gardner, a leading English authority on Greek art, ventures
to speak of the "puritanism" of the Dorians. While in
America humanists are attacked as Puritan, in France they
are attacked as Catholic, and Mr. T. S. Eliot has been attacked as both. Even though American historians do not
agree as to what the distinguishing virtues and vices of the
seventeenth-century Puritans were, it may be suggested that
one of their plainest virtues was the possession of a certain
faith, now extinct. Their successors, wanting this faith,
cannot well be said to have even the Puritan defects of that
virtue. Sometimes those dire opposites of the humanists,
the promoters of Uplift, are called Puritans. For my part,
I think of our Uplifters rather as misguided humanitarians,
followers not of Calvin but rather of that other Genevan,
Rousseau.

What the naturists are really driving at, when they fight
this phantom Puritan, this Feathertop, is regimentation or
discipline. Now, humanism does wish to emphasise discipline, whenever, as to-day, it needs to be emphasised. It
has no desire to measure conduct quantitatively, according to
the familiar formula, as three-fourths of life, but it does
desire to show that the quality of all life is higher or lower
according as our power of vital restraint is exercised. Humanism conceives that the power of restraint is peculiarly
human, and that those who throw down the reins are simply
abandoning their humanity to the course of animal life or

the complacency of vegetables. It conceives, further, that the attainment of the ideal of completeness of life, of a human nature rounded and perfect on all its sides, is fatally frustrated at the start unless the ideal of centrality or self-control is introduced as the regulating principle. The substitution of *intensity* as the regulating principle, which is proposed by many modernists such as Aldous Huxley, provides for quantity but not quality of life, and tends to defeat the ideal of completeness, because certain parts of human nature, if not disciplined, will always thrive at the expense of other parts. This fact was glimpsed even by Walter Pater, notwithstanding his doctrine of the intense moment, when he wrote: "For us of the modern world, with its conflicting claims, its entangled interests, distracted by so many sorrows, with many preoccupations, so bewildering an experience, the problem of unity with ourselves, in blitheness and repose, is far harder than it was for the Greek within the simple terms of antique life. Yet, no less than ever, the intellect demands completeness, centrality."

Many other modernists reject the ideal of completeness itself as making for a dull uniformity, and propose instead the ideal of diversity. Life is "full of a number of things," one of them prattles, remembering his *Child's Garden*, but forgetting that humanism itself aims at diversity—not by urging men to be queerly "different," each in his own infantile way, but by urging them to develop with mature reasonableness the diversities latent within themselves and thus to work toward a many-sided human type. Humanism believes, with Goethe, that "every one must form himself as a particular being, seeking, however, to attain that general idea of which all mankind are constituents." There have been enough humanists in the world to prove that in fact (and not only in theory) this image of a dull humanistic uniformity is merely another scarecrow. It is not the hu-

xiv

manists, certainly, who look forward to a millennium in which all men and women will be superbly alike! If they speak more of the past than of the future, it is because the wisdom of the ages is on record and the wisdom of the future a hope devoid of useful content. But they unreservedly agree with critics who protest that "beyond anything that has yet been said by the academic humanists, there is work for the humane imagination to do."

This does not exhaust the attacks on the humanists. They are reproached by romanticists for being romantic, but I let that pass. More sensibly, they are ridiculed by irreligionists for being religious, but I let that pass also. Something should be said, however, of still another attack—the objection, by impressionists, that they employ words and phrases as catchwords and labels in disregard of the elusiveness of truth. To offer this objection, surely, is to object to the use of language itself. If words are not more or less arbitrary labels for things and ideas and the relationship of things and ideas, all language is pure nonsense. When Mr. Van Wyck Brooks fifteen years ago, in *America's Coming-of-Age*, called for "catchwords" as well as a "programme," he showed a sounder instinct than he and his followers have displayed since: they have found no programme, and are increasingly averse to catchwords. No doubt the truth *an sich* is hopelessly elusive, but the attainment of provisional or human truth is the reward of courage and labour. We cannot afford to shirk the task of achieving a reasonably clear and consistent terminology, even though every definition is by nature an affirmation that tends to shut out some portion of absolute truth. Whenever words become too hard and exclusive, humanism is concerned with reconsidering their frontiers; but whenever, as to-day, they become so vague and fluid as to imperil human communication, humanism aims to achieve a clear relation of labels to thought.

# PREFACE

If the object of this book, on the one hand, is to indicate the fundamental needs of America as the dominant world power and inadequate model of civilisation in the twentieth century, on the other hand its object is to inquire into the fundamental needs of humanism—to work toward a set of definitions and a terminology neither too rigid nor too loose, to consider the requirements of humanism in the various activities of modern thought and life, to determine the special tasks that confront humanism in this latest moment of time, and to enlist the interest and efforts of that "rather considerable leaven of intelligent people" who, as the *Forum* has said editorially, "cannot view with indifference the general decay of standards and the resultant chaos into which our intellectual and moral life has been plunged." The publication of a symposium addressed to this public was first proposed, years ago, by Percy H. Houston, and to him as well as to G. R. Elliott and Robert Shafer, advisory editors in this undertaking, cordial thanks are due for many valuable suggestions, although I am alone responsible for the form which the book has finally assumed. The contributors are for the most part between thirty and forty-five years of age (perhaps three or four are over, and three or four under these limits). One-third of them, as it happens, hold or have held important editorial positions. The academic group comprises several professors of English literature, one of French and comparative literature, one of the fine arts (also director of an art museum), and one of physics (also dean of a graduate school). The youngest contributor, a student and athlete, represents that rapidly growing part of the rising generation which is turning from aimless revolt to the quest of standards. In consequence of a diversity in occupations, as well as in temperament and personality, the authors of the book display numerous divergencies in outlook, in emphasis, and especially in tone. While all of them,

xvi

for example, are lovers of the law of measure or "Golden Mean," some of them seek the way of quiet firmness or "sweet reasonableness," even in this blatant age, while others conceive that modern excesses must be

"Scorch'd by a flaming speech on moderation."

As the reader will soon perceive, the contributors agree in certain broad, fundamental opinions. Without exception they have sought to work their way free of the dogmatic incrustations that threaten to corrode even what is sound in characteristically modern thought. None of them, I think, can be suspect of a secret attraction to those pseudo-scientific and humanitarian short-cuts to truth and morality that lead in fact to pure scepticism and anarchy. All of them perceive that a naturistic humanism is finally a paradox. Some of them might be termed "pure" or "mere" humanists, others are religious humanists. Each has been free to speak his own mind, and is responsible only for what he has himself said. If the reader chances to conceive, as I personally do, that Irving Babbitt is at the centre of the humanistic movement, some of the other authors will appear to be near the periphery, although they too may seem near the centre from some other point of view. The authors of this symposium, in a word, have no desire to form a closed school, or party, or cult, or religion. They would agree that the *ism* in humanism is at present a necessary evil. They are here temporarily assembled for the sole end of offering suggestions toward that new integration of values which may yet justify modernity.

NORMAN FOERSTER.

*January,* 1930.

# Contents

*The essence of Elizabethan as of other humanisms is the understanding of man and the definition of the sphere of properly human activity. The philosophical mind of Shakespeare's age began the work of reflection by cleaving the universe along three levels. On the lowest level is the natural world, which is the plane of instinct, appetite, animality, lust, the animal passions or affections; on this level the regulation is by necessary or natural law. On the middle level is the human world, which is regulated and, in a sense, created by the will and knowledge of man; working upon the natural world; but governed by reason, the special human faculty; and illuminated more or less from the level above. On the third level is the supernatural world, which is the plane of spiritual beings, and the home of eternal ideas.*

—STUART P. SHERMAN: "ON CONTEMPORARY LITERATURE."

# HUMANISM
# AND
# AMERICA

# The Pretensions of Science

## LOUIS TRENCHARD MORE

### I

Since the time when the Whigs of England fastened the specific title of *Pretender* on the son and grandson of James II, the word has retained in our speech a sinister significance. For us a pretender is one who makes a false claim to a title. But in speaking of the pretensions of science, humanists do not mean precisely this. No humanist would deny that science has a legitimate field of its own when investigating the phenomena of the objective world and attempting to find law and order in the flux of events. Nor would he deny that it has added much to our security and power and has increased our opportunities for a richer life and character.

Science has its legitimate pretensions to power; but false claims are now being advanced on all sides under the shelter of its name, and it is these false claims which the humanist is concerned to expose. While our modern pretenders are unfortunately far greater in number than the two descendants of James, they do fall into two classes. The first includes those men of science who are not content to work in their limited field, but are really metaphysicians who have created a fictitious world of the imagination made out of æthers, electrons, and mathematical symbols, and have confused it in their own and others' minds with the sensible world of brute fact. This class does comparatively little direct harm, as it merely creates some confusion in the orderly domain of

3

science; but, indirectly, it has given a stimulus and specious authority to the pseudo-scientists. The second class comprises those who are claiming that the phenomena of the subjective world also lie in the field of science and have imposed on the age the pseudo-sciences of psychology and sociology. They would have us believe that all truth is scientific and that the conclusions of self-examination are but guess-work. By mere verbal analogies they have linked the study of man's intellectual and spiritual nature to the physical world of mechanical matter and motion. It is the false claims of these pseudo-sciences which must be exposed and renounced in order that humanism may come again into its own as the arbiter of character.

As in the Middle Ages canting simulation of goodness, as well as honest virtue, was covered by the word religion, so to-day vague speculation, as well as accurate experimentation, is proclaimed as science. By a curious throw-back we are apparently using the word "science" in the primitive sense of "all knowledge," as the Greeks used it. And they, in spite of their acumen, had not been able to differentiate between the two equally valid methods of learning by objective experimentation and by personal experience. We have seemingly forgotten that one of the greatest achievements of the Renaissance was to discover this difference of method and to limit "science" strictly to the investigation of objective phenomena. Even Descartes, who attempted to create a purely mechanical world, excluded the processes of thought as something foreign to the scientific method.

It was the biologists of the nineteenth century, intoxicated with the delusion that the magic word evolution was a key to unlock all the mysteries of the universe, who foisted on the world the idea that man is but a complicated physical and chemical machine, and who sought to discredit the dualistic philosophy of the Renaissance physicists. And of all

4

the biologists, Huxley, the militant propagandist, was the one who did the most to degrade humanism into the pseudo-sciences of psychology and sociology. He first correctly emphasised the fact that there is but one scientific method which is best exemplified by the subject of mechanics. But —and in this lies the source of his mischief to clear thinking —*he then defined science as merely organised common sense*. One has only to analyse this definition to discover its speciousness and its confusion of thought. His definition has been almost universally accepted, although it undoes all the lessons taught us by the religious thinkers of the Middle Ages and the scientific experimentalists of the Renaissance; and its effect has been to drive theoretical science back into the hypothetical metaphysics of the Greeks.

It is merely a truism to say that our contact with the objective and subjective worlds is based, directly or indirectly, on our sense-perceptions; and, to be intelligibly transmitted from one person to another, such data must be common to many individuals. Also, it is an inevitable tendency of the mind to organise all facts or to link them together. Thus Huxley really classes all sound knowledge as science. But, since this sound knowledge, according to him, can be attained only by following the method of mechanics, which is the interpretation by the mind of the spatial and temporal relations between sensible bodies, his inference is clear that the phenomena of consciousness, the individual mind, and our social relations, are to be interpreted as problems of matter and motion.

Yet what, actually, is the process of exact science? The answer to this question should show us whether or not the term does have any precise and limited significance, and whether or not fundamental confusion must result from the attempt to make it synonymous with all knowledge.

Exact science, then, is first of all based on the naïve belief in an objective and real world whose events are connected in an orderly and prescribed manner, and occur independently of our thought or will. The phenomena of this objective world appeal to us through our sense-organs by some form of action, which we call energy, and are interpreted by our minds. We speak of this interpretation as observation; but to be scientific we must also select the phenomena to be observed, in order that we may classify their similarities and their dissimilarities. In the course of time, we have found such precision in many of our classifications and such regularity in the past actions of phenomena, that we are able to predict future events. Those predictions, which from past experience we find to have been accurately verified, we formulate as laws. For example, we have observed the actions of so many falling bodies that we have formulated the law of gravitation. It would be an error to say that a body fell, yesterday, because of this law; that event was simply one of the observed facts from which the law was deduced; but it is quite proper to predict that such a body will fall, to-morrow, in accordance with the law of gravitation. To sum up, the scientific method is limited to experimental observation and the formulation of laws; its value lies in the fact that, by its cultivation, we have done much to allay our apprehensions for the future and thus have abated the edge of superstition; and we also have vastly increased our power over our environment, or, in the much misunderstood aphorism of Francis Bacon, we have found science to be valuable for its fruits.

In a general way, we may say that the scientist should follow in his investigations the phenomena of the objective world only until their special forms of energy are absorbed by our nervous system. It is in the province of the humanist to study the phenomena of the subjective world after these stimuli have been translated into emotion and thought.

6

If a scientific prediction, or law, is to be something more than a vague statement of what will probably occur, we feel the necessity of measuring the quantity of the event; that is, our minds are not satisfied until we are able to express it mathematically. Since the only measurable attributes, concerning which our opinion of more or less is definite, are geometrical lengths, the aim of all science is, and must be, to express its laws in the language of mechanics; for that subject alone deals exclusively with simple, sensible masses and their geometrical relations in space. We have then the paradox that while mathematics is the goal of science, in that it is the ideal method, or language of expression, it is not itself a science since it is concerned with subjective ideas and is not limited by the restrictions of sensible bodies. Modern men of science may rebel against this fact; but even the newer, and more dubious, of the pseudo-sciences are forced to substantiate their claims with the support of factitious mathematical formulæ and tables and to simulate the mechanistic method. The inevitable tendency of science is to investigate all phenomena quantitatively, and to view the whole universe as a vast and measurable machine.

If the phenomena of life are to be classed as an exact science, it is necessary to postulate that the living organism, also, is a machine,—a thing of various material parts, acting on each other by mechanical forces. Such a postulate is pure *fiat*, for we have found no common factors between what we call vital actions and mechanical and physical forces. Biology is, at best, confined to the discovery of qualitative classifications, and the mutual chemical and physical reactions of the organism; and life is so complex and so variable that very few of its phenomena can be predicted with any accuracy. For example, the so-called law of heredity is often cited, but we have made scarcely any progress towards predicting variations in even an immediately succeeding generation.

7

Even if a general law of progressive evolution were granted to have been established, no one could foretell by it the future variations of any species.

If the scientific method is badly strained when applied to even the simplest forms of life, it completely fails when used to elucidate the phenomena of the mind. The fundamental definition of science excludes the processes of consciousness from its field, for it assumes that objective phenomena are to be interpreted by the mind. If we attempt to study the mind objectively, then we come face to face with the absurd paradox of a thing investigating itself by means of itself. And the gibe cast at the scientific psychologists, that they propose to study the mind by first denying its existence, is only too well founded.

The possibility of a scientific method is based on a rational interpretation of objective phenomena. Psychology, as a science, would be a solemn version of *Alice Through the Looking Glass* in which real persons are viewed and analysed by their images, or rather by some other intelligence, such as a dog or an inhabitant of Mars. The futility of such a process should be apparent if we recollect that an animal's mental processes can themselves be estimated and expressed only as a vaguer and more rudimentary sort of human mind.

## II

Our modern idea that science embraces all kinds of knowledge is, as I have mentioned before, a curious reversion to the Greeks. In spite of the fact that they formulated the great deductive laws of physics, such as cause and effect, conservation of matter, etc., and developed an extraordinarily fruitful science of geometry, they remained indifferent to the experimental method. They developed almost no apparatus for experimentation, established no standards of measurement, and their arithmetical symbols were so awkward that only the simplest calculations could be made. They never succeeded in disentangling subjective and objective ideas. Plato could anticipate the modern conception of natural law in his aphorism that God geometrises, but at the same time he vaguely identified the human soul with the stars and endued the universe with life. Democritus pictured the world as an aggregation of atoms, differing only in size, shape, and motion; yet he also tacitly ascribed to them a will or desire to move which was only less pronounced than in those finer particles which constituted the souls of men. Also the four classic elements,—earth, water, air, and fire,—which combined in different proportions to form all material bodies, were actuated by the animistic principle that each element sought its own place. One could multiply these examples of classical thought which confused mechanical forces with the vital attributes of will and desire.

The failure of the Greeks to develop an objective and experimental method was intensified by the domination of the Christian religion during the Middle Ages. The emphasis of thought was placed on the problems of human character. At a time when men were taught that our environment was a trap set by the powers of evil to allure our souls to eternal damnation, there could be little stimulus to study the laws of nature or to apply them to increase our interest in a temporal life. It is customary for historians to condemn the Church for having crushed science, but no concerted opposition was necessary in a society which saw no advantage in gathering its fruits. It was an axiom that truth was the direct consequence of intuition and revelation, that God had revealed in the Bible, and through His living Church, all the knowledge necessary for man's guidance in a transitory state. To neglect such a certainty for the perceptions of our fallible and sinful senses, and to construct a world from them according to our

9

reason, would be to fall into the sin of the pride of the intellect. Furthermore, in a society small in numbers and in area, where the greater number were believed to have been created to minister to the comfort of the few, little need was felt for mechanical power and industry. The only science which seemed to be worth cultivating was one which was believed to foretell human events and to affect our spiritual life.

It had been generally accepted from ancient times that the stars influenced our lives and foretold the future. Such knowledge was eagerly sought by a society which was principally concerned with religion and was, at the same time, a prey to superstitious fear. It is not surprising that astrology was seriously cultivated. If we grant the postulate that the stars do affect us, then we must admit that astrology was a true science. The positions and the motions of the planets and stars were observed and recorded as accurately as possible, and deductions were made according to rules and laws believed to have been verified by experience. Nor does it seem to me much more credulous to believe that our character is determined by the relative positions of the planets, than to assume, as do Mr. Watson and the modern behaviourists, that our thoughts are caused by the relative positions and motions of the material atoms which happen to compose the substance of our brains. The astrologists had, at least, the great advantage of dealing with real bodies which we can observe, while these psychologists have for their use only the hypothetical and machine-made atoms of the chemist which they can never hope to observe. There is little to choose between the superstition that the planets foretell our characters and the superstition that atoms constitute thought; both lead to equally foolish and irrational practices. And there is the less excuse for the psychologist, since he has had the benefit of a longer past experience than had the

10

astrologer to convince him of the futility of identifying mind and matter.

The only other science which aroused popular interest was alchemy. The basis of this subject was the postulate that all matter was composed of the four elements combined in various proportions. By the use of chemical reagents, the combinations of these elements could be altered and a given substance be thus changed into another. Alchemy is generally associated with the attempt to transmute metals and, in particular, to change lead into gold, because the natural cupidity of their patrons made it advisable for the alchemists to hold that prospect before them in order to obtain a livelihood. In principle, alchemy is but little different from modern chemistry. Our most recent theory still holds that the difference between lead and gold is due only to the numerical relations of a single element, the electron. The difference between chemistry and alchemy does not lie in either their fundamental hypotheses or their methods, but in our vastly superior technique of experimentation and accumulated knowledge. The nature of the modern electronic atom is essentially as fictitious as was the nature of the mediæval elements.

Besides exciting the hope of wealth, alchemy was important as an aid to health and longevity. Since health required that the four elements of the body should be preserved in their proper balance, illness, and even death, were but the temporary or permanent loss of their right proportions. Alchemists, convinced of this truth, were led to seek for a sovereign substance, the philosopher's stone, which would have the power to restore this disturbed balance and give to its fortunate owner permanent health and life.

It is a mistake to suppose that the Church oppressed these sciences—many of its most orthodox fathers and saints eagerly studied them. The abuses due to the rampant charlatanry of many of their practitioners were repressed, but their serious doctrines were fused into the religion of the time much as, in our day, the clergy have tried to harmonise Christianity and biological evolution. In fact, as we shall see, the most determined opposition which the new Copernican theory of the solar system had to overcome was the fusion of Christian dogma with Aristotelian astrology and alchemy.

It was natural that the first fruits of the new science of the Renaissance should have been in astronomy and mechanics. The accumulated observations of the astrologers had vastly increased the complexity of the Ptolemaic system, and the discrepancies between the observed and calculated positions of the planets had become glaringly evident. When the great treatise of Copernicus was finally published as he lay on his death-bed, it is altogether probable that no one suspected that it marked the beginning of a new philosophy. He had merely proved that the calculations of astronomers were greatly simplified by assuming that the sun, instead of the earth, was the fixed centre of the solar system, and that the earth and other planets revolved about it in circular orbits. It must remain a mooted question whether Copernicus believed that his discovery was only a mathematical device; his book states explicitly that he, as a Catholic, still subscribed to the belief that the earth was actually the fixed centre of the universe as the Church and the Aristotelians both taught to be a necessary article of faith. At all events, it was not until Galileo some sixty years later invented the telescope and turned it on the heavens, that men saw the significance of the discovery. The eye of the telescope penetrated the depths of the solar system. It proved that the planets were not pure celestial matter but were mere masses like the earth. Their brilliance was not a divine fire but ordinary sunlight reflected from their dull surfaces; they, like the earth, were inanimate bodies revolving about the sun and the Copernican system became a fact instead of a mathematic device. It is not extravagant to assert that, with the acceptance of Copernican astronomy, the whole mediæval conception of nature gave place to a reliance on experimental evidence.

The work of Galileo in founding the science of mechanics was fatal to the mysticism of the contemporary alchemists. Instead of the elements with their natural places, their likes and dislikes, their hierarchy of nobility, and their subserviency to planetary influences, he laid down the universal principle that all natural actions were due to mechanical forces whose only function was to alter the motions of bodies and whose amount was measurable in mathematical symbols. His significant work for us was an uncompromising war waged against the scientific dogmatism of the Aristotelians on the clear-cut issue that knowledge of the objective world could be obtained only by experimental evidence, and not by subjective preconceptions. Understood rightly, he had reinstated the Platonic dualism of two worlds, one of matter, and the other of the mind or spirit.

It is significant that during Galileo's lifetime, so swift was the movement, Descartes saw the trend of the new science and its inevitable effect on philosophy and religion. In his *Système du Monde,* he pictured a universe of matter and motion and nothing else,—a machine. From matter he tried to strip every sensible attribute except extension, or its mere geometrical position and extent. All phenomena became for him merely phases of motion. With the courage of his conviction, he even tried to imagine plants and animals to be mechanically acting automata. One thing only he could not include in this mechanism,—and that was *thought and consciousness.*

The cosmogony of Descartes has long since crumbled to

dust, but the gap he made between the subjective and objective worlds has never been closed in spite of incessant later attempts. And these early creators of science, as something distinct from humanism, were quite conscious that they were engaged in a revolution which could end only with the overthrow of the dogmatic science of the Middle Ages, sheltered by the authority of Aristotle and the Bible. Galileo, Descartes, Pascal, and Bacon all declared explicitly that the old order must pass. From their day to ours, we have more and more regarded the universe as a machine, a combination of inert matter and moving forces, acting not as we may desire, but according to invariable laws which we have personified as Nature. Man was left, by the physicists, as a unique outsider who could interpret this machine in terms of his sensations and mind, but could neither alter nor avoid its fateful operation.

Only one step further was needed to identify all science with mechanics and to compress the scientific method within the limits imposed by mechanical laws. This fundamental principle was Newton's discovery of the universal attraction of matter. According to this law, a single kind of force, depending only on the amount of matter and the distance between bodies, operated to hold the stars in their paths and to cause all the chemical and physical activities of atoms. With its discovery, the mechanistic theory was complete and dominant, and science had, in principle, gone as far as it can ever go. But, what is even more important, Newton grasped in his early years the fact that the scientific method is limited to the experimental investigation of objective phenomena, those which can be classified, measured geometrically, and formulated in laws which predict future events. He held with absolute consistency and restraint that what is once accomplished by this method is permanent. The experimental laws of gravitation, of the pressure of gases, and all others of like nature, are true within the limits of accuracy of our observation and measurement. If these improve, such laws do not fail, their mathematical expression is merely made more precise. They belong to the permanent acquisitions of the mind.

### III

To attempt to explain the nature of matter, or heat, or light, the mechanism by which they act, or the method by which their energy is translated into sensation and thought, this, however, is to pass into the realm of metaphysics, or what Newton excellently called hypothesis. All such speculations are, at best, transitory, and, instead of predicting new lines of work, they lag behind the sure and steady advance of experimentation; they are constantly being revised to explain new phenomena after they are discovered. A convincing illustration of this criticism can be found in the history of the hypotheses of the nature of light. Physicists commonly assert that the corpuscular hypothesis retarded the advance of the subject of light for a century; their answer was to replace it by an equally metaphysical hypothesis of mechanical waves in an æther. After incessantly patching up this new conception during the next century, they are again returning to a corpuscular hypothesis, even more metaphysical and incomprehensible than its prototype. It seems impossible for us to learn that the trouble does not arise from the weakness of any particular variety, but lies in the nature of hypothesis, itself. We have created fictitious æthers, atoms, and electrons which bear no resemblance to sensible bodies; light is alternately a stream of corpuscles, or waves, or quanta of energy, or even a mathematical symbol; space is declared to be impenetrable except along certain curves; and time is confused with space. What one age proposes as a great advance is flung aside by the next which makes a new hypothesis whose only fate is to be rejected. So far have these speculations been carried that the dogma is seriously maintained that a false scientific hypothesis is valuable because in some mysterious way it leads to the discovery of truth.

As we have advanced in sober experimental science, these hypotheses have become more and more abstruse and more and more dogmatic until the most recent of these dreamers, Whitehead, Eddington, Einstein, have pictured a phantasmagoria, instead of a world, as non-sensical as the hallucinations of the mediæval monk driven mad by the fevers of asceticism.

Such models of the structure of matter may, indeed, be useful to give substance to our thought and a language for our ideas. They have something of the same sort of relation to real objects that portraits do to living persons. But there is this important point to be remembered. A skilful painter has seen and studied the person and can make so faithful a likeness as to create the illusion of reality. But the man of science is attempting to picture things which can never be seen, for atoms lie in the realm of the infinitely small, whose very existence is problematical. Models of atoms, of æthers, or of space have about the same degree of authenticity as the posthumous portrait of a person whom no one then alive had ever seen. Men of science are too prone to confuse the thing and the model in their own minds, and they have certainly been so careless in their teaching that even very highly educated laymen accept these hypotheses as facts. Is it not true that the world pretty generally takes the hypothetical explanation of gravitation by Einstein, which involves the concept of a fictitious space of more than three dimensions and the fusion of time with space, to be equally as scientific, and therefore equally as true, as the experimental law of the attraction of bodies? Do not many accept as a demonstrated fact one or another of the many hypotheses advanced by biologists to explain the cause of the observed variations in species? And having failed to distinguish between scientific fact and fiction, we have incorporated this mass of speculation into our philosophy of life and especially into our religion. We are worse confused than the Deists of the eighteenth century who believed that the mind of God could be defined by learning the facts and laws of Nature; we now propose that the intellectual and spiritual attributes of Man be framed in the hypotheses of dogmatic Science.

That the scientific method, as evolved from physics and chemistry, is not applicable to the problems of life has been the settled conviction of virtually all the investigators in those sciences. In fact, in order to achieve their results they have had to assume that life is a perturbation which cannot be included in a mechanical and mathematical world, and that so far as possible sense-perceptions must be excluded as criteria of laws. However, it has not been so clear to many of them that the mechanical method imposes definite, and rather narrow, limitations even upon the study of physical and chemical problems. These limitations were clearly defined in the seventeenth century during the protracted controversy between Newton on the one side, and Hooke and Huygens on the other, as to the nature of light and the *modus operandi*, or mechanism, of its transmission. The question involved was clear-cut; and it will pay to discuss it in some detail because it settled once for all, I think, the distinction between science and humanism.

Theoretical physics, from the very beginning, has been a synthesis of phenomena in terms of mechanics; that is, in terms of substance and motion. For example, the physical properties of heat, sound, and light are expressed by the same mathematical formulæ which express the motion of a

17

wave in water. To distinguish between them, we assign different names to the substances involved, as a molecule of air, a corpuscle of light, or an æther. But whatever names we may give to them, or however we may try to distinguish them, we assign to all of them the common attribute of mass, or inertia, which is the only essential coefficient in a mechanical equation. And we use for all these different phenomena the same formula of motion, the quotient of the distance by the time. These quantities, mass and motion, when combined give us the law of mechanical energy, and our synthesis rests on the single fact that heat, sound, and light may be changed into mechanical motion, and may be produced by it. This energy is then their common and mutable factor.

But the objective phenomena of heat, light, and sound are cognisable to us through three separate sense-organs and are perceived as temperature, sight, and tone. These sensations are fundamentally different and, in fact, to confuse any of them with another is one of the surest indications of insanity. Thus the world as depicted by the physicist does not correspond with our world of sensation; nor does he attempt to do more than to discuss a restricted set of attributes, and not even those which really distinguish heat, light, etc., as such.

Newton, in his earliest published work, made evident this essential difference between the fields of physics and psychology. By means of a prism he refracted a beam of white sunlight into a continuous spectrum. He then placed a screen, containing a narrow slit, behind the prism in such a way as to permit only a very thin ray from the spectrum to pass on, and through, a second prism fastened parallel to the first prism. (I call it a homogeneous light ray to distinguish it from its psychological analogue, colour.) No matter what portion of the spectrum was used for the second prism, there was no further change of colour; the ray merely suffered a second angular deviation equal to that produced by the first refraction. He also recombined the whole spectrum by a reversed prism and obtained a single ray parallel to the original ray and pure white in colour. As a result of his experiments, he announced the following law: a primary ray of light is one which has a definite and specific angle of refraction by a prism, and each such primary ray is, to the eye, a primary colour. White is therefore a mixture of an indefinitely large number of primary rays, each possessing a different angle of deviation when passed through a prism; and when so separated each primary ray is seen by the eye as a primary colour.

The experiments of Newton were accepted as correct by Huygens and Hooke, probably the two most eminent physicists of the time. But they objected to his definition of a primary colour and to his conclusions. They had found previously, by their own experiments, that certain pairs of complementary colours, such as a certain red and a certain blue, gave to the eye the same sensation of white as did clear sunlight. They had defined them as the two primary colours which, by different proportions of mixture, would produce all other colours, including white. They therefore objected that it was unnecessary and cumbersome to assume an infinite number of primary rays when two were quite sufficient. By no process of reasoning could these two opinions be either reconciled or controverted. They involved fundamentally different criteria. White produced by the combination of a continuous spectrum and the white produced by a combination of red and blue were one and the same to Hooke and Huygens because their criterion of identity was the sensation of sight, and it must be the same for all psychologists who deal with subjective light. To Newton, the two whites were altogether different. The one examined by a prism gives a continuous spectrum, and the other gives two separated bands of blue and red. What, then, to the physicist is a fundamental dissimilarity is to the psychologist complete identity. How then can psychological sensations be studied by physical methods?

To show that this is not an isolated case, but that this gulf runs between the entire fields of physics and psychology, I can give an artificial example. While I deprecate the pseudo-scientific pictures, now fashionable, of the state of prehistoric man and of the condition of the earth before its habitability, I am able to imagine a world in which the eye had never developed, so that all life was blind. I am sure the word colour would never have been coined in such a world and that there could be no psychology of sight, but I also know that the blind race could develop a physical science of light because very many of its phenomena can be, and are now exclusively, studied by such apparatus as thermometers and electric galvanometers which can be read by touch. Or, to cite an everyday example, is not the mere fact, that the sensation produced by pepper on the tongue cannot be distinguished from that of heat, sufficient to make us hesitate before trying to study the sensations objectively, to synthesise the objective and subjective worlds, or to try to investigate them by the same method?

The history of physics, since the time of Maxwell, shows a record of vain efforts to reconstruct a materialistic monism. These attempts have failed because they involved a supposititious æther and atom which could no longer satisfy the growing body of experimental facts about radiant energy. After Maxwell predicted the existence of electro-magnetic radiation, an æther or atom possessing the ordinary attributes of matter became an absurdity.

But our childish, or at least youthful, reluctance to admit our limitations is so great that we proceeded to repeat the hypothetical method once more by substituting an energiastic monism. Unmindful of Pascal's dictum that man cannot investigate the world of either the infinitely small or the infinitely large, we are replacing a material atom and æther by Planck's hypothesis of discrete and disembodied *quanta*, or atoms, of energy. Already there have arisen four insuperable difficulties.

The hypothesis affirms action without specifying something to act, unless the word *energy* is given all the physical attributes of matter. In which case a *quantum* of radiant energy is merely our old friend, a corpuscle of light, masquerading under a new name. Again, it substitutes the principle of discontinuity of action for continuity, and one is puzzled to know from what the *quantum* originates and in what it ends. And again, it creates the dilemma that light is simultaneously corpuscular and vibrational, since without the latter quality none of the phenomena of interference is explicable. Lastly, it drifts into a pure philosophy of idealism.

My discussion would not be complete without a reference to the theory of relativity. It is significant that the earliest serious critique of Newtonian physics was made by Bishop Berkeley. With the greatest ingenuity and skill, he pointed out that objects can become known to us only *by* the mind and that since light, sound, and motion are interpreted by the mind as essentially different, they cannot be synthesised by any experimental and objective process. So far Berkeley's critique is thoroughly valid. He proceeded, however, to make the *non-sequitur* that objects exist only *in* the mind. If we accept this postulate, the logic of idealism is irrefutable; few, however, will accept it. Idealism fails because it ignores brute fact, and we accept the answer of Dr. Johnson who made his objection by merely kicking a large stone in his path.

Einstein also began with a critique of Newtonian dynamics

to prove that the conclusions we can draw from electro-dynamics are as limited and as relative as those from mechanics. From this denial of our ability to obtain real or absolute knowledge he, like Berkeley, has proceeded to construct a positive philosophy of the absolute. Relativity, as it has now been interpreted by such disciples as Whitehead and Eddington, is merely idealism under a new guise. The objective world of sensation and experience is illusion, and truth exists only in a set of subjective mathematical formulæ of cosmic *events*. The relativists openly rejoice that mathematics has come into its own kingdom and is no longer to be the handmaiden of physics, no longer to be restricted by the limitations of the sense-perceptions. Euclidean geometry, which is limited to the three dimensions of tactual space, has been replaced by a geometry of hyper-space, the properties of which no one can be cognisant of. Subjective time is eliminated, and objective time is conflated with space. They, too, deny the validity of the senses, as did the mediæval schoolman, and picture a topsy-turvy world. They are labouring under the delusion that the limitations of logic can be avoided by the simple substitution of mathematical symbols for words, forgetting that mathematical symbols are as meaningless as words when they are detached from facts. They fail to see that the equation is but a form of the syllogism. One can trace all through their argument the old and familiar fallacy of the ambiguous middle. They are quite reckless, as it suits their convenience, in confusing physical space of three dimensions with mathematical space of an unlimited number; neither do they distinguish time as a subjective sequence of events from time as a measurable component of velocity. The relativists are as rash as those sociologists who see a real connection between physical energy of motion and mental energy of thought and so deceive themselves with the notion that they are scientific.

22

A note of uncertainty is beginning to show itself, however, for thoughtful physicists are seeing the *impasse* into which their unbridled hypotheses have led them. Abstruse mathematical analysis is again proving to us, what Pascal, Newton, Lagrange, and philosophy had demonstrated in a simpler way, that the mechanistic method can, at best, only picture an objective world as it seems to us, and not as it is. As a recent physicist confesses: "The physicist thus finds himself in a world from which the bottom has dropped clean out; as he penetrates deeper and deeper it eludes him and fades away by the highly unsportsmanlike device of just becoming meaningless. No refinement of measurement will avail to carry him beyond the portals of this shadowy domain which he cannot even mention without logical inconsistency. A *bound* is thus forever set to the curiosity of the physicist. What is more, the mere existence of this bound means that he must give up his most cherished convictions and faith. The world is not a world of reason, understandable by the intellect of man, but as we penetrate ever deeper, the very law of cause and effect, which we had thought to be a formula to which we could force God himself to subscribe, ceases to have meaning." [1] The answer to this naïve confession is simple enough: there never was a *bottom* to his hypothetical world, as he could have foreseen if he had acquainted himself with the warning of the more profound men of science, philosophers, and humanists.

The writer adds that this failure, now proved, "must forever keep the physicist humble." But there is no cause for him to think lowly of himself for what he has accomplished and for what he may achieve. He should, rather, be modest and restrict himself to what can be done legitimately by the scientific method. I fear, however, that in spite of such

[1] "The New Vision of Science," by Professor P. W. Bridgman, *Harper's Magazine*, 1929.

occasional confessions, the physicists are neither humble nor modest, but are merely bewildered. The false pretensions of science must be wholly abandoned, and the problems of our destiny be examined by a wise judgment drawn from human experience, before we can hope for a sane and humanistic philosophy.

# Humanism: An Essay at Definition

IRVING BABBITT

## I

The art of defining is so indispensable that one needs to define the limits of definition itself. A very eminent humanist, Erasmus, showed his awareness of these limits when he complained of the attempts of the theologians of the Reformation to formulate deity that every definition was a disaster. Though the humanist does not seek to define God and is in general chary of ultimates, he is wont in more mundane matters to put the utmost emphasis on definition. This Socratic emphasis would seem especially needed at a time like the present which has probably surpassed all previous epochs in its loose and irresponsible use of general terms. Unless this tendency is corrected, the day may come when, outside of words that stand for the measurements of science or the objects of sense, communication between men will be well-nigh impossible. The exchange of ideas regarding those aspects of life that fall outside the merely quantitative and material may become as difficult as economic exchanges would be with coins that have no definite value.

This growing debasement of the intellectual coinage may be illustrated from the word humanism itself. The boundaries of a genuine humanism are broad and flexible. It is plain, however, that the word is being appropriated for points of view that cannot be brought within these boundaries, however generously extended. As a preliminary to pointing out some of the more serious of the resulting confusions it would seem desirable to build up the historical background. For what a word actually has meant should surely throw light on what it ought to mean.

As is well known, the word humanist was applied, first in the Italy of the fifteenth century, and later in other European countries, to the type of scholar who was not only proficient in Greek and Latin, but who at the same time inclined to prefer the humanity of the great classical writers to what seemed to him the excess of divinity in the mediævals. This contrast between humanity and divinity was often conceived very superficially. However, the best of the humanists were not content with opposing a somewhat external imitation of the Ciceronian or Virgilian elegance to the scholastic carelessness of form. They actually caught a glimpse of the fine proportionateness of the ancients at their best. They were thus encouraged to aim at a harmonious development of their faculties in this world rather than at an other-worldly felicity. Each faculty, they held, should be cultivated in due measure without one-sidedness or overemphasis, whether that of the ascetic or that of the specialist. "Nothing too much" is indeed the central maxim of all genuine humanists, ancient and modern.

In a world of ever-shifting circumstance, this maxim is not always of easy application. Whoever has succeeded in bridging the gap between the general precept and some particular emergency has to that extent achieved the fitting and the decorous. Decorum is simply the law of measure in its more concrete aspects. For every type of humanist decorum is, in Milton's phrase, the "grand masterpiece to observe." Actually this observation may rest on deep insight, as it did in the case of Milton himself, or it may degenerate into empty formalism. The adjustment of which I have spoken between the variable and the permanent elements in human experience requires spiritual effort and most men are spiritually indolent. For genuine adjustment they tend to substitute outer conformity so that decorum itself finally comes to seem a mere veneer, something that has no deep root in the nature of things. Moreover the notions of decent behaviour to which men have conformed at any particular period have always been more or less local and relative. It is easy to take the next step and assume that they have been *only* local and relative, an assumption subversive not merely of decorum but of humanism itself. Humanism, one of our modernists has argued, may have done very well for other times and places, but under existing circumstances, it is at best likely to prove only a "noble anachronism." A similar objection to humanism is that it has its source in a psychology of "escape," that it is an attempt to take flight from the present into a past that has for the modern man become impossible. But humanism is not to be identified with this or that body of traditional precepts. The law of measure on which it depends becomes meaningless unless it can be shown to be one of the "laws unwritten in the heavens" of which Antigone had the immediate perception, laws that are "not of to-day or yesterday," that transcend in short the temporal process. The final appeal of the humanist is not to any historical convention but to intuition.

It does not follow that the humanist is ready to abandon history to the relativist. The main conventions that have prevailed in the past reveal important identities as well as differences. These identities cannot be explained as due to their common derivation from some previous convention. The Chinese made an independent discovery of the law of measure.[1] An important task, indeed, that awaits some properly qualified scholar, preferably a Chinese, is a comparison

[1] For an outline of Chinese humanism, see the article by Chang Hsin-Hai in the *Hibbert Journal* for April, 1928 ("The Essentials of Confucian Wisdom").

of Confucian humanism with occidental humanism as it appears, for example, in the *Ethics* of Aristotle. The announcement was made recently in the press that a Harvard astronomer had discovered the "centre of the universe" (more strictly the centre of our galactic system). In the meanwhile the far more important question is being neglected whether human nature itself has any centre. One's faith in the existence of such a centre increases when one finds the best commentary on Pascal's dictum that the great man is he who combines in himself opposite virtues and occupies all the space between them, in a Confucian book the very title of which, literally rendered, means the "universal norm" or "centre." [2] Here and elsewhere the Confucian books reveal a deep and direct insight into the law of measure. Legge's translation of the Chinese word for decorum (*li*) as "the rules of propriety" has been rightly censured as unduly prim and formalistic; though it must be admitted that a formalistic element is very marked at times even in the older Confucian writings.

Practically the assertion of a "universal centre" means the setting up of some pattern or model for imitation. The idea of imitation goes even deeper than that of decorum, but is an idea that humanism shares with religion. Humanism, however, differs from religion in putting at the basis of the pattern it sets up, not man's divinity, but the something in his nature that sets him apart simply as man from other animals and that Cicero defines as a "sense of order and decorum and measure in deeds and words." [3] It dwells on the danger of any attempt to pass too abruptly to the religious level; it holds, if I may be pardoned for quoting myself, that the world would have been a better place if

[2] See *The Conduct of Life*, translation of the *Tsung Yung* by Ku Hung Ming (Wisdom of the East series), p. 55.

[3] "Unum hoc animal sentit quid sit ordo, quid sit quod deceat, in factis dictisque qui modus." *De Officiis*, Lib. I.

28

more persons had made sure they were human before setting out to be superhuman. The virtue that results from a right cultivation of one's humanity, in other words from moderate and decorous living, is poise. Perfect poise is no doubt impossible: not even Sophocles succeeded in seeing life steadily and seeing it whole. The difference is none the less marked between the man who is moving towards poise and the man who is moving away from it. Since the break with the somewhat artificial decorum of the eighteenth century most men have been moving away from it. It would not be easy to argue with any plausibility that the typical modernist is greatly concerned with the law of measure; his interest, as a glance at our newspapers should suffice to show, is rather in the doing of stunts and the breaking of records, in "prodigies, feats of strength and crime," [4] the very topics that, according to the traditional report, Confucius banished from his conversation. "Let us confess it," says Nietzsche, speaking not merely for the rank and file but for the leaders, "proportionateness is foreign to us." It is foreign to us because we no longer refer our experience to any centre. With the growth of the naturalistic temper, the normal has come to have less appeal than the novel. The pursuit of poise has tended to give way to that of uniqueness, spontaneity, and above all intensity. "The last remnant of God on earth," says Nietzsche himself, "are the men of great longing, of great loathing, of great satiety." Once grant that there is no constant element in life and one might agree with Walter Pater that a man's highest ambition should be "to burn with a hard gem-like flame," to get "as many pulsations as possible into the given time." [5] Æsthetic perceptiveness is an excellent thing, but thus to set it up as an end in itself is almost at the opposite pole from humanism. Yet

[4] See *Analects* (Wisdom of the East series), p. 109.
[5] "Conclusion" to his volume *The Renaissance*.

Pater has been called a humanist.  One might so regard him if one accepted his view that the distinctive humanistic trait is an all-embracing curiosity.[6]  Humanism appears primarily, not in the enlargement of comprehension and sympathy, desirable though this enlargement may be, but in the act of selection, in the final imposition on mere multiplicity of a scale of values.  Matthew Arnold, with his striving for centrality, has far better claims to be regarded as a humanist than Pater—and that in spite of his inadequacy on the side of religion.  The model that Arnold sets up for imitation in the name of culture is a constant corrective of everything that is one-sided and out of proportion.  "I hate," he says, speaking not only for himself but for all true humanists, "all over-preponderance of single elements."

## II

We have seen thus far that the word humanist has two main meanings—an historical meaning in its application to the scholars who turned away from the Middle Ages to the Greeks and Romans, and a psychological meaning, as one may say, that derives directly from the historical one: humanists in this latter sense are those who, in any age, aim at proportionateness through a cultivation of the law of measure.  Keeping this definition in mind, we should now be prepared to deal with the confusions in the use of the word of which I spoke at the beginning.  These confusions have arisen from its misapplication to various types of naturalists and supernaturalists, especially the former.

For example, the eminent orientalist, M. Sylvain Lévi, has in a recent book used the term humanism in speaking of persons as far apart as Buddha and Rousseau.[7]  Buddha, it

[6] For Pater's definition of humanism see the end of his essay on Pico della Mirandola (*The Renaissance*).

[7] See *L'Inde et le Monde*, pp. 32, 165.

is true, had his humanistic side: he recommended that one follow a *via media* between asceticism and self-indulgence. But, unlike Confucius, he is in his primary emphasis not humanistic, but religious. The association of humanism with Rousseau is especially unjustifiable. Rousseau was, in the current sense of the word, a highly vital individual, but he cannot be properly regarded as either religious or humanistic. He attacked both humanism and religion in their traditional forms, and instead of working out some modern equivalent for these forms, helped to usher in the era of free naturalistic expansion in the midst of which we are still living. He was above all for free temperamental expansion. He was himself emotionally expansive to a degree that was incompatible not only with artificial but with real decorum. He encouraged the humanitarian hope that brotherhood among men may be based on emotional overflow. In general the most serious confusion in the use of the word humanist has arisen from its appropriation by the humanitarians. Walt Whitman was, for instance, highly Rousseauistic in his notion of brotherhood. We should therefore know what to think of the assertion of Mr. Lewis Mumford that Walt Whitman was a true humanist; also of the assumption of the term by the left-wing Unitarians and other Protestants who have been moving towards humanitarianism.[8]

The humanitarian has favoured not only temperamental expansion; he has also, as a rule, favoured the utmost expansion of scientific knowledge with a view to realising the Baconian ideal. Perhaps indeed the chief driving power behind the humanitarian movement has been the confidence inspired in man by the progressive control physical science

[8] See, for example, the symposium entitled *Humanist Sermons* edited by C. W. Reese (1927). On page 60 of this volume one encounters the statement that "all Americans are humanists"! For a fuller elucidation of the distinction between the humanist and the humanitarian see the opening chapters of my book *Literature and the American College* (1908).

has enabled him to acquire over the forces of nature. It goes without saying that the humanist is not hostile to science as such but only to a science that has overstepped its due bounds, and in general to every form of naturalism, whether rationalistic or emotional, that sets up as a substitute for humanism or religion. In the case of such encroachments there is not only a quarrel between the naturalist and the humanist, but a quarrel of first principles. When first principles are involved the law of measure is no longer applicable. One should not be moderate in dealing with error. I have pointed out elsewhere the danger of confounding the humanistic attitude with that of the Laodicean.[9]

The reason for the radical clash between the humanist and the purely naturalistic philosopher is that the humanist requires a centre to which he may refer the manifold of experience; and this the phenomenal world does not supply. In getting his centre the humanist may appeal primarily to tradition, or as I have said, to intuition. In the latter case he will need to submit to a searching Socratic dialectic the word intuition itself—to distinguish between intuitions of the One and intuitions of the Many. Otherwise he will run the risk of not being a modern but only a modernist. The contrast between modern and modernist is not unlike that between Socrates and the sophists. Both modern and modernist are under compulsion to accept in some form the ancient maxim that man is the measure of all things.[10] Only, the measure of the modern is based on a perception of the something in himself that is set above the flux and that he possesses in common with other men; whereas the perception with which the modernist is chiefly concerned, to the subversion of any true measure whatsoever, is of the divergent

[9] See my book *Democracy and Leadership*, p. 25.
[10] For the different meanings that this maxim may have see the last chapter of my book *The Masters of Modern French Criticism*.

32

and the changeful both within and without himself. The present menace to humanism, it has been said, is less from its enemies than from those who profess to be its friends. Thus Mr. F. C. S. Schiller of Oxford proclaims himself a humanist, and at the same time seeks to show that the true humanist was not Socrates but that precursor of recent "flowing" philosophers, Protagoras.

It should be noted that many of our votaries of change and mobility are more emotional than Protagoras or any other Greek sophist. They tend to make, not their own thoughts, but their own feelings the measure of all things. This indulgence in feeling has been encouraged by the sentimentalists who have discovered in feeling not only the quintessentially human element, but, as I said in speaking of Rousseau, the ultimate ground of fraternal union. In our own time, partly perhaps as a result of the psycho-analytical probing of the sources of the emotional life in the subconscious, there is a growing distrust of the sentimentalist. To be sure, one may, according to the psycho-analyst, turn the emotions to good account by a process of "sublimation." Why not escape still more completely from one's complexes and infantile survivals by adjusting oneself to the cosmic order that is revealed to the scientific investigator in his laboratory? One may thus cease to be ego-centric and become truly mature and disinterested. This is the attitude that Mr. Walter Lippmann recommends in *A Preface to Morals*, and it is this attitude that, by a flagrant misuse of the word, he terms "humanism." It is well that a man should adjust himself to the reality of the natural order and, as a preliminary, should strive to be objective in the scientific sense; but humanism calls for an adjustment to a very different order that is also "real" and "objective" in its own way. It insists in short that there is a "law for man" as well as a "law for thing," and is in this sense dualistic. Mr.

33

Lippmann's attempt to base ethics on monistic postulates is, from either a religious or humanistic point of view, a revival of the stoical error. Yet he would have us believe that any one who has become disinterested after the scientific fashion has got the equivalent not only of humanism but of "high religion." By thus dissimulating the gap between the wisdom of the ages and the wisdom of the laboratory, he is flattering some of the most dangerous illusions of the present time. He escapes from the main humanitarian tendency to give to feeling a primacy that does not belong to it, only to encourage its other main tendency to accord to physical science a hegemony to which it is not entitled.

It is self-evident that humanitarianism of the scientific or utilitarian type, with its glorification of the specialist who is ready to sacrifice his rounded development, if only he can contribute his mite to "progress," is at odds with the humanistic ideal of poise and proportion. The religious pretensions of humanitarianism of this type are even more inacceptable, at least if one understands by religion anything resembling the great traditional faiths. The Baconian has inclined from the outset to substitute an outer for an inner working—the effort of the individual upon himself—that religion has, in some form or other, always required. The result has been to encourage the acquisitive life and also the pursuit of material instead of spiritual "comfort." A typical example of this utilitarian trend is Professor T. N. Carver's *Religion Worth Having*, in which he so exalts the "productive life" that religion is all but identified with thrift. At this rate it may soon be possible to get one's religion securely tucked away in a safe-deposit drawer! One should, however, be grateful to Professor Carver for not having called himself a humanist.

It does not seem possible to supply from the sentimental or Rousseauistic side of the humanitarian movement the elements that are, religiously speaking, absent from its utilitarian side. The nature to which the Rousseauist invites one to return, is, as I have sought to show elsewhere, only a projection of the idyllic imagination. In the state of nature or some similar state thus projected, in other words in Arcadia, man is "good." Practically this has meant that there is in the natural man an altruistic impulse that may prevail over his egoism. The upshot of this myth of man's natural goodness has been to discredit the traditional controls, both humanistic and religious. Humility, conversion, decorum, all go by the board in favour of unrestricted temperamental overflow. The crucial question is whether the immense machinery of power that has resulted from the efforts of the utilitarians can be made, on this basis of unlimited expansion, to serve disinterested ends. Everything converges indeed on both sides of the humanitarian movement upon the idea of service. If it can be shown that there has been no vital omission in the passage from the service of God to the service of man, one may safely side with all the altruists from the third Earl of Shaftesbury to John Dewey. Unfortunately a formidable mass of evidence has been accumulating (the Great War was for many a convincing demonstration) that, in the natural man as he exists in the real world and not in some romantic dreamland, the will to power is more than a match for the will to service.

The benefits that have ensued from the major concentration upon the natural order that has been under way since the Renaissance have been numerous and dazzling. We are still celebrating these benefits under the name of progress. It is no longer possible, however, to allay the suspicion that the price which has been paid for progress of this type has been a growing superficiality in dealing with the still more important problems of the human order. "Nothing is more certain," says Burke in a well-known passage, "than that our manners, our civilisation, and all the good things which are connected with manners and with civilisation, have, in this European world of ours, depended for ages upon two principles; and were indeed the result of both combined; I mean the spirit of a gentleman and the spirit of religion." The whole debate would seem to narrow down to the question whether it is possible to secure on utilitarian-sentimental lines a valid equivalent for Burke's two principles. As for the "spirit of a gentleman," its decline is so obvious as scarcely to admit of argument. It has even been maintained that in America, the country in which the collapse of traditional standards has been most complete, the gentleman is at a positive disadvantage in the world of practical affairs; he is likely to get on more quickly if he assumes the "mucker pose." [11] According to William James, usually taken to be the representative American philosopher, the very idea of the gentleman has about it something slightly satanic. "The prince of darkness," says James, "may be a gentleman, as we are told he is, but, whatever the God of earth and heaven is, he can surely be no gentleman."

As for the "spirit of religion," I have already glanced at its humanitarian substitute. The humanitarian maintains that the spirit that appears in Christianity will, if disengaged from mere dogma, be found to be something very similar to his own spirit of service. One should at least be able to understand the position of the person who has become convinced that there is a supernatural element in genuine Christianity, lost in the passage from the old dispensation to the new, for which mere altruism is no substitute, and who therefore takes his stand on the side of tradition. Dogmatic and revealed religion, he argues, was alone capable of rescuing the ancient world from a decadent naturalism. It alone

[11] See "The Mucker Pose" by James Truslow Adams, *Harper's Magazine*, November, 1928; reprinted in *Our Business Civilisation* (1929).

affords an avenue of escape from the analogous situation that confronts the world to-day.

## III

The relation of the humanist to this religious traditionalist can scarcely be defined too carefully. Between the humanist and the humanitarian, I have said, there is a clash of first principles. Between the humanist and the authentic Christian, on the other hand, there is room for important co-operation. To be sure, many of the leaders of the early Church were satisfied with nothing short of a stark supernaturalism and inclined to reject the genuinely humanistic elements of the ancient civilisation along with its naturalistic errors. But the orthodox attitude has, in spite of the difficulties of reconciling otherworldliness with a merely secular wisdom, come to be one of friendliness to the classical humanities.[12] Mr. T. S. Eliot is probably close to this attitude when he maintains that humanism is of very great value, but only in subordination to the historical Church. As an independent doctrine, at least in any large way, it is, he maintains, ineffective. A broad survey of the past does not, however, confirm the view that humanism is thus either precarious or parasitical. The two most notable manifestations of the humanistic spirit that the world has seen, that in ancient Greece and that in Confucian China, did not have the support of Christianity or any other form of revealed religion. Take again the humanism of seventeenth-century France: the ideal of the finely poised gentleman who "does not plume himself on anything" was often allied with Christianity ("devout humanism"), but it was also found among

---

[12] For the early hostility of certain Christians to Graeco-Roman culture and the final reconciliation between this culture and the Church, see E. K. Rand's *Founders of the Middle Ages*, *passim*. *Cf.* also P. E. More's "Paradox of Oxford" (*Shelburne Essays*, Vol. IX).

37

the free-thinkers ("libertines") who were hostile to every form of belief in the supernatural.

In general, why should not the humanist, it may be asked, devote himself quietly to his own task—that of effecting an adjustment between the law of measure and the ever-novel emergencies of actual living, and at the same time refuse to take sides too decisively in the great debate between the naturalists and the supernaturalists? If pressed too hard by the supernaturalists in particular, why should he not reply in the words of Pope:

> "Presume not God to scan;
> The proper study of mankind is man"?

One must, however, admit an element of truth in the assertion of Plato that things human cannot be properly known without a previous insight into things divine. Another thinker, Pascal, who had this religious insight in a high degree, though combined with a form of dogma peculiarly alien to most modern men, declared that unless man has the support of the supernatural, unless in short he attains to true humility, he will fall fatally either into the stoic pride or else, through the intermediary stage of scepticism, into the epicurean relaxation. The whole question bristles with difficulties: one thinks of the immense and, on the whole, salutary influence that two Roman humanists, Cicero and Horace, have exercised on occidental culture, though, to adopt Pascal's classification, the humanism of Cicero leaned unduly to the stoical side, that of Horace to the epicurean. Yet I believe that the humanist will finally be forced to recognise that there is truth in Pascal's contention, that he will have to take sides in the debate between naturalists and supernaturalists, however much he may deplore the frequent failure of both of these fell antagonists to do justice to the immense

38

range of human experience that is subject primarily to the law of measure.

For my own part, I range myself unhesitatingly on the side of the supernaturalists. Though I see no evidence that humanism is necessarily ineffective apart from dogmatic and revealed religion, there is, as it seems to me, evidence that it gains immensely in effectiveness when it has a background of religious insight. One is conscious of such a background, for example, in Sophocles, who ranks high among occidental humanists, as well as in Confucius, the chief exponent of the humanistic idea in the Orient. The phrase religious insight is in itself vague. Is it not possible to give the phrase a definite content without departing from the critical attitude? One may be helped to such a definition by asking oneself what element has tended to fall out of the life of the modern man with the decline of the traditional disciplines. According to Mr. Walter Lippmann, the conviction the modern man has lost is that "there is an immortal essence presiding like a king over his appetites." But why abandon the affirmation of such an "essence" or higher will, to the mere traditionalist? Why not affirm it first of all as a psychological fact, one of the immediate data of consciousness, a perception so primordial that, compared with it, the deterministic denials of man's moral freedom are only a metaphysical dream? One would thus be in a position to perform a swift flanking movement on the behaviourists and other naturalistic psychologists who are to be regarded at present as among the chief enemies of human nature. One might at the same time be in a fair way to escape from the modernist dilemma and become a thoroughgoing and complete modern.

The philosophers have often debated the question of the priority of will or intellect in man. The quality of will that I am discussing and that rightly deserves to be accounted

39

superrational, has, however, been associated in traditional Christianity not primarily with man's will, but with God's will in the form of grace. The theologians have indulged in many unprofitable subtleties apropos of grace. One cannot afford, however, as has been the modern tendency, to discard the psychological truth of the doctrine along with these subtleties. The higher will must simply be accepted as a mystery that may be studied in its practical effects, but that, in its ultimate nature, is incapable of formulation. Herein the higher will is not peculiar. "All things," according to the scholastic maxim, "end in a mystery" (*Omnia exeunt in mysterium*). The man of science is increasingly willing to grant that the reality behind the phenomena he is studying not only eludes him, but must in the nature of the case ever elude him. He no longer holds, for example, as his more dogmatic forebears of the nineteenth century inclined to do, that the mechanistic hypothesis, valuable as it has proved itself to be as a laboratory technique, is absolutely true; its truth is, he admits, relative and provisional.

The person who declines to turn the higher will to account until he is sure he has grasped its ultimate nature is very much on a level with the man who should refuse to make practical use of electrical energy until he is certain he has an impeccable theory of electricity. Negatively one may say of the higher will, without overstepping the critical attitude, that it is not the absolute, nor again the categorical imperative; not the organic and still less the mechanical; finally, not the "ideal" in the current sense of that term. Positively one may define it as the higher immediacy that is known in its relation to the lower immediacy—the merely temperamental man with his impressions and emotions and expansive desires—as a power of vital control (*frein vital*). Failure to exercise this control is the spiritual indolence that is for both Christian and Buddhist a chief source, if not the

40

chief source, of evil. Though Aristotle, after the Greek fashion, gives the primacy not to will but to mind, the power of which I have been speaking is surely related to his "energy of soul," the form of activity distinct from a mere outer working, deemed by him appropriate for the life of leisure that he proposes as the goal of a liberal education. Happiness, which is for him the end of ends, is itself, he tells us, "a kind of working." Here is a difference, one may note in passing, between a true humanist like Aristotle and the epicurean who also has his doctrine of moderation and so often sets up as a humanist. It is no doubt well, as the epicurean urges, so to indulge in present pleasures that they may not be injurious to future ones. To employ the trivial illustration, it is well to avoid overeating at dinner lest one impair one's appetite for supper. But the meaning of the Aristotelian working is that one should not be content with transitory pleasure at all, but should be striving constantly to rise from a lower to a higher range of satisfactions. The energy of soul that has served on the humanistic level for mediation appears on the religious level in the form of meditation. Religion may of course mean a great deal more than meditation. At the same time humanistic mediation that has the support of meditation may correctly be said to have a religious background. Mediation and meditation are after all only different stages in the same ascending "path" and should not be arbitrarily separated.

This question comes up especially in connection with the rôle of enthusiasm. Humanism is not primarily enthusiastic, whereas religion is. There is a touch of enthusiasm even in Aristotle, in general one of the coolest and most detached of thinkers, when he comes to the passage from the humanistic to the religious level. "We should not," he says, "pay heed to those who bid us think as mortals, but should, as far as may be, seek to make ourselves immortal." At the same

41

time it must be admitted that even a true religious enthusiasm is hard to combine with poise and that this true enthusiasm has many counterfeits. "For one inspired, ten thousand are possessed," wrote the Earl of Roscommon, having in mind the religious zealots of the English seventeenth century. The neo-classic gentleman was therefore as a rule distinctly unfriendly to the enthusiast. The humanist, however, should not deny enthusiasm but merely insist on defining it. He cannot afford to be an enthusiast in Rousseau's sense; on the other hand, he should not neglect the truth of Rousseau's saying that "cold reason has never done anything illustrious."

Though one should, in my judgment, side with the oriental as against Aristotle and the Greeks in giving priority to the higher will over mind,[13] especially if one attaches importance to the supreme religious virtue, humility, it yet remains true that this will must be exercised intelligently. Granted that the existence in man of a power of control may be affirmed, quite apart from any dogma, as a psychological fact, the individual must nevertheless go beyond this fact if he is to decide rightly how far he needs to exercise control in any particular instance: in short, he needs standards. In getting his standards the humanist of the best type is not content to acquiesce inertly in tradition. He is aware that there is always entering into life an element of vital novelty and that the wisdom of the past, invaluable though it is, cannot therefore be brought to bear too literally on the present. He knows that, though standards are necessary, they should be held flexibly and that, to accomplish this feat, he must make the most difficult of all mediations, that between the One and the Many. The chief enemies of the humanist are the pragmatists and other philosophers of the flux who simplify this problem for themselves by dismissing the One,

[13] See Ch. V of *Democracy and Leadership* ("Europe and Asia"); also Appendix A ("Theories of the Will").

42

which is actually a living intuition, as a metaphysical abstraction.

Whatever reality man achieves in his dealings with either the human or the natural order, is dependent, I have tried to show elsewhere, on the degree to which he establishes a correct relationship between the part of himself that perceives, the part that conceives, and the part that discriminates. The part that conceives, that reaches out and seizes likenesses and analogies, may be defined as imagination; the part that discriminates and tests the unity thus apprehended from the point of view of its truth may be defined as analytical reason; the part that perceives is, in the case of the humanist, primarily concerned with the something in man that is set above the phenomenal order and that I have already defined as a power of control. One may say therefore that standards result from a co-operation between imagination and reason, dealing with the more specifically human aspects of experience, and that these standards should be pressed into the service of the higher will with a view to imposing a right direction on the emotions and expansive desires of the natural man. The supreme goal of ethical endeavour, as Plato pointed out long ago, is that one should come to like and dislike the right things.

## IV

Humanism, even humanism of the distinctly individualistic type I have been outlining, may, as I have already suggested, work in harmony with traditional religion. In that case there must be a careful determination of boundaries. Though humanism and religion both lie on the same ascending path from the naturalistic flux, one must insist that each has its separate domain. It is an error to hold that humanism can take the place of religion. Religion indeed may more readily dispense with humanism than humanism with re-

ligion. Humanism gains greatly by having a religious background in the sense I have indicated; whereas religion, for
the man who has actually renounced the world, may very
conceivably be all in all. On the other hand, the man who
sets out to live religiously in the secular order without having recourse to the wisdom of the humanist is likely to fall
into vicious confusions—notably, into a confusion between
the things of God and the things of Cæsar. The Catholic
Church has therefore been well inspired in rounding out its
religious doctrine with the teaching of Aristotle and other
masters of the law of measure. It can scarcely fail to recognise that the position of the positive and critical humanist is
sound *as far as it goes*. It follows that the Catholic and the
non-Catholic should be able to co-operate on the humanistic
level. A like co-operation should be possible between the
humanist and the members of other Christian communions
who have not as yet succumbed entirely to humanitarianism.

I have tried to show that the weakness of humanitarianism
from both the humanistic and the religious point of view is
that it holds out the hope of securing certain spiritual benefits—for example, peace and brotherhood—without any ascent from the naturalistic level. The positive and critical
humanist would seem to have a certain tactical superiority
over the religious traditionalist in dealing with the defects of
the humanitarian programme. In the battle of ideas, as in
other forms of warfare, the advantage is on the side of those
who take the offensive. The modernists have broken with
tradition partly because it is not sufficiently immediate, partly
because it is not sufficiently experimental. Why not meet
them on their own ground and, having got rid of every ounce
of unnecessary metaphysical and theological baggage, op-
pose to them something that is both immediate and experimental—namely the presence in man of a higher will or
power of control? I use the word experimental deliberately

44

by way of protest against the undue narrowing of this word by the scientific naturalists to observation of the phenomenal order and of man only in so far as he comes under this order. One should also protest against the restriction of the term reality to observation of this type. Some of the most monstrous mutilations of reality that the world has ever seen are being perpetrated at this moment—for example, by the behaviouristic psychologists—in the name of the "real." At all events everything in the modernist movement will be found to converge either upon the rôle of feeling or upon the rôle of experiment, and the final question raised in either case is that of the will. As a result of the combined influence of the various types of naturalists, the present age is at once more emotional and more mechanical than any other of which we have historical record. By mechanical I refer primarily not to the multiplication of machines in the outer world but to the mechanising of mind itself. An effective procedure is, as I have said, to meet the mechanist on his own ground and point out to him that he is unduly dogmatic, if he holds that his hypothesis is absolutely valid even for the natural order, and that, if he goes further and seeks to make it cover the whole of experience, to impose a deterministic nightmare on the human spirit itself, he is abandoning the experimental attitude for an even more objectionable form of dogmatism.

Similarly one should meet the emotionalist on his favourite ground of immediacy. Inasmuch as the higher immediacy has been largely associated in the Christian occident with the operation of God's will, the substitution for it of the lower immediacy has meant practically the setting up of a subrational parody of grace. In order to make this parody plausible, the emotionalist has had recourse to the usual arts of the sophist, chief among which are a juggling with halftruths and a tampering with general terms. I have commented elsewhere on the way in which words like "virtue" and "conscience" have been so twisted from their traditional meaning as to eliminate the dualistic element that both humanism and religion require. If there is to be any recovery of the truths of dualism, at least along critical lines, a battle royal will need to be fought over the word "nature" itself; here, if anywhere, one needs to practise a Socratic dichotomy.

The half-truth that has been used to compromise religion in particular is that, though religion is in itself something quite distinct from emotion, it is in its ordinary manifestations very much mixed up with emotion. I give an example of this error in its latest and fashionable form. In a very learned and, in some respects, able book,[14] the Rev. N. P. Williams seeks to show that St. Augustine's experience of grace or, what amounts to the same thing, his love of God, was only a "sublimation" of his "lust." St. Augustine was a very passionate man and his passionateness no doubt enters into his love of God. But if it could be shown that the love of God was in St. Augustine or any other of the major saints merely emotion, sublimated or unsublimated, religion would be only the "illusion" that Freud himself has declared it to be. The psycho-analytical divine, who is, I am told, a fairly frequent type in England, is about the worst *mélange des genres* that has appeared even in the present age of confusion.

One may be helped in escaping from this confusion by considering, so far as possible from a strictly psychological point of view, what the exercise of the higher will has actually meant in genuine religion. One must admit at the outset the difficulty of determining what is genuine religion. Religion, not merely to-day but always, has been subject to extraordinary perversions. It has ever been the chosen do-

[14] *The Ideas of the Fall and of Original Sin* (Bampton Lectures for 1924). See p. 331.

main of self-deception and "wishful" thinking. When one reflects on the fanaticism, casuistry, obscurantism, and hypocrisy that have defaced the history of Christianity itself, one is tempted at times to acquiesce in the famous exclamation of Lucretius.[15] Yet one must insist that religion is in its purity the very height of man. As to where this pure religion is to be found, we should keep in mind the saying of Joubert that in matters religious it is a bad sign when one differs from the saints. Let us then turn to the saints in whom there is some authentic survival of the spirit of the Founder. This spirit surely appears in the author of the *Imitation* when he writes: "Know for certain that thou must lead a dying life; and the more a man dies to himself the more he begins to live in God." Moreover the author of the *Imitation* is at one here not only with Christ but with Buddha, the chief source of sanctity in the Far East.

The point on which Christ and Buddha are in accord is the need of renunciation. It should be abundantly plain from all I have said that the higher will is felt in its relation to the expansive desires as a will to refrain. The humanist does not carry the exercise of this will beyond a subduing of his desires to the law of measure; but it may be carried much further until it amounts to a turning away from the desires of the natural man altogether—the "dying to the world" of the Christian.

With this background in mind, we should know what to think of the humanistic and religious claims of the modernist movement. This movement has, from the eighteenth century and in some respects from the Renaissance, been marked by a growing discredit of the will to refrain. The very word renunciation has been rarely pronounced by those who have entered into the movement. The chief exception that occurs to one is Goethe (echoed at times by Carlyle).

[15] "Tantum religio potuit suadere malorum."

47

Any one who thinks of the series of Goethe's love affairs prolonged into the seventies, is scarcely likely to maintain that his *Entsagung* was of a very austere character even for the man of the world, not to speak of the saint. The humanitarians in particular, whether of the utilitarian or of the sentimental type, have put slight emphasis on the inner control of appetite. They have encouraged, either directly or through the ineffectiveness of the substitutes they have offered for this control, a multiplication and complication of desires that is in flat contradiction with the wisdom of the ages. Judged by the standards of the great traditional faiths, the religion of "progress" or "service" or "humanity" merely illustrates on a vast scale the truth of the old Latin adage that "the world wishes to be deceived." The various naturalistic philosophies that have been built up on the ruins of tradition should, at all events, whatever their merits or demerits, be made to stand on their own feet. It should be one's ambition to develop so keen a Socratic dialectic, supported by such a wealth of historical illustration, that it will not be easy for the Walter Lippmanns of the future to propose some form of naturalism as the equivalent of "humanism" and "high religion."

In his attempt to show the inadequacy of humanism apart from dogmatic and revealed religion, Mr. T. S. Eliot has painted a picture of the humanist exercising in a sort of psychic solitude self-control purely for the sake of control. It is evident however that the real humanist consents, like Aristotle, to limit his desires only in so far as this limitation can be shown to make for his own happiness. This primary reference to the individual and his happiness is something with which we are nowadays rather unfamiliar. Our preoccupation, one is almost tempted to say our obsession, is, at least in our official philosophy, with society and its supposed interests. A study of humanism from the sociological point

48

of view would call for a separate essay. I may, however, indicate briefly the main issue: the individual who is practising humanistic control is really subordinating to the part of himself which he possesses in common with other men, that part of himself which is driving him apart from them. If several individuals submit to the same or a similar humanistic discipline, they will become psychically less separate, will, in short, move towards a communion. A group that is thus getting together on a sound ethical basis will be felt at once as an element of social order and stability.

No doubt a still more perfect communion may be achieved on the religious level. There are however differences of dogma and ecclesiastical discipline that make a meeting on this plane difficult even for the various denominations of Christians. If one's survey is extended, as it should be in these days of universal and facile material communication, to include Mahometans and Hindus and Chinese, the obstacles in the way of a union among men that is primarily religious are seen to be well-nigh insuperable. It might, for example, be conducive to the peace of the world if everybody, East and West, accepted the authority of the Pope. The chances of such universal acceptance are, however, short of some very "visible upset of grace," practically negligible. One can scarcely remind oneself too often that the great traditional faiths, notably Christianity and Buddhism,[16] have their humanistic side where closer agreement may be possible. If the leaders of the various national and cultural groups could bring themselves to display in their dealings with one another moderation, common sense and common decency, they would accomplish a great deal—vastly more than they have been accomplishing of late. The difficulties in the way of an understanding, even on this humanistic basis, not to speak of any deeper religious understanding,

---

[16] Confucianism is of course primarily humanistic.

49

have been augmented by the fact that large numbers in the Christian occident as well as in the orient, especially in China, are falling away from their traditional disciplines into spiritual anarchy. The dangers of this anarchy, combined, as it is, with the accumulation of a formidable mass of machinery that, in the abeyance of any higher will, is likely to be pressed into the service of the will to power, are appalling.

The first step, if there is to be an effective opposition to spiritual anarchy of the current type, must be, as I remarked at the outset, right definition. The idea is becoming fairly widespread that there is needed at present a reaction from the romantic movement and that this reaction should assume a religious or a humanistic character. This idea will not in itself take us very far. Even Benedetto Croce, whose philosophy would seem to be in its underlying postulates almost at the opposite pole from a genuinely religious or humanistic position, has declared that we need a "new Christianity" or a "new humanism," if we are to escape "from intellectual anarchy, from unbridled individualism, from sensualism, from scepticism, from pessimism, from every aberration which for a century and a half has been harassing the soul of man and the society of mankind under the name of Romanticism."

Occasional humanists may appear under existing conditions, but if there is to be anything deserving to be called a humanistic movement, it will be necessary that a considerable number of persons get at least within hailing distance of one another as to the definition of the word humanism itself and the nature of the discipline that this definition entails. This preliminary understanding once established, they could then proceed, in the literal sense of that unjustly discredited term, to work out a convention. Their next concern would almost inevitably be with education. Education is, as Professor Gass has remarked, the one altruistic activity of the humanist. The reason is that if the humanistic goal is to be achieved, if the adult is to like and dislike the right things, he must be trained in the appropriate habits almost from infancy. The whole question should be of special interest to Americans. Economic and other conditions are more favourable in this country than elsewhere for the achievement of a truly liberal conception of education with the idea of leisure enshrined at its very centre. In the meanwhile, our educational policies, from the elementary grades to the university, are being controlled by humanitarians. They are busy at this very moment, almost to a man, proclaiming the gospel of service. It will be strange indeed if dissatisfaction with this situation is not felt by a growing minority, if a demand does not arise for at least a few institutions of learning that are humanistic rather than humanitarian in their aims. One is at all events safe in affirming that the battle that is to determine the fate of American civilisation will be fought out first of all in the field of education.

NOTE.—For a humanistic view of the field of education, the reader may be referred to an article by Irving Babbitt, "President Eliot and American Education," in the *Forum*, January, 1929, or to his book on *Literature and the American College: Essays in Defence of the Humanities* (Houghton Mifflin Co., 1908). See also Norman Foerster's recent book, *The American Scholar: A Study in Litteræ Inhumaniores* (University of North Carolina Press, 1929).—Editor.

# The Humility of Common Sense [1]

PAUL ELMER MORE

## I

It is a nice question to ask whether belief in the absolute irresponsibility of the artistic temperament has engendered the modern ideal of absolute art, or the contrary. Which is first, the complacency of conceit or of theory? For myself I am willing to leave the solution of such a problem to the Demon himself, who alone knoweth his own mind; but from the *Æsthetic* [2] of Signor Croce, the most epoptic hierophant of the demonic mysteries in these days, I can see how nearly the two absolutes are related, and can get some glimpse of the procedure of the metaphysical mind at its highest point of activity.

Now Signor Croce, though really himself a child of Hegel, makes good sport of the theoretical æstheticians in the train of Kant and Hegel who define art as pure hedonism, or pure moralism, or pure conceptualism; and so far he does well. You might suppose he was taking the ordinary and sensible point of view, viz., that art must of course give pleasure, and must be psychologically moral (not pedantically so), and must contain ideas, but that it is a false sort of simplification to define art itself therefore *as* pleasure,

---

[1] Sections IV and V of the title essay in *The Demon of the Absolute* (New Shelburne Essays, Vol. I), 1928; reprinted with the kind permission of the author and of the Princeton University Press. Section IV (I, as here reprinted) concerns "The Fetish of Pure Art" and section V (II) "The Fetish of Pure Science."

[2] *Nuovi Saggi di Estetica*, 1920.

52

or *as* morals, or *as* ideas. If such were the motive behind Croce's antipathy to the Teutonic æsthetics of the last century, he would seem, as I say, to be pleading for the liberty of common sense against the absolutism of the Demon; but he too quickly dispels any such illusion. "Art," he declares, "which *depends* on morals or pleasure or philosophy *is* morals or pleasure or philosophy, and not art at all." Now what kind of logic is this that argues: Because art is not pure pleasure, therefore pure art is absolved from the need of giving pleasure; because art is not pure morals, therefore pure art is absolved from any concern with morals? One might as well say, e.g., that cookery which is relished for the pleasure it gives *is* pleasure, and not cookery at all; therefore cookery has nothing to do with pleasure. It is the old story of Luther's drunken man on horseback: prop him up on one side and over he flops on the other. Because one absolute is not true, therefore the contrary absolute must be true; because art which gives pleasure is not definable simply as pleasure, therefore art is a hieratic abstraction entirely independent of pleasure.

But if such a theory of art would seem to be buzzing in a metaphysical vacuum, it is not without its very practical aspect, whether as cause or effect. "The artist," says Signor Croce, coming down abruptly to earth, "is always above blame morally and above censure philosophically." There you have it, the claim to irresponsibility, so dear to our militant gentlemen of the press, vested in the authority of an awesome name. I do not suppose many of our emancipated writers are deeply versed in the thin dialectic of æsthetics, but they understand pretty well what is meant when they are told that in their work as creative artists they need not concern themselves with the ethical laws supposed to govern life or with the dull maxims of truth.

It may be a question, as I have said, whether the great

Neapolitan has risen from the popular lust of irresponsibility to his theory of independent art or has condescended to the lower level from the heights of abstract reasoning. In either case the next step, from a definition by negation to a definition by affirmation, carries him into an altitude beyond the reach of any earthly telescope. Art, he has shown, is absolutely not pleasure or morals or philosophy; it just absolutely *is*—but is what? In the answer to this question I seem to hear no human voice but the very diction of the Demon. Otherwise I cannot understand whence the avowed foe of Kantian and Hegelian abstractions has derived his positive definition of art, which of all abstractions is the most abstract and of all absolutes the most absolute. "Art is intuition," he says, that and nothing else; not the vision of something, mind you, but pure vision. Or, if you desire more words in your definition, you may have it thus: "An aspiration inclosed in the circle of a representation, that is art; and in it the aspiration exists solely by the representation, and the representation solely by the aspiration." Which words, if they mean anything, signify, I suppose, that art is of the spirit of pure creativeness, a reaching out towards a goal which is non-existent until visualised by the very act of reaching out. Such a definition may engage the attention of metaphysicians; in my common-place mind, frankly, it draws blank. I do not comprehend what is meant by aspiring towards that which is non-existent until we visualise it by aspiring.

Croce is the pope of the new school, and as such ought to be immune from the questioning of the lay intelligence. For a more accessible exposition of the ideas stirring the young modernists, I turn to the distinguished critic and philosopher of Spain, José Ortega y Gasset, and in particular to his essay published under the significant title of *The Dehumanization of Art*.[3] Unless I mistake his language, Señor

[3] *La Deshumanización del Arte*, Madrid, 1925.

54

Ortega finds little satisfaction æsthetically in the extreme products of the movement he describes. But he believes that it is not the function of a critic to value works of art in accordance with his own taste or distaste. And especially to-day, when more than ever before it is a characteristic of art to divide mankind sharply into those who comprehend and those who do not, the business of criticism should be to enter into the intention of the artist, and not to judge his work from some alien point of view, least of all to condemn. Well, Señor Ortega in a sense comprehends; he states the various theories adopted by the *jóvenes* to justify their adventurous ways with admirable perspicuity and precision—and with that final confusion at the back of his mind which enables him to speak as one who belongs intellectually to the movement, however practically his taste may lag a little behind its utmost advance.

The central thesis of Señor Ortega's book, which at once justifies his title and summarises the most advanced attitude towards art, is exactly this: "To rejoice or suffer with the human lot which a work of art may incidentally suggest or present to us, is a very different thing from the true artistic pleasure. More than that: this occupation with the human element of the work is essentially incompatible with pure æsthetic fruition." [4]

That clearly is the voice of the Demon once more, appealing to the same lust for an irresponsible absolute as inspires the Crocean æsthetics. And now art is to be not only independent of morals but in its essence divided altogether from human nature; and if it still aims to please, its pleasure is of a kind peculiar to itself and unrelated to the coarse fodder of life. Suppose, to take the illustration given by

[4] *Alegrarse o sufrir con los destinos humanos que, tal vez, la obra de arte nos refiere o presenta, es cosa muy diferente del verdadero goce artistico. Más aún: esa ocupación con lo humano de la obra es, en principio, incompatible con la estricta fruición estética.*

Señor Ortega, a notable man is lying at the point of death. His wife will be standing by his bed, a physician will be counting his pulse, while elsewhere in the house a reporter awaits the news and a painter is engaged to depict the scene. All four persons—wife, physician, reporter, painter—are intent upon the same fact, but with varying degrees of intimacy and with different kinds of interest. To the wife the event is an occasion of grief and anxiety; she is, as it were, a part of it; whereas to the artist, at the other extreme, the situation is entirely divested of human sympathy or sentiment: "his mind is set solely on the exterior, on certain lights and shadows, certain chromatic values." And so it happens that if the natural emotions felt on such an occasion by the wife, the physician, and even to a lesser degree by the news-reporter, are what the ordinary man (the "philistine" or "bourgeois" of the older romantic jargon) regards as the real stuff of life, then art to the ordinary man is removed to a sphere of incomprehensible unreality. "An artistic object," says Señor Ortega, "is artistic only in the measure in which it ceases to be real." Hence, in the scene just described, the actual death-bed and the artist's picture of it are two things "absolutely different (*completamente distintos*)." We may interest ourselves in one or the other; in one case we live with, or in, the event, in the other case we "contemplate" an object of art as such, with æsthetic pleasure perhaps, but with no human emotions. Just in so far as the picture shows any feeling for, or awakens in the beholder any response to, the significance of death, it falls below the high function of art. The tragedy of loss, the frustration of ambition, the humility of surrender, the consolations of hope, the victory of love, the sanctities of religion,—any shadow of these resting upon the canvas will detract from the purity of æsthetic pleasure. The artist and the connoisseur in the presence of death find only an occasion for certain lines and colours. And further, as our power of contemplation becomes more refined, we cease to discern (or, if we are artists, to paint) even the unreal representation of a real event; a picture will cease to depend on, or suggest, any subject whatsoever. For art is like a window through which we look out upon a garden. The ordinary man sees only the flowers and leaves beyond, and is so absorbed in these as to be quite unaware of the pane of glass, the more so as the glass is purer and clearer. But with effort we can make ourselves conscious of the medium through which we are looking; and as our vision is thus concentrated on the glass, the garden fades into a confused blotch of colours or even passes out of conscious perception altogether.

That is Señor Ortega's vivid metaphor for the Crocean theory of art as pure intuition—which he professes to reach, however, by no theorising of his own but from study of the actual practice of certain of the *jóvenes*. For those who believe in the divine mission of art the elevation of society might seem to lie in obeying the command of Mr. Skionar in Peacock's *Crotchet Castle:* "Build sacella for transcendental oracles to teach the world how to see through a glass darkly." It all sounds rather funny to me. But I hope I am not laughing at an unfair caricature. What else in fact is the meaning of those sapient critics, who might join me in repudiating the language of metaphysics, yet insist that in judging a picture we shall pay no heed to the subject represented but consider it as pure representation, or who say that the value of a work of art depends not at all on the character of the human experience put into it but only on the sincerity of self-expression?—as if there were some mystical virtue in self-expression even when the self has no experience worthy to be expressed. It is, in fact, pedantic talk of this sort in the mouths of respected critics that indicates how far the depredations of the Demon have extended into the realm of common sense.

As for the creators, so called, there may be a young votary of art here and there who is trying honestly to put these abstractions into practice; and for him, I should suppose, the goal of dehumanisation and derealisation will have been attained when his pictures are simplified to a cunning design of line and colour with no suggestion of a definite subject, or still further to a spread of pure colour with no design at all; his music to a pure tone without melody or even variation; his poems to a succession of beautiful words unsullied by sense. That would seem to be the nearest practical equivalent to seeing a pure pane of glass. One wonders why the pilgrim of vacuity should be so slow and hesitant in his progress towards so easy a mark. Perhaps he foresees that absolute art, so reached, will cease to be art at all. Perhaps he has a foreboding that the prize if obtained would not be very valuable. It is hard to imagine the pleasure or profit to be derived from concentrating one's attention upon a pane of transparent glass until one sees nothing through it; most of us would prefer to retain our impure perception of the flowers in the garden beyond. Despite the majestic logic of youth we persist in thinking that such a picture as Leonardo da Vinci's Last Supper is a truer work of art than the deftest whirl of colours ever painted; that the *Æneid* is richer in poetical joy than *Kubla Khan* (not to mention the latest lyric from the American colony in Paris); that Bach's Mass in B Minor is still a miracle and a rapture of sound. Yet all these—the painting and the epic and the mass—are brimming with human emotion and with a brooding sense of the eternal values of life. They are great for various reasons, no doubt; but certainly among those reasons is the fact that they are not art at all as the modernists would have us believe.

58

The simple truth is that the effort to create pure art is nothing more than idolatry to a fetish of abstract reason—unless you prefer to ticket it as empty conceit—and could never engage the practical interest of any but a few witless cranks. There is a profound confusion in Señor Ortega's interpretation of what is happening among the mass of the younger artists, as indeed there is often in their own statement of what they are endeavouring to do. They may be seeking an absolute, but it is not an absolute of purity in any sense of the word.

Now I grant at once that there is a difference between art and life, that the attitude of the painter, to return to the old illustration, is not identical with that of the wife in the house of mourning. There is in art a change, a transmutation, a something taken away and a something added. "Art," said Goethe, "is art only because it is not nature." And Aristotle, perhaps, had the same truth in mind in his famous theory of the purgation of the human passions. In that sense we can accept a maxim that comes from Japan: "Art lies in the shadowy frontiers between reality and unreality." [5] The point I would make is the falseness and futility of the logical deduction that art can therefore dispense with the stuff of humanity or nature, or can weigh anchor and sail off into a shoreless sea of unreality. What has actually happened is this. Always the great creators have taken the substance of life, and, not by denying it or attempting to evade its laws, but by looking more intently below its surface, have found meanings and values that transmute it into something at once the same and different. The passions that distract the individual man with the despair of isolated impotence they have invested with a universal significance fraught with the destinies of humanity; the scenery of the material world

[5] *Masterpieces of Chikamatsu, the Japanese Shakespeare,* translated by Asataro Miyamori, p. 48.

they have infused with suggestions of an indwelling otherworld. And so by a species of symbolism, or whatever you
choose to call it, they have lifted mortal life and its theatre
to a higher reality which only to the contented or dust-
choked dwellers in things as they are may appear as unreal.
That, for instance, is precisely what Perugino has achieved
in his picture of a death-scene entitled the Mystic Crucifixion,
where pain and grief and the fear that clutches the individual
heart in its hand of ice have been transmuted into a drama
of divine redemption through suffering, while the tender
burgeoning of spring thrown up against the far-off juncture
of earth and sky gives hints of a mode of existence in joyous
and infinite freedom. Even the lesser creators, those who
in innocence of spirit have undertaken merely to reproduce
what they see, may have done so with a clarity and largeness
of vision capable of working a magic alchemy of which they
themselves perhaps never dreamed.

That was the tradition of agelong practice; it is what
we mean, or ought to mean, by classical. And then, after
the devastating materialism of late eighteenth-century
philosophy there came a change of ideals. The veritable
feeling for the otherworld and for spiritual values was lost,
while at the same time the new school, stirred with vague
aspirations, was not satisfied with a simple and, in its way,
wholesome naturalism. Above all these prophets of the
romantic movement, as we designate it, revolted from the
restrictive rules of an art which was neither classical nor inno-
cently naturalistic, but pseudo-classical, and which had developed from one side of the Renaissance. They too perceived that no great art was possible without escape from
the levelling tyranny of natural law, and, being unable to
transcend nature, seeing indeed no higher reality into which
nature could be raised, they sought freedom by sinking below
nature. In painting, as Mr. Mather has shown with fulness

60

of knowledge and admirable acumen, this process of escape meant "a successive elimination of academic authority, imagination, memory, fidelity to nature, and nature itself. It would seem as if the last sacrifice had been made; but no. In all these rejections and in the most grotesque experiments the painter had retained his seriousness and self-respect. This too went by the board in a brief moment after the War, when the Dadaists bade the artist create in a mood of joyous bluff, meanwhile mocking himself and his world. The oft-repeated demonstration is complete once more—the latter end of expansive Romantic individualism is Romantic disillusionment and Romantic irony." [6]  And the same history might be given of modern music and literature, though in the case of the latter the disinvolution, by reason of the medium employed, is more complicated. For instance the liberation of art from the moral obligations of life, so vaunted by Mr. Cabell and others of the left wing in America as a new achievement, is really contemporaneous with the romantic movement. At least as far back as 1837 we find George Sand declaring that by almost universal consent the arts have become accomplices in this strange tendency towards "amoralism." Now conscientious theorists may hold that amoralism is a step in the direction of freedom; in practice it became commonly a mere euphemism for immorality, not to say vulgar indecency. The climax of the movement in that direction was reached in the realism of Zola and others who, quite frankly and systematically and "scientifically," made human nature coterminous with the bestial in man. Art may have been emancipated from one set of bonds, but it was wrapt and enfolded and constricted in a bondage tenfold straiter. It may have been dehumanised in the sense that it had repudiated the government of reason which to the older humanists was the distinguishing trait of man as man;

[6] *Modern Painting*, by Frank Jewett Mather, Jr., p. 375.

61

it certainly was not purged of its attempt to evoke passions which on a lower plane are *menschlich allzu menschlich*.

As a matter of fact the radical writers of to-day who are accomplishing anything of magnitude are still predominantly of that school of realism. But a few restless souls, those in particular whom Señor Ortega has in mind, driven on by the despotic Demon of the Absolute, have not been content to abide in this halfway house. They see clearly enough that art has not been purified by such realism, but mixed and muddied by deliberate opposition to the ethical interpretation of life; they will detach art from even that poor remnant of deliberation which made a selection among the elements of composite human nature with a certain regard, though an inverted regard, for moral values. They hold deliberation to be the foe of liberation. Hence the later theory, exemplified in English by James Joyce, that art shall not reproduce a picture of life as the humanist sees it, or even from the inverted point of view of the realist, but for its subject matter shall descend to what they call the pure "stream of consciousness." The hero of fiction shall have no will, no purpose, no inhibition, no power of choice whether for good or evil, but shall be merely a medium through which passes an endless, unchecked, meaningless flux of sensations and memories and emotions and impulses.

And so the limit of elimination has been reached—at least the practical limit, since below the stream of consciousness there would seem to remain nothing to represent save bottomless inanity. But this fact is to be noted: though the process of evolution may seem to have been carried on in the name of absolute art, the actual goal attained is an absolute of quite another order; there has been no true liberation, but a progressive descent in slavery. As, successively, one after another of the higher elements of our composite nature has been suppressed, a lower instinct has taken its place. The submergence of the humanistic conception of man as a responsible creature of free will has been accompanied by an emergence of the romantic glorification of uncontrollable temperament; this has been supplanted by a realistic theory of subjection to the bestial passions, and this, at the last, by an attempt to represent life as an unmitigated flux, which in practice, however it be in literature, means confinement in a mad-house. The practitioners of the newest art call themselves *surréalistes*, super-realists; they flatter themselves, they are sub-realists. Art may be dehumanised, but only in the sense that, having passed beyond the representation of men as undifferentiated from animals, it undertakes to portray them as complete imbeciles. To speak of the works produced by the boastful modern school as pure art is, from any point of view, mere bluff. By their fruits you shall know them. Turn the pages of the little magazine published in Paris under the title of *transition*, wherein Mr. Joyce and a group of denationalised Americans and Americanised Frenchmen collaborate to their own mutual satisfaction: you will there find what the Simon-pure article is in theory and practice. For instance a certain M. Louis Aragon,—described by his admiring introducer as "an intellectual on a lifelong holiday, a twentieth-century pilgrim with a pack of words on his back," etc.,—expounds the theory thus:

Reason, reason, o abstract day-phantom, I have already driven you from my dreams. And now I am at the point where they are ready to blend with the realities of appearance. There is no longer room only for me. In vain reason denounces the dictatorship of sensuality. In vain it puts me on guard against error. Error is here the queen. Come in, Madame, this is my body, this is your throne. I pat my delirium as I would a beautiful horse. . . . Nothing can assure me of reality. Nothing, neither the exactness of logic nor the strength of a sensation, can assure me that I do not base it on the delirium of interpretation.

63

And so M. Aragon, concluding "that only the syllables of reality are artistically usable," exemplifies the new style:

> *Ité ité la réa*
> *Ité ité la réalité*
> *La réa la réa*
> *Té té La réa*
> *Li*
> *Té La réalité*
> *Il y avait une fois LA RÉALITÉ.*

Such is the manifesto of Super-realism, "the Freudian period," as the addicts of the stream of consciousness call it, "to the realistic misconception." Their title, I have said, is a pretty mistake for sub-realism; but they are not mistaken in their claim to have reached a kind of absolute. At least I cannot imagine what lower level of imbecility may still be honoured with the name of art.

(If any votary of "pure art" chances to read this essay, he will say: So Keats and Milton were treated by critics of their age.)

## II

One of the hardest things for a student to learn, which yet, if he could but know it at the beginning, would save him from endless perplexities and perhaps from final despair, is just the simple fact that *brain-power is no guarantee for rightness of thinking*, that on the contrary a restlessly outreaching mind, unchecked by the humility of common sense, is more than likely to lead its owner into bogs of duplicity if not into the bottomless pit of fatuity, that, to repeat the phrase of Bacon, himself a shining example, the *intellectus sibi permissus* is the easiest of all dupes for the Demon of the Absolute. There has been no more powerful intellect for the past hundred years than Kant's; I doubt if any writer ever filled the world with more confusion of thought or clouded the truth with a thicker dust of obscurity. And it is in this spirit of distrust, not incompatible with a kind of admiration, that I criticise the works of one who to-day has reached the pinnacle of fame as a thinker.

Professor Whitehead's philosophy spans the double field of religion and science; and in each of these, I presume to say, he has come by the circuitous ways of abstract reasoning to conclusions that in a lesser man would be regarded as preposterous. If such a statement shocks you or sounds disrespectful, take yourself the argument of his *Religion in the Making* and strip it to the bones. You will find that it proceeds from the definition of religion as "the longing for justification," and is directed by the fact that "to-day there is but one religious dogma in debate: What do you mean by 'God'?" Upon this basis, then, Mr. Whitehead undertakes to find such a meaning for the word "God" as will satisfy man's "longing for justification." Such a simplification of the religious problem will strike some inquirers as high-handed, but I let that pass; it has at least whatever merits appertain to simplicity. And I admit ungrudgingly that in the course of his lectures Mr. Whitehead makes many shrewd observations on the deeper mysteries of human life. Memorable passages might be quoted, for instance such sentences as these, that touch the Crocean metaphysic on the quick: "To be an actual thing is to be limited," "Thus rightness of limitation is essential for growth of reality," "Unlimited possibility and abstract creativity can procure nothing."

But in the end how does Mr. Whitehead reply to his own question: "What do you mean by 'God'?" For convenience' sake I quote this summary of his answer from a eulogistic article in the *Hibbert Journal* for July 1927:

All being does this [*i.e.*, "comes to a focus in each thing"] because it is its nature so to do. *This inherent nature of all being is*

*God.* All being does this because it is organised according to the principle of concretion. All being does this because of a certain order or character which pervades it. That order pervading the universe that makes it concrete is God. God is not himself concrete, says Whitehead, but he is the principle which constitutes the concreteness of things.

That is to say, in still simpler language: An individual object is not cut off from the universe, but stands in some relation to all other objects and owes its character to this relationship; this is so because it is the nature of things to be so; such is the law of "concretion," and the "principle of concretion" is God.

Now, apart from the final clause, a plain man might suggest that the argument, so relieved of the obscurantism of metaphysical jargon, is more true than original—true to the point of insipidity. As for the conclusion, no doubt, so left in its native jargon, it comes with the shock of originality; but has it sense? Will any man admit that the God whom he worships and to whom he prays—and without worship and prayer the use of the word "God" is a pure solecism— is no more than the "principle of concretion" in the universe? Has such a definition any bearing on religion as the "longing for justification"? Is it anything more than a phantom of abstract science surreptitiously substituted for the object of faith? The fact is that between the last clause of the argument and what precedes there is a sheer hiatus. It is the age-old fallacy of metaphysics: you take a word used in ordinary speech ("God") with a perfectly clear connotation; you define the word in a manner to suit your convenience ("the principle of concretion"); you prove that there is something in the nature of things corresponding to your definition, and then casually assume that your proof holds good of the word in its popular sense. It is the oft-repeated adventure of the Absolute: you wrap a common-place up in abstract terminology, and then in that fog of language you find yourself precipitated into an abyss of nonsense (that the "longing for justification" is satisfied by belief in "the inherent nature of all being").[7]

But this is by the way. Our present topic is rather Mr. Whitehead's philosophy of science, which is his real concern, and in which the terms "God" and "religion" are manifestly unwarranted intrusions. Here, again, to the student of contemporary thought Mr. Whitehead's *Science and the Modern World* must be in many ways a welcome book. His comments on the connexion between the poets and the physical theories of their day are illuminating and bring to the subject a knowledge not often found in the literary critic. And I for one am much beholden to him for his treatment of the ghastly relic of materialism bequeathed to us by our fathers—I would almost say his indecent burial of it, were the epithet indecent applicable to the disposal of a corpse which has remained too long above ground. And very cleverly he directs his attack to the two points where the mechanistic philosophy is most vulnerable—its apparent simplicity and its presumptive regard of facts.

There was indeed at first sight a seductive simplicity about the theories of Huxley and his militant brothers. It is so easy to say that the world is nothing but a machine nicely constructed of atoms, running smoothly and undeviatingly under the mechanical laws of motion; to deny that anything new or incalculable ever breaks in to disarrange the regularity demanded by science; to dispose of the passions and appetites and the very consciousness of man as mere products

[7] There are passages in Mr. Whitehead's books in which the word "God" is used properly, even nobly, with its religious connotation; and indeed, as Professor A. E. Taylor has shown in the *Dublin Review* for July 1927, part of the difficulty in grasping his argument is owing to this intellectual double-dealing. But in the end the conception of God as a physical law, or impersonal principle, quite wins out.

67

of atomical reaction. It was the kind of simplification that promised to solve for us all the annoying problems of life, exactly the kind of bait that the Demon of the Absolute loves to dangle before a mind unprotected by the humility of common sense. Certainly if ever any group of men had a cosmic footrule in their pockets, it was this particular group of mid-Victorians who married the atheistical philosophy of the eighteenth century to the physical discoveries of the nineteenth. Unfortunately, what seemed a process of simplification has led step by step to such a complexity of adjustments to keep the machine going that long ago the plain man, if he dared, would have scouted the whole conception as a fantastic dream. And here Mr. Whitehead, by virtue of his standing as a mathematician, speaks with an authority for which the plain man must be very grateful. "The physical doctrine of the atom," he says, "has got into a state which is strongly suggestive of the epicycles of astronomy before Copernicus." In all conscience, is it not true that to accept the more recent developments of scientific mechanism requires about the same sort of credulity as was demanded of the theologian in the Middle Ages when asked to debate the number of angels who could stand together on the point of a needle?

And as the mechanistic theory, when used to explain the inner workings of matter, instead of simplifying science, breaks down under a weight of infinite complications, so, when applied to the nature of man, it shatters itself on what Mr. Whitehead rightly calls certain "stubborn and irreducible facts"—the most stubborn and irreducible of these facts being, as every unperverted mind knows, that we are not pure machines, and that any argument which would subject the human will and consciousness to the mechanical laws of motion is void because based on false premises. Against the high-handed assumptions of Darwinian materialism and the fanatical dogmatism of its votaries (relics of which still circulate in the backwaters of the biological laboratory), as against all forms of complacent obscurantism, whether theological or scientific, "Oliver Cromwell's cry echoes down the ages: 'My brethren, by the bowels of Christ I beseech you, bethink you that you may be mistaken.'"

It is the bare truth that one must rake the records of history to discover a more complete and abject subservience to the Demon of the Absolute than that of the philosophy, falsely called science, of the period now closing. And, as I say, any one who clings to common sense must be thankful to Mr. Whitehead for lending his authority as a scientist to the unlocking of these shackles. But then, why should so masterly an intellect, again like Luther's drunken man, topple over on the other side into a contrary but equally impossible absolutism? Why? "The only way of mitigating mechanism," he says, "is by the discovery that it is not mechanism." And so, instead of admitting humbly that mechanism is mechanism while beside it there exists something of a totally different nature, and that the ultimate nexus between these two fields of experience surpasses our comprehension, he must demonstrate mechanism out of the world altogether. In his philosophy there will be no more solid obstinate material things such as go to the making of machines, but only "events." Time and space, which used to be regarded as modes of perception, become internal components of things; value, which used to be a name for our conscious estimation of what we could do with things or for their effect on our spiritual life, now proves to be "the intrinsic reality of an event." There is, you see, an entire reversal of the mechanistic hypothesis. Formerly it was held that the human soul obeys the same laws as a stone; now we are to believe that a stone is of the same nature as the soul. In either case we avoid the discomfort of a paradoxical dualism

69

and reduce the world to a monism which may plausibly call itself science, though as a matter of fact Mr. Whitehead's theory, if carried out, would simply abolish science.

And it is clear enough that the new monism is open to precisely the same criticism as was that of the mechanists which it looks to supplant. Aiming ostensibly to simplify, it really renders the nature of things incomprehensibly complex. Promising to release us from the known paradox of a world composed of two irreconcilable classes of things, it ends by forcing a perfectly arbitrary paradox upon us in its definition of inanimate objects. To define a stone as an event consisting of a bundle of time, space, value, and relationships, does not seem to me to be moving in the direction of lucid simplicity. "What is the sense," Mr. Whitehead asks, "of talking about a mechanical explanation when you do not know what you mean by mechanics?" And the question is entirely pertinent, if by the word "mechanics" we mean slyly to imply something more than the observed actions and reactions of material bodies in motion. Mr. Whitehead therefore discards the "traditional scientific materialism" for an "alternative doctrine of organism," that is, for a "theory of *organic mechanism.*" Well and good. But is it unkind to ask the use of talking about an organical explanation when you do not know what you mean by "organism," or to hint that no very clear idea will be evoked by joining together two unknown quantities, "organism" and "mechanism," and calling the world an "organic mechanism"?

And again, what of the "stubborn and irreducible facts," in whose name Mr. Whitehead attacks the rationalism of the Huxleyites and their predecessors of the eighteenth century? If we are to cast away their imposing structure of logic as unreasonable for the simple reason that, after all is said, we still know that the human mind (or soul, if you please) is something other than a stone, shall we swallow the contrary theory, which has not even the virtue of logic, and which transfers human qualities to a stone? Aristotle made the proper and sufficient distinction long ago, when he said that a stone obeys laws and a man forms habits: you may throw a stone into the air a thousand times and it will continue to do the same thing, whereas a man learns by experience. But alas for those "stubborn and irreducible facts"! How bravely we all summon them to our aid! How desperately we run from them when they appear!

But if this merging together of the animate and the inanimate in a new naturalism makes a travesty of the inorganic world, its real menace is that, equally with the older naturalism, it reacts to deprive humanity of what is distinctly human. The solid objects of "our naïve experience" have been made organic by a kind of relaxation into fluid composites of time and space and value and relationships; they have evaporated into a semblance of psychical events (the very term "events" indeed is little more than an awkward translation of Berkeley's "ideas in the mind"), and the peculiar note of an event is its transitoriness: "one all-pervasive fact, inherent in the character of what is real, is the transition of things, the passage one to another." Thus it happens that the organic and the inorganic worlds flow together in an indistinguishable flux, wherein the soul also, dissolved by association into a complex of relationships, loses that central permanence of entity which used to be held to mark the dignity of man. Nor, if we look beyond, is there anywhere "an ultimate reality" to which we can appeal "for the removal of perplexity," but only an endless concurrence of events. "In the place of Aristotle's God as Prime Mover [itself a conception, one might suppose, far enough removed

from "our naïve experience" into the abyss of abstraction],
we require God as the Principle of Concretion"—not a person, not an entity of any sort, nor even a law apparently, but
a mere name for the fact that concrete groups of qualities
are everlastingly forming and reforming in the infinite
vortex of existence. A cynic might distinguish between the
old naturalism and the naturalism now proposed to take its
place by saying that under the régime of the former true
science might flourish but no humanism or religion, whereas
the metaphysical naturalism of Mr. Whitehead would leave
us neither true science nor humanism and religion, but only
mathematics. The Demon of the Absolute, whether he appears as the advocate of a mechanical fatalism or of the universal flux of relativity, is brother germane to Apollyon, the
Destroyer.

The curious thing in all this farrago of insight and error is
the superstitious hold of the word science on a mind otherwise so awakened. Mr. Whitehead perceives that one scientific hypothesis swallows up another—as indeed he could
not fail to see that his own hypothesis turns its predecessor
upside down; he admits with engaging candour that one and
all they rest on a "naïve faith" which cannot be verified and
is "indifferent to refutation"; yet he clings fanatically to the
scientific attitude as possessing a monopoly of truth and honesty. "When," he says, "Darwin or Einstein proclaim[s]
theories which modify our ideas, it is a triumph for science.
We do not go about saying that there is another defeat for
science, because its old ideas have been abandoned. We
know that another step of scientific insight has been gained."

I suspect that an utter confusion of thought has arisen
here from the ambiguity of a word—as has happened im-
memorially with metaphysicians better and worse than Mr.
Whitehead. Science as an accumulation and classification and

72

utilisation of observed facts may go on from victory to victory; but science as a name for such hypothetical theories of time and space, matter and motion and life, as those broached by the Darwinians of the nineteenth century, or the Einsteinian relativists of the twentieth, is not a progress in insight but a lapse from one naïve assumption to another in a vicious circle of self-contradicting monisms. It really is not easy to understand the state of mind of one, cognisant of the history of thought, who urges us to seek relief from the present *débâcle*—Mr. Whitehead himself places our intellectual and spiritual level lower than it has ever been since the Dark Ages—by introducing the hypothetical method of science into religion. This is his analysis of the present condition of the popular mind: "A scientific realism, based on mechanism, is conjoined with an unwavering belief in the world of men and of the higher animals as being composed of self-determining organisms. This radical inconsistency at the basis of modern thought accounts for much that is half-hearted and wavering in our civilisation." My reading of history is different. I should assert that our vacillating half-heartedness is the inevitable outcome of the endeavour, persistent since the naturalistic invasion of the Renaissance, to flee from the paradox of life to some philosophy which will merge, no matter how, the mechanical and the human together. I should assert that the only escape from our muddle is to overthrow this idol of Unity, this Demon of the Absolute, this abortion sprung from the union of science and metaphysics, and to submit ourselves humbly to the stubborn and irreducible fact that a stone and the human soul cannot be brought under the same definition.

> There are two laws discrete
> Not reconciled,—
> Law for man, and law for thing;

The last builds town and fleet,
But it runs wild,
And doth the man unking.

For legitimate science one may have the deepest respect. But to scientific absolutism masquerading as religion, one may say justly and truly what was said so unjustly and cruelly to Keats: Back to your gallipots!

# The Pride of Modernity

## G. R. ELLIOTT

## I

In European literature from Homer down to Milton and Racine (not to speak of Oriental literature) pride, wrong pride, is represented as far and away the chief of human evils. Such is not the case with the comparatively brief stretch of literature that ensues. Of course there are sharp exceptions to the rule. But speaking by and large recent literature—if that of the past two hundred years may so be termed in view of the long eras behind it—has not held up pride as the towering villain of the human drama. That villain has become more and more shrunken and shadowy. The *hubris* of the Greeks, the proud presumption against the high gods that constituted for ancient writers the crown of human errors, seems now an old, unhappy, far-off thing, quite hopeless for literary purposes in the opening twentieth century. Even more hopeless seems the lineal successor to *hubris*, the Pride that led the seven deadly sins in mediæval pageantry, and doomed the heroes of humane tragedy in the Renaissance.

The surface reason for the fading of pride on our literary scene is obvious enough. Pride used to be considered not only the most immoral but also the most dramatic quality of human life. But recently life, or our imaginative way with life, has assumed a non-dramatic air. The interminable series of the falls of proud heroes and princes, historical or legendary, that runs through the bulk of the world's litera-

75

ture—well, this series seems now to have terminated. Democracy's interest in such personages is lackadaisical. I heard a bright American undergraduate refer to them as "those old guys that used to get bumped off quick." And one must bear in mind that America, if still a bright undergraduate, is widely representative of modern civilisation. Yesterday a remote collection of insignificant states, she is now becoming an international state of mind and, more significantly, of imagination. In this state of imagination the old proud-falling potentate cuts a small figure. Recently, to be sure, many princes have fallen, in fact the majority of them; but they have fallen softly. The downfall of a business corporation is far more noisy and generally disturbing; but a corporation is impersonal and undramatic. As for pride, doubtless some American presidents have shown promising tragic signs of it, but of course these had to be nipped in the bud. A prince, even so powerful and autocratic a prince as the American president, cannot fall proudly and dramatically when he has to fall regularly every four years.

Pride is not popular with democracy either as a vice or as a virtue. Even a just pride in oneself is publicly regarded as not justifiable. Self-esteem must be submerged in party loyalty; and party loyalty, in turn, must whitewash its rising arrogance with humanitarian sentiment, with eloquent devotion to the welfare of men in general. To be sure, intelligent persons dislike the blatancy of this sentiment. Most of them nevertheless are actually in accord with the very heart of it. They wince and shrug at the slogan trumpet of "Service to Mankind," but they quietly salute the flag. They bow in spirit to the reigning standard of "Social Value." Tacitly accepting it as prime motive they deprecate their own self-esteem. They abet the general feeling that pride as the

76

ruler of this world, good and evil pride alike, has modernly been deposed: it is a thing of the past.

This feeling, more than any other feature of modernity, constitutes our break with the past. It has inspired the general conviction that the modern age, so far from being merely one phase, even the most important phase, of human history, has brought about a permanent alteration in the basic conditions of human history. And here again the majority of the leaders of opinion, while disavowing the popular view in its blatant extreme, have been moulded in spirit by the accumulating pressure of it. At the same time our knowledge of the *facts* of the past has continued to increase. Popular biographies and surveys have circulated through a vast reading public. Hence has arisen what may be termed the modern historical paradox. The opening twentieth century has a wider speaking acquaintance with the past, and a fainter grip of its essential reality, than was ever the case before. The past is quite vivid to us, and quite unreal. Its main motif, its pride, is a dramatic ghost.

Recently Lytton Strachey's keen book on Queen Elizabeth and her Essex, and Francis Hackett's glowing story of Henry Eighth and his wives, have made the pageant of the sixteenth century brilliantly alive for us. But in the end the pageant is more a pageant than ever; the past is more utterly past. The scene sparkles along before our eyes in sharp and multitudinous detail. Above all, the persons are amazingly human, as they loom toward us in vivid "close-ups." Yet in the end they are human foreigners. They belong to a remote clime, and our attitude toward them is ironic and superior even when most sympathetic. In fact they seem to us *amazingly* human just because we are surprised that they can be human at all. For the central motive of their lives, their pride of spirit, is or seems to us entirely out of date.

77

Their ordinary desires were the same as ours; we see that more fully every day. But the power of their pride, which swamped or swept before it all those common desires, like the gale that ruled their little sailing-ships on the Atlantic, is obsolete. It appears almost as strange and superstitious, when we pause to reflect upon it, as the spasmodic fits of humility that made those proud ghosts grovel at the feet of their kings and gods. We think we have changed all that.

But so deep-going an alteration in human nature, such a huge discrepancy between present and past, is disconcerting to the mind. It must needs be reduced and accounted for. Our emotional conviction of the obsolescence of pride, like every other strong and persistent feeling harboured by human beings, must needs be rationalised. And the rationalisation is now in progress. Pride has seemed to our imagination very unreal in the present; therefore our reason is demonstrating that it was also quite unreal in the past. Historical science aided by other sciences has undermined the pride of the past. It appears now that proud princes, as well as proud nations and empires, fell of old not by reason of pride but by reason of economics—or the lack of economics. Or else there were geographical, ethnological, biological, or psychological causes. The last-mentioned category is the most effective of all for eliminating moral factors from human history. For example, only an old-fashioned reader may still fancy that Henry the Second, by conquering the violence of his pride, could have refrained from causing the slaughter of Becket. That, to be sure, was the subsequent opinion of Henry himself. But, psychologically speaking, Henry and the old-fashioned reader are mistaken. Henry was subject to certain stimuli and certain complexes that completely determined, and completely explain, his extraordinary behaviour before and after the murder of the archbishop.

78

Emerson, looking back mildly from Concord upon the greedy and murderous pride of old days, found human history very tiresome because it was so very bad. To-day many disillusioned persons are finding it still more tiresome because it seems to them neither bad nor good. It is non-moral, and therefore non-dramatic. Never does it hang dramatically in the fearful balance of the free human will between a false pride and a right humility. It merely moves back and forth like the waves and currents of the sea. History, unhappily, just happens.

Perhaps, however, this ultra-modern view of history, in which pride seems so unreal, is itself the offspring of a very real pride. Modern pride is not of necessity less real than ancient pride just because, so far, its way is less conscious and dramatic. After all it takes time to dramatise ourselves to ourselves; and the modern age, so modernists say, is not yet in full swing. They say that the modern theatre has merely made a beginning and that in the future it will do great things. If so, I would claim that the greatest of those great things must be an adequate dramatisation of modern pride. But we cannot wait for that. If we did, it would never come. It cannot come until there is general recognition of the fact that pride is still the grand protagonist in the human drama; and that under its drab modern dress it has lost not a whit of its ancient sinew.

Pride is most virulent, indeed, when it wears plain clothes, when it hides itself from itself. Self-blindness, not dramatic display, is and always has been the very heart of it. Precisely when pride is most insidious is it least dramatic. Recognition of itself, which is the preliminary step toward cure, is also the preliminary step toward dramatic manifestation. Pride was very dramatic in old literature just because it was unearthed from its very *un*dramatic lair in old human nature. Discovery is the essence of drama. Life is

79

intensely dramatic as soon as its least discoverable motive is discovered, as soon as its "last infirmity," its most hidden pride of spirit, is shown in action.  Therefore if a superficial glance persuades us, as I said at the beginning, that pride has faded in modern literature because modern life is non-dramatic, a deeper search informs us that modern life *seems* non-dramatic because the meaning of pride has faded in our thought.  We need to rediscover the truth of the truism that pride is the most insidious and blinding of all human qualities.  Then we may discover the way of modern pride.  We must see how utterly non-dramatic pride can be before our poets may show us how intensely dramatic modern life is. We cannot envisage the drama of modern life in its full reality, we cannot touch the very heart of its tragedy, until we realise the peculiar blindness of modern pride.

## II

For example.  Some twelve years ago President Wilson announced on behalf of the United States, or was quoted as announcing, that we were "too proud to fight."  Soon afterwards we were fighting, not without martial pride, in the greatest war of all time.  The irony of this sequence was too broad to escape notice.  Yet the notice was comparatively slight.  And the whole matter has faded with ominous speed from the imagination of a public debauched with the most adulterous mixture of pacific and pugnacious prides that the world has ever known.  The Wilsonian remark was easily smiled into oblivion.  The full dramatic irony of the situation, and the tragedy behind it, cannot appear until that proud utterance is recognised, not as the passing whimsy of a single person or party or nation, but as a vivid symbol of the modern spirit at large.  It may fairly be regarded, indeed, as the verbal apex of the whole bad pyramid of modern pride—

the pride of quick and direct solutions, the pride of immediacy.

The basis of that pyramid is religious. No doubt the superstructure owes much to our triumphantly swift results in science, industry, and humanitarian reform. But the pride of practical achievement, thoroughly wholesome in its proper *locale*, would not have formed a modern Babel unless assembled and underpinned by modern religion. And modern religion, while denouncing more and more the various arrogancies of our material civilisation, has not unearthed the deep foundation which it itself has provided for them. As religion is properly the founder and guardian of human humility, so religious pride is the prime evil. We see this very easily in the past. We know that the most blinding and hateful pride that grew among the ancient Greeks and Romans was not the pride of city-state, of empire, of symmetric culture. It was the arrogance of the religious philosophy of the Stoics, their assumption of a pseudo-divine impassivity of spirit. Likewise the mediæval glorification of chivalry, and even of ecclesiastic and theological edifice, is as nothing to modern eyes in comparison with the spiritual presumption that grew in mediæval asceticism. We see how vicious it was for the Stoic to be proud of his pride, and for the monk to be proud of his humility. We have not yet seen how vicious it is for the modern citizen to be proud of being neither proud nor humble.

He is spiritually proud of having escaped from spiritual pride. He believes he has left that historic vice far and forever behind. In his leisure hours he has learned all about it, he thinks, from interesting books, periodicals, preachers, lecturers, travels, historical moving-pictures, and maybe survey courses in college. He is amused and in better moments saddened at the tremendous dramatic display of religious pride in old times,—unaware that this evil never *displayed* itself to the hearts it mastered, nor does to-day. What, then, can he know of real humility? "Why," I was recently asked by a sincerely puzzled undergraduate whose psychological interests had led him to scrutinise certain ancient documents, "why were the old Christians always jawing about humility?" The modern man is conscious, explicitly or implicitly, of possessing a new form of humility much superior to the old. He is proud of his freedom from the fearful self-abasement of his benighted ancestors. He is certain that his own brand of humility, his kindly modesty in relation to nature and to other men, is far more reasonable and real. Reality, indeed, is his keynote. He believes he sees the facts of human nature with a plain and full reality, or immediacy, that was impossible to men of old, distracted as their vision was by the extremes of pride and humility. He has done away with those two "mighty opposites." His realism, his direct contact with life, has antiquated their histrionic conflict. He is superior to that primitive battle in the human breast. He has emerged from that cave warfare into the light of immediate reality. He is "too proud to fight."

And this pride of immediacy, as I have called it, is at bottom religious. It was founded by the Protestant Reformation. More broadly speaking, it grows from that urgent religious revolution still going on which was publicly begun by the Protestant revolt of the sixteenth century. It goes on in Catholic and Protestant realms alike and has many modes, ranging all the way from the glittering wit of French Catholico-Modernism to the rash eloquence of the Protestant pulpits of New York. Revolution it is with a vengeance, not re-formation. And if it be true that the modern intelligence under the influence of science is coming to see the natural need of ordered evolution, instead of destructive revolution, in all human affairs, then we should see this need primarily in religion. Here the cost of revolution is heaviest.

For the mischief of the revolutionary method—namely, that it externalises the issue—is greatest in that sphere which should be of all the most internal. The mental surfaces of religion are thrown into false prominence as the insignia of controversy. Sacred rites and dogmas, through the protective devotion of the loyalist and the pointed hostility of the rebel, are externalised. The imaginative flexibility properly belonging to them is congealed into a stiff surface that hides their inmost meaning, human and divine. Instead of vital human organisms, nourished in their growth and change by something of the divine circulation, they become fixed mechanisms; to be maintained in running order or else discarded altogether—windmills, pumping the living water direct to the household of faith, or suddenly assaulted into junk-heaps by quixotic insurgents.[1] Loyalists and rebels, in reaction from each other, attribute to their own doctrines an impossible immediacy of truth. Thus both parties foster the pride of spiritual immediacy.

Obviously, however, it is not the conservative but the protestant or modernist pride of immediacy that, for the time being at least, has won the day. Indeed it has flourished like a weed in the very midst of our best achievements. The great achievement of modern times is the general realisation that life is of necessity experimental, that change is a constant law for us, and that the human spirit is more important than human customs and institutions however sacrosanct. Hence our pride of freedom, freedom from the past. And

---

[1] Recently I attended on successive Sundays an extremely Catholic and an extremely Protestant celebration of the Holy Communion. The solemnity of the former was injured by the priest's sermon, which evinced the pumping process, the "defence-mechanism," referred to above. At the other service, the mound of bread-cubes that appeared on the table below the pulpit, alongside a pitcher of grape-juice, was suggestive, I fear, of the above mentioned junk-heaps. For the minister interrupted his readings from old sacramental liturgies to explain how much the ceremony rightly meant to his sect, and how much it wrongly meant to the Catholics.

this pride is proper and sound in so far as it is a proud gratitude for the general dissemination of a truth that the great saints and sages, under all dispensations, knew—the experimentality of life. But our pride is rank and noxious when we imagine we know this truth as well as the saints and sages knew it, if not better. To be sure, we know it more widely in a certain sense than they did, having discovered with the aid of science many exterior illustrations of it which were unknown to them. We know it with a wide and superficial immediacy. But they knew it with a profound immediacy.

They knew the basal experimentality of life because they knew it was basifixed. They knew the depth and height of change because they knew the permanency below and above it. They knew the Permanency that does the experimenting, the Changeless that enables us to know change. Of this we have lost hold. And the main source of our modern spiritual catastrophe, the cancerous growth that disguises itself and induces the thronging diagnosticians to limit their attention to secondary symptoms and remedies, is the ancient evil in modern form, blind spiritual pride. The modern imagination has more and more lost hold of the changing Permanency as the modern mind has more and more developed its arrogance of change, its pride of immediacy. This very pride keeps us from seeing the permanence of the law of pride and humility in human nature. We patronise the wise men of old—confident writers on "personal religion" in American magazines patronise them—assuming that when they signalised spiritual pride as the *permanent* root of human ills, they were speaking only for an age and not for all time, at any rate not for our time.

This pride means a false emphasis on "personal religion" over against institutional religion. "Personal religion" now comprises a vast variety of creeds. Many of these are asserted by their proponents, sometimes angrily asserted, to be not religious at all, but they really are religious in the broadest or lowest extension of this term. A few years ago newspaper reporters discovered in a western state a not insane man who claimed that the earth was flat. As to the long story of geodesy, he said it meant little to him, for he had "a science of my own." Nowadays many a person has in the same way "a religion of my own." But this phenomenon, unlike the other, is too popular just at present to have any comic news-value. It would start a public laugh only in the thirteenth or, who knows, in the thirtieth century. To-day many persons who religiously swallow the authority of science, who religiously believe that Einsteinism is true and wish they could understand what it means, reject all authority in religion.

They say that Jesus himself rejected it, and patronise Him as the first of the moderns. They isolate Him from the religious organism to which he was deeply attached; which shaped his principles no less than his images; and through which indeed, during the long preceding centuries of Hebrew history, his sublime nature itself had been (if this may be said without irreverence) gradually "evolved." Thus they affix to Him a singularity no less miraculous, no less disruptive of the laws of human nature and history, than that attributed to him by popular orthodoxy; but far better calculated to debauch with blind pride the souls of his worshippers or, as the case may be, his modern rivals or superseders. They have learned from Him, not wisely but too well, that the Sabbath was made for man and not man for the Sabbath. They hug the false inference which he so sternly and constantly rejected, namely, that man was made to disuse instead of to use the Sabbath, to win spiritual maturity by discarding institutional religion. Jesus discarded revolution. He continued and reformed a great re-

ligious tradition. He made it capable of feeding itself—
and us—upon the best of Greek as well as Hebrew thought.
He made it nobly catholic in the very process of nourishing
his individual soul upon it. He was crucified because he
was more deeply true to it than the modernists, as well as
the loyalists, of his day. Our modernists, however, deem
that his hand was raised and pierced to direct us to bite the
hand that fed us.

The gnawing pride of religious individualism cloaks itself
in the assumption that the individual has transferred his
reverence *entire* from the traditional deity to "the present
God" as Emerson called Him, or to the present Reality as
successors of Emerson often prefer to call It. But actually
that transfer is never accomplished. The reverence never
arrives entire. Always some of it, often most of it, leaks
away unnoticed during the transshipment. Therefore this
exchange is never attempted by the greatest men of religion,
nor advocated by the truest realists or humanists. Jesus and
Socrates both found the "Father's business" in the Temple,
in the moral and imaginative organism of orthodox religion,
and never more so than when they were doing their best to
cleanse it of thieves. They were wrongly accused of an intention for which some of our modern spiritual leaders have
been wrongly praised, the intention of destroying the Temple in order to rebuild it on their own insights, as it were in
three days. No doubt all men of deepest insight are strongly
tempted, in their first maturity, by this pseudo-divine impatience with tradition. They yearn to show immediately
that the Power within them is more reliable than the "pinnacle of the Temple." [2] But they perceive the spiritual
pride of this yearning, its tempting of God, and they forth-
with school themselves to the divine patience. They recognise that the Temple is essential for *their own* fullest de-

[2] Luke IV, 9-13.

velopment. They do not patronise it diplomatically for the public welfare while deprecating it for themselves. They see that the fullest type of spiritual life is attainable only through the unbroken "tension," [3] the constant critical inter-action, between personal and institutional religion, between individual inspiration and a rich tradition. They know that their own humility, like that of the multitudes whom they influence, must grow and bear fruit in the kind of temple that George Herbert saw, the temple which is at once, and mysteriously, within and without. In short, the greatest leaders of the spirit faced the pride of spiritual immediacy and subdued it.

But Emerson did not. He only partly faced it, and he very considerably succumbed to it.[4] He fell, and modern spirituality fell with him. The greatness of this default in so great a man is admitted very reluctantly by those of us who have loved him from youth. When they were begin-ning life, he told them what a happy day it was for the youth when he discovered that "the above" was the same as "the within." He did not tell them that "the within," on the same happy day, begins to leak down through an unseen pride to "the below." He told them that "I the im-perfect adore my own Perfect." He was not careful to ex-plain to them how very imperfect is this Perfect—or else, how scantily It is my own.

Emerson's effect on young men is most significant, I think, in the case of Matthew Arnold. In Arnold's Oxford days, Newman impressed him with a sense of the laborious diffi-culty of spiritual truth. But that sense was considerably soothed and weakened, I think, by the cheery, confident

[3] This word is borrowed from the late Baron Friedrich von Hügel, in whose life and writings the truth of it is powerfully and beautifully illustrated.

[4] His crucial period in early maturity, his "temptation in the wilderness," is examined in my article "On Emerson's 'Grace' and 'Self-Reliance'" in the *New England Quarterly*, Vol. II, No. 1, 1929.

voice that came to him from across the Atlantic; throwing
into contrast the melancholy beauty of Newman's voice and
relegating its religious message to a past which, however
alluring in its beautiful melancholy, seemed now so utterly
past. Arnold lost Newman for religion while continuing
to patronise him for beauty and culture. He did not discern how greatly Newman, on account of his fresh and profound humility, joined with a mind unsurpassed in the
modern age for analytic penetration, was needed by this age
as a "friend and aider of those who would live in the spirit."
Therefore Arnold left the way open for T. H. Huxley to
persuade the oncoming generation, in the blundering pride
of his naturalistic sophistry, that Newman's way with truth
was in the main sophistic.[5] I am very far from wishing to disparage Arnold, as I am accused of having done in previous
papers. It is just because he was so great and influential a
critic, such a fine stronghold of humanism in the midst of the
nineteenth century, that his deficiency in this matter is costly
to-day. His tendency to a certain superior ease, not free
from presumption, in his treatment of religious truth was
doubtless due in good measure to the influence of Emerson.
Hence when Arnold came to America in the eighteen-
eighties he could tell us how matchless Emerson was as a
modern "friend and aider of those who would live in the
spirit" without telling us how deficient this friend was in the
pertinent and prime requisite of spiritual humility.

Just here, perhaps, some readers are priding themselves
on never having cared for Emerson, in other words on never
having been young. But maybe they have absorbed some
jots and tittles of his toxin by way of Arnold and the college
professors, or of Huxley and the scientific metaphysicians,

[5] See the essays on Newman, Arnold, and Huxley in Robert Shafer's
*Christianity and Naturalism*, 1926.

or of Whitman and the current poets. By de-personalising his individualism in a rare and not unspecious fashion, Emerson could send it seeping through an extraordinary variety of individuals. To-day wherever two or three, or two or three hundred, are gathered together in the name of God (modern)—in the name of the Over-Soul or the Under-Soul, of Reality, Nature, Humanity, Hinduism, Good Will, Progress, World Peace, World Religion, Individual Freedom, yes and even Enlightened Disillusion—there is Emerson in the midst of them. To be sure it is but a shade, a distorted shade, of the master. Yet it reminds us what a crooked, widening shadow is thrown forward through the years by a hidden grain of pride in a master mind. Emerson's spiritual pride was veiled by his personal modesty, which was the tolerant deference and flexibility of the modern spirit at its brightest. His luminous nobility of nature and the underlying soundness of his humanism [6] enabled him to give unexampled force and radiance to the proud errors he inherited from the eighteenth-century naturists and the great Romantic poets. It was he, above all, who made naturism seem deeply natural and Romantic irresponsibility nigh divine.

He disclaimed responsibility for his words, yet spoke as one having authority. He claimed the moody freedom of a Romantic poet together with the plain weight of a prose prophet of common sense. He consummated the noxious amalgam that his predecessors in prose and verse had prepared: he *solidly* confused poetic immediacy of experience with the immediate presence of Truth. Admirers, half perceiving his confusion, have wholly excused it on the ground of his unique constitution—just as he did! If gold rust, what will iron do? If Emerson could be vitally yet complacently muddled, what of the Emersonians? If the

[6] See the chapter on him in Norman Foerster's *American Criticism*, 1928.

modern outlook is now confused and unhappy, one reason is that the chief modern sage was confused and at the same time spiritually proud.

The balefulness of his confusion was concealed from him by the subtle mingling of his pride into his modesty. He was too modest to believe that his individual outlook could become a public tragedy, and too proud to doubt that his individual inspirations were universally valid. He attributed these too much to deity and not at all to Rousseau. He disavowed all predecessors and all disciples. In his study or along the woodpath he deemed he was alone with the Soul; never realising how much the thoughts that arose in him were determined by the souls who had influenced his soul and by the souls whom his soul wanted to influence. His solitude of the Soul was thronged with unacknowledged souls. He dislimned them all into deity. His religious predecessors had loudly demolished one religious form after another to leave no barrier, so they thought, between the soul and God. He, the last great Protestant, serenely set fire to the limits of the soul itself. With suave and awful presumption, he melted all souls into God. The outcome is a new barrier between them and Him, a cool, unobtrusive glaze of pride.

The modern pride that Emerson helped so much to crystallise, wears a lucent, modest air. It looks like a lens turned directly upon Reality. But it has the opaqueness of a mirror and is turned upon ourselves—if only by the grace of God we could see our reflections in it. Its surface seems plain, undramatic, when compared with the ancient modes of *hubris*,—until one perceives therein the swarming shapes and conflicts of the modern tragedy.

Dramatic enough is the way this pride, during the past two hundred years, has worked out cogently from its religious centre to its secular circumference, in recent years with catastrophic speed. In religion it has meant more and more a blind emphasis upon the *immediacy* of spiritual values—as though their close presence to Everyman were the same, or almost the same, as his real possession of them. Modern religionists have debased the great doctrine of the Immanence of God and, therewith, the doctrines of divine love, the brotherhood of man, the goodness of the human heart, and the "positiveness" of morality. The results for Everyman are now glaring.

Deity, from Everyman's modern viewpoint, is fast disappearing into human nature; or into that mystic conglomerate of man and the universe which is either called Nature or, as Mark Twain might say, is "the same gentleman under another name." New names are being invented for It daily by pseudo-science. Advanced Protestant theology lies at the proud foot of this conqueror. Forgetting that modern religion at the first did help to wound herself, the more conservative type of theist blames science for harming religion. The up-to-date theist blames religion for not equalling the flight of science, unaware how terribly religion has maimed her wing with pride. A common type of minister deprecates the spread of atheism while confidently advocating the very doctrine that fosters it. If he is shrewd enough to glimpse his dilemma, he can justify himself with Emersonian blandness by pointing out that the abuse of an excellent idea is not a good ground for the disuse of it—the excellent idea being a conceited, facile, and slippery sentiment of divine immanence.

This immanentism has proudly pawed down holy truths to the everyday level of Everyman. And he, finding that when thus muddied they sour the daily bread of his happiness, is now rejecting them wholesale; thereby exhibiting the destructive aspect of that divine justice, that relentless Love of Perfection, which his pastors have hidden behind a gross version of the divine love for men. Our religious leaders,

announcing promiscuously the perfect love that casteth out
fear—a doctrine which the holiest saints approached with
awe—have succeeded in casting out the true fear that belongs
with our imperfect love. They have speciously disparaged
"negative" in favour of "positive" morality. With Emersonian impatience they have shrugged at the *definite* moral
precepts of the ages, as trite and rather forbidding antiquities,
while advocating an *indefinite* moral sentiment, as the prime
discovery and panacea of the modern age. They have
slurred the divine negation, the "Everlasting No," which,
acting down through the poor human conscience, constitutes
the great *unadulterable* factor of positive morals and, in the
end, the most positive provision against positive unhappiness.

This proud religious blindness has opened the highway
for blind secular naturism. The one has played into the
hands of the other; the blind has led the blind toward the
pit of spiritual anarchy. Consider, for example, the quick
succession and interplay of these three phases of the modern
spiritual drama: first, the Protestant notion of immediate
justification by faith in Christ; second, the humanitarian
notion of justification by faith in mankind; and third, the
cynical notion of justification by faith in nothing—except
primitive desire. In the third act of the tragedy, as in the
other two, the leading motive is a specious emotional immediacy fed by subconscious pride. For the Nothing that
modern sceptics are devoted to (its finest dramatic representation is in the works of Thomas Hardy) includes a con-
cupiscent Something by the exercise of which, so they feel,
we may be saved—or at least vitally damned. Hence our
very disillusion to-day is flown with pride. Our current disillusionists, not humbled by the fact that the modern rejection
of moral severity is eventuating in a febrile weakness of the
vital human appetites, continue to disparage that severity
and to advocate, as our only hope, a romantic resurgence of

those appetites. They yearn for a flood-tide between rotten banks; fancying, apparently, that "sinners plunged beneath that flood lose all their guilty stains," immediately. They hymn a spurious Primitive as their Protestant forbears hymned a spurious Christ.[7]

Consider, too, the dramatic inevitability with which the "psychists" and the "legislationists," so to call them, have come swarming more and more into the breaches that modern religion has made in the human conscience. The psychists are proudly animated with the old Sophist hope of reducing that mysterious citadel and of rearranging the whole soul on modern rational lines. They are teaching the oncoming generation to *think* in a fashion indicated in the following remark made to me by a thoughtful youth: "When a fellow tries to do the right thing, he has a satisfaction that seems at the time very real; but of course, as soon as he *thinks,* he sees that this satisfaction isn't real at all." At a recent American congress of thinkers, one of them explained how religion and morality are being taken over and saved, in so far as worth saving, by psychology. He was confident of tucking the setting sun, quite immediately, into his grandstand.

The legislationists, on the other hand, would save the fading rays by immediate public measures, national and international. In a world dim with unprecedented bloodshed, misty with subtle suspicion and self-seeking, and darkening ever more with impiety and lust, they would produce by political or social machinery the lights of peace, good will, purity, and temperance. They are busily wiring a twilight world for incandescent goodness. They would arrest and soften with electric legislation the awful working-out of divine laws. The leader in this project is an ideal figure of

[7] An interesting critique bearing on this subject is "The Modern Distemper" by Professor Ralph Barton Perry in the *Saturday Review of Literature,* June 1, 1929.

Columbia. But under grave scrutiny the radiant figure reveals a good many lineaments of her who was the leader of the seven deadly sins. One recalls with something of a shiver the queenly "progress" of Lucifera in her pleasant twilight—oblivious of the dead men's bones thick under foot and the "foggy mist" all along the way.[8]

Columbia, the progressive modern spirit, is too proud to face the fearful carnage of human values and the foggy confusion of principles brought about by the modern *heart*. Kindly persons after criticising various modern ills, take comfort by concluding that, after all, the modern age is sound and right at heart. But here, precisely, is the source of all those ills. The modern heart has gone wrong. The chief leaders of imagination during the past two centuries assumed that modernity meant a real change of heart, a change for the better; that owing to the long schooling of the past and the new lights of the present, the human heart could now afford to relax its old combat with itself. This assumption is parroted to-day, with varying degrees of subtlety, by preachers, philosophers, educators, youngsters, legislationists, artists, Rotarians, and disillusionists. At the same time they are demonstrating conclusively that the old human heart, unregenerate, is still with us. They are showing its ancient and amazing capacity for inventing new ways of disguising old Duty,—the kind of duty that means a daily, painful, but not inglorious battle within the heart itself. They are showing us how inglorious human thought and art can become, how shallow, cheap, and in the end intolerable, when the human *heart* has become "too proud to fight."

[8] Spenser's *Faerie Queene*, Book I, canto 4. This great poetic fable would be studied in our schools and colleges with deeper emotion if its application to modern pride were not screened off by modern pride itself.

## III

This catastrophe, when fully recognised, can point us to fresh hope and faith. We may win afresh the old faith which goes hand in hand with a certain disillusion, a certain kind of scepticism, foreign to our current disillusionists. This faith, says Newman, "looks for no essential improvements or permanent reformations in the dispensation of those precious gifts which are ever pure in their origin, ever corrupted in man's use of them." [9]

So far, the moral corruption of the twentieth century has not produced the flagrancy of conduct that characterised a good many earlier ages. "My *ideas* of life have become so rotten," thus a Pragmatised and Behaviourised youngster confessed to me, "that I wonder my *life* is not rottener." He looked startled when I told him to give his ideas time. However, it appeared that, partly in spite of and partly by means of his marked self-consciousness, he had attained to some veracity of inward unhappiness. We may hope that his case is quite typical. In other words, our self-conscious modern age has provided a wide and unprecedented demonstration of the fact that the chief danger to human happiness is immorality of *ideas*. Previous ages have done lip-homage to high moral standards while grossly violating them in practice. The modern age has proudly assumed that it has grown far beyond such hypocrisy. Meanwhile it has developed the subtler hypocrisy of cultivating depraved and specious ideas while shrinking from the *full* consequences of them in conduct. The result is that life looks dully undramatic, culture and art degenerate, and thoughtful persons who are harmless enough in their acts have a real misery in their spirit. Surely, therefore, we have now a chance to learn afresh the *inward* relentlessness of the Moral Laws; particularly that

[9] From *Parochial and Plain Sermons*, 1880, Vol. II, No. XXXI.

"precious gift" which we have so bitterly corrupted, the law of humility. We may now perceive that the universal proverb "Pride goes before a fall" is no less applicable to our age than to the old aristocratic ages; and that, far from being merely a maxim of external prudence, it is the folk-sign of an *inward* region of cause and effect that we, with all our self-consciousness, have scarcely penetrated.

We may find again the inward and yet superhuman rigour of the Laws. We may learn that they are supernatural without being ever *un*natural; always immanent in us and yet, in a mystery beyond the reach of our science, always transcendent of us. Browning's Paracelsus, embodying the modern mixture of romance and science, complained in regard to his own catastrophe that "God's intimations fail in clearness rather than in force." Precisely so; but there is no use in whining about it. The human task is to clarify and obey, as well as we can, Laws which we did not invent; which no man, except when stupified by pride—either his own pride or the pride of his teachers, relentlessly visited upon him to the third and fourth generation—can conceive to be merely human inventions.

Those Laws fail in human clearness, certainly, but not in force. They came to send a sword into the earth, more than Peace. They have been the cause of agony and misery for millions of innocent or ignorant people; and no man has succeeded in making clear the full ground of this. From the standpoint of human justice, those Laws are fearfully general, vague, and incalculable. Yet our truest happiness, and indeed our truest originality, depend on a constant effort to elucidate them and apply them afresh to each new generation and individual. This task is of course, in a worldly sense, an impossible one. New sins and difficulties, or rather old sins and difficulties in inexhaustibly new modes, appear at every step. Salvation for the individual never becomes easier; and the social frame is so built, beneath our building, that it cannot be saved. Old seers and new scientists are true to a deep human instinct in prophesying that some day the world will be destroyed by fire, collision, or decay; will "dissolve like an insubstantial pageant faded." Our surest Comfort, at the opposite pole from modern comfortableness and not divisible from right conduct, is in knowing that those Laws, while "ever corrupted by man's use of them" are indeed "precious gifts ever pure in their origin." Clough, that fine religious humanist who faced the modern situation without blinking, had a sound humility when he wrote:

> "I steadier step
> When I recall
> That though I slip
> Thou dost not fall."

The fresh humility that we need must be built up patiently by religion and by humanism; each working in its own way and carefully respectful of the other, even (perhaps *especially*) when these two approaches are equally employed by one person.

Religion is normally theistic, and therewith mediatorial and sacramental. Otherwise she is not catholic and, *in the long run,* loses her right humility. This should be evident enough from the long history of religion, Christian and non-Christian, past and present. Theism decays continually, but by reason of its own sins rather than the virtues of opposing doctrines. Pantheism, deism, and all the others flourish in its decadencies, more or less parasitically, but cannot take deep root in human humility. I do not mean that theism is true because it works, but that it works because at its best it is our truest mode of conceiving the Eternal One. Voltaire's epigram, "God created man in His own image and man promptly returned the compliment," is superb and lasting

97

because the doctrine here parodied is lasting and sublime. The parody is catholically critical because the doctrine itself is deeply catholic. Modernism, when strictly criticising catholic doctrine, is helpful; when frankly rejecting it, respectable; when blandly attempting to reduce it to poetry, baneful—baneful in its hidden pride—and, I trust, hopeless. Not similarly hopeless is Latin Fundamentalism; by which I mean the attempt of Latinised theology, no matter in what branch of the Christian church it appears, to define religious mysteries with a literalism that is too precise to be accurate. Most hopeful is the work of a small and quiet group of theologians, belonging to various churches, who are resuming and carrying forward the thwarted hope of the great Christian humanists of the Renaissance. They are striving for a non-revolutionary, a firm and organic, development of Christian doctrine; that is, for a real catholicity. It is they, studious, ethical, open-eyed, and humble who are rebuilding the foundations of the Temple.

Yet the Temple, or let us say "the church militant here upon earth," is at its best inadequate. The man of good sense has always found and will always find it necessary to take the church with a grain of salt, even though the salt loseth its savour without the church. Good sense is a distinct foundation; and humanism is built upon it. Humanism may be theistic or *non*-theistic; it is unsound when it is anything between. When non-theistic, it falls short of the full truth that is in the human imagination. The pre-eminent example of course is the sublime religious humanism of the Buddha. However, if it be true that the primitive Hindu pantheon had 330,000,000 gods, doubtless the Buddha had several million good reasons for not being a theist. Theism at its worst fosters, as nothing else can, the proud imaginations of the human heart. Humanism, which in one of its most important functions is a criticism of religion, is essential for

98

sound religious humility. Religion needs the humility derivable from the consideration that happiness may be obtained without religion. Humanism is the study and practice of the principles of human happiness *uncomplicated* by naturistic dogmas on the one side and religious dogmas on the other. When religion, as at present, has degraded "God's love" and abolished "God's anger," humanism will insist that the former doctrine (though at its best supreme) is no less *metaphorical* than the latter, and not less subject to unconscious superstition. When religion assists irreligion in softening God's laws, humanism will insist that a rediscovery of their severity is essential for right humility and happiness.

Just here I am forced to express the hope that those estimable critics, Mr. T. S. Eliot and Mr. Walter Lippmann, will at one point counteract each other's influence upon the public. Mr. Eliot, aiming toward humane religion, tends to reduce humanism to a mere balance of mind, a ghost of the Arnoldian culture, subservient to anglo-catholicism. Mr. Lippmann, aiming toward religious humanism, tends to reduce deity to "an ideal of the human personality," [10] a rather ghostly ally of practical morals. Each is somewhat swayed by the modern desire for immediate measures.

Providentially, however, a more catholic attitude has already been erected by two older critics, Baron Friedrich von Hügel and Professor Irving Babbitt—the two most potent and distinguished personalities, though not the finest writers, that have so far appeared in English literature of the twentieth century. The one, a devout Roman Catholic of England, has indirectly done much for the best interests of humanism. The other, a rigorous moral humanist of New England, has indirectly done much for the best interests of religion. Their extraordinary scholarship is guided by a

[10] *A Preface to Morals*, p. 326.

99

sound humility of spirit. In their writings, neither ventures further than his equipment warrants into the other's field, and they do not contradict each other in fundamental points. They agree in the conviction that now, for the sake of religion itself, the way of humanism must be clearly discriminated from the way of religion. Mr. Babbitt has urged that religion at its best is far above, and at its worst far below, a sound humanism. Baron von Hügel has urged that Christians should face now, more frankly and fully than they have ever faced before, the fact that the ethical or humane way has a distinct and *divinely ordained* validity of its own for those who cannot honestly follow the religious way; and that the full health of each way depends upon the health of the other.

This truly catholic attitude, which is essential for modern humility, is not palatable to the pseudo-catholicity of the modern mind. We have fancied, especially in America, that expert reason aided by democratic tolerance could soon discover the underlying relationships between the different ways of salvation, thus federating these in a single "concern," a sort of efficient successor and substitute for the universal infallible church of the Middle Ages. Behind this enterprise stands the overweening assumption of modern philosophy that the universe itself is a single organism with a large variety of inter-assimilable aspects, such as religion and science, love and morals, good and evil, God and Nature. Tennyson would not have been so shocked by his rediscovery of the perennial fact that God and Nature are at strife if he had not been so infected by the modern notion that they ought not to be,—that properly they belong in a universal banking trust whose members, however they may quarrel on the surface, never suffer a real severance of business relations. Nor would our current disillusionists feel so badly about the inevitable dissolution of that trust if their grandfathers had not credited it so heavily. Let us now recognise pride as the grand sponsor of that trust—the pride of unity and immediacy, or of universal "continuity" as the late T. E. Hulme would say. Let us humbly admit that the universe is faulted, geologically speaking, deeper and higher than our knowing. What of ultimate plan and unity its strata may have, God only knows.

Our youths who have learned to smile with a weary superior air at the traditional division of reality into God, Man, and Nature, would breathe more freely and begin again to taste the vital zest of the universal drama, if we would now teach them that this traditional division is *less naïve* than the theory of universal continuity; is better grounded in universal human experience; and, above all, is more truly accordant with the profound division which any thinking man may find within himself to-day when he is sufficiently self-reliant and experimental to plumb beneath the surfaces where our ephemeral psycho-physicisms weave and flutter. Recently humanism, in its attempt to fulfil and deepen the experimentality of the modern spirit, has of necessity placed its chief emphasis upon that inward division. It has insisted that the *opposition* between the higher and lower wills within us, whether they be called "divine" and "natural" or what not, is essentially inexplicable by expert reason and is nevertheless, from the present standpoint of human happiness, the most important feature of the universe arrived at by free and full experimentation.

This humane *dualism* strikes at the very heart of modern pride, the pride of spiritual *monism*. It sets a true immediacy over against a false immediacy. It assigns a central value to the paradox established by the immediate experience of Everyman when he tries (in the terminology of common sense) to be "at one with himself" by keeping his "better self" above his "worser self." It depreciates the expert reasonings and romantic emotions which, overriding that vital paradox of good sense, would leap immediately at spiritual unity and continuity. Consequently the humane dualism, more than any other doctrine of recent criticism, has met with angry rejection or obfuscating comment. A good example of the latter is afforded by a generous and intelligent reviewer who comments as follows upon the dualistic humanism of Milton: "Milton, after all, had not read Darwin; we have . . . Milton's energetic dualism was based on religious conceptions which are genuinely outlived; the power behind his allegory of the soul was his belief that the world was shaped and created for mankind; and, conceiving of ourselves now so much more humbly than he did, we cannot set our lives on such a stage. . . . We cannot invent an opposition we do not feel." [11]

The above, in a representative modern fashion, confuses modesty and humility. The modern modest dogma that the world was not "shaped and created for mankind" has shown itself, when all its implications are considered, no less deficient in real humility than the conceited belief that the world was created for human comfortableness. This belief was far more radically repudiated by Milton than by us. Only with the aid of modern pride can we be sure that his *basic* religious ideas have been "*genuinely* outlived" and that we, having read Darwin, conceive of ourselves "much more *humbly* than he did." He, to be sure, was no adept either in Darwinian or in Emersonian modesty. As a man among men he had strong intellectual and even personal pride. But above it he had true spiritual humility; which may consist with, and derive support from, that virtue too much obscured by modern modesty, namely "self-esteem, founded on justice and right, well managed." This kind of self-

[11] From a review of my book *The Cycle of Modern Poetry* in the *Times Literary Supplement* (London), June 20, 1929.

reliance enabled Milton to assign full value to the moral division he found within himself. His "energetic dualism," as the reviewer calls it, his dramatic sense of the *real* opposition between the nature of lust, pride, and Chaos and the nature of purity, humility, and Peace, was not "based on" transient religious concepts. It was "based on" the duality he found at the centre of himself as well as at the centre of European experience, Christian and pagan. He would have found it also at the centre of ancient Buddhism, if he had known this as we know it to-day. But, says my reviewer, "we cannot invent an opposition we do not feel." Very true. Nevertheless, with the aid of right self-esteem and humility, with a patient critical reverence for what is best in ourselves and in accumulated tradition, European and Oriental, we may not only "feel" but realise, in thought and conduct, an opposition we did not invent.

Only thus can we proceed to a spiritual use of our scientific modesty. Over against the self-flattery of religious superstition, science has revealed the indifference of a vast physical universe. Here is wholesome seed for a fresh humility. But so far its growth in the modern spirit is blighted; blighted much less by the old superstitions which the modern religionist enjoys attacking than by the new superstition which he himself has fostered—the bastard ideal of love. This ideal, religiously derived from an illegitimate mixture of two fallibles, democracy and St. John, infects to-day the blood of many who, rejecting St. John and perhaps also democracy, believe loudly in Sex; or who, tired of Sex also, believe in nothing because it seems the sole alternative to the spurious all-immanent divinity of modern love. This love, though masquerading as powerful and strenuous, is essentially soft. It has succeeded in masking the Cross, not only the Christian but the universal Cross, in soft flummeries. The hard universe of science disowns it. And so does the

severity of the divine Laws. If we learn again to revere
these in their full severity as we find it in history (especially
recent history) and in ourselves, to bow before their awful
beauty with a love that fears to call itself worthy of casting
out fear, then the outward laws can again become real images
of the inward Laws.

Outward nature with her unfathomable self-subsistence,
her rigorous detachment from the egoistic delusions of the
human heart, and her firm satisfactions for those who seek
only to know and follow her laws, can again be seen as a
real though very distant representation of the Divine Nature
itself. The dual nature of man, freed from the intervolv-
ing vapours of old metaphysical dualisms and new metaphysical monisms, guarded from insidious loves, and cultivated with renewed moral vigour, can be seen again as the
isthmus between Time and Eternity: our firm and fruitful
land between unfathomable, unmixing, but not unkindly
seas.

# Religion Without Humanism

## T. S. ELIOT

I must rely, in these few pages, upon a brief summary of the limitations within which I believe humanism must work, which I published in the *Hound and Horn*, June, 1929. In that paper I stated my belief that humanism is in the end futile without religion. Here I wish to put forward briefly a view which seems to me equally important, the counterpart of the other, and one which ought to be more welcome to humanists. Having called attention to what I believe to be a danger, I am bound to call attention to the danger of the other extreme: the danger, a very real one, of *religion without humanism*.

I believe that the sceptic, even the pyrrhonist, but particularly the humanist-sceptic, is a very useful ingredient in a world which is no better than it is. In saying this I do not think that I am committing myself to any theological heresy. The ideal world would be the ideal Church. But very little knowledge of human nature is needed to convince us that hierarchy is liable to corruption, and certainly to stupidity; that religious belief, when unquestioned and uncriticised, is liable to degeneration into superstition; that the human mind is much lazier than the human body; and that the communion of saints in Tibet is of a very low order. If we cannot rely, and it seems that we can never rely, upon adequate criticism from within, it is better that there should be criticism from without. But here I wish to make a capital distinction: criticism, infidelity and agnosticism must, to be of value, be *original* and not inherited. Orthodoxy must be traditional, heterodoxy must be original. The attitude of Voltaire has value, because of its place in time; the attitude of Renan has value, in its historical perspective; Anatole France I can only consider as a man who came at the most unfortunate date for his own reputation—too late to be a great sceptic, and too soon to be a great sceptic. There must be more orthodoxy before there can be another Voltaire. And precisely I fear lest humanism should make a tradition of dissent and agnosticism, and so cut itself off from the sphere of influence in which it is most needed.

For there is no doubt in my mind that contemporary religious institutions are in danger from themselves; that they have with few exceptions lost the "intellectual," except that pernicious kind of intellectual who adopts dogma merely because doubt is out of date. Nowhere is this more obvious than in America. All the religious forms which have some ancestry, and many which have none, flourish there; but among persons whom I have known, there is hardly one who had any connection (not to say any conviction) with any of them.

But America is not isolated in this respect; it merely shows us under a magnifying glass what occurs everywhere. The two dangers to which religion is exposed are apparent everywhere—and they are both cases for which "humanism" or "culture" might be called in: *petrified eccleciasticism*, and *modernism*.

The great merit of the Catholic Church, from the worldly point of view, is its catholicity. That is to say, it is obvious that every religion is effectively limited by the racial characters of the people who practise it, and that a strictly racial or national religion is certain to hold many irrelevances and impurities, from lack of an outside standard of criticism. When the Catholic Faith really is catholic, the aberrations of one race will be corrected by those of another. But it is

106

obviously very difficult even for the Roman Church, nowadays, to be truly catholic. The embarrassment of temporal powers, the virulence of racial and national enthusiasms, are enormous centrifugal forces. The great majority of English speaking people, or at least the vast majority of persons of British descent; half of France, half of Germany, the whole of Scandinavia, are outside of the Roman communion: that is to say, the Roman Church has lost some organic parts of the body of modern civilisation. It is a recognition of this fact which makes some persons of British extraction hesitate to embrace the Roman communion; and which makes them feel that those of their race who have embraced it have done so only by the surrender of some essential part of their inheritance and by cutting themselves off from their family.

But if one feels that the culture of the Roman Catholic Church to-day is imperfect—and also in danger of splitting up into various local and national bigotries and political factions which will retain only the name and the observances of catholicism—one cannot get any satisfaction from what happens outside of that church either. The Roman Church in America has little contact with some of the most valuable elements in American culture; it not only lacks humanism, but is in danger of adding vulgarity. In England it is negligible. But both in England and America, Protestantism is in still worse case. It can be, and usually is, equally vulgar; it can be equally narrow and bigoted; with the alternative that when it is not narrow and bigoted it is liberal, sloppy, hypocritical and humanitarian. The Roman Church is dangerous in one direction; the Protestant Churches are dangerous in two directions.

I have already said what I think of humanism without religion; I respect it, but believe it to be sterile. Religion without humanism produces the vulgarities and the political compromises of Roman Catholicism; the vulgarities and the fanaticism of Tennessee; it produces Mrs. MacPherson; and it produces liberal uplift; and it produces the Bishop of Birmingham. For it is the chief point of this short paper, that religion without humanism produces the opposite and conflicting types of religious bigotry (liberalism in religion is a form of bigotry). We have Cardinal O'Connell; the late W. J. Bryan; and we have the cultivated divines of the most radical wing of Unitarianism. The sum of *disjecta membra* is completed by the humanists.

I have examined several popular theological works by Anglican clergy of the liberal school.[1] It would I am sure be difficult to convince any of these worthy people that they were humanitarian without being humanist. Humanitarians (and among them we must include anti-humanitarians like Dean Inge, a sentimentalist *à rebours*) are often highly cultivated people who have read many books; some of them, in England at least, can read Latin and Greek; the Bishop of Birmingham took honours in mathematics. Yet in surrendering dogmatic faith they are at the same time surrendering their humanism. It is from such people that we hear most about "science and religion"; it is such people who pay, and lead the flock to pay, that exaggerated devotion to "science" which the true humanist deplores.

It is curious that whilst on the one hand the liberal theologian tends to pay homage to an illusory divinity called "science" the advanced scientist tends to pay homage to an equally vague "religion." People seem to suppose that by science yielding points to religion, and religion yielding points to science, we shall quite soon arrive at a position of comfortable equilibrium. What will be "real" will be the technical progress of science, and the material organisation

[1] E.g., *Should Such a Faith Offend?*, by the Bishop of Birmingham; *I Believe in God*, by Maude Royden; *The Impatience of a Parson*, by H. R. L. Sheppard.

of the churches: we shall still have professors of physics and we shall still have clergy, and nobody will lose his job. Scientists and clergy alike seem to speak nowadays as if they were in terror of the spectre of unemployment: "I will not make exaggerated claims," they both seem to say, "lest I may be discovered to be superfluous."

But this apparent approximation of science and religion, which we discover in such theological works as those I have mentioned, and in such popular scientific works as those of Whitehead and Eddington, is a delusion. The meeting is a mere cancellation to zero. Nothing positive is attained by reciprocal surrender. The theologian says "of course dogma is not truth," and the scientist says, "of course science is not truth." Every one is happy together; and possibly both parties turn to *poetry* (about which neither scientist nor theologian knows anything) and say "*there* is truth, in the inspiration of the poet." The poet himself, who perhaps knows more about his own inspiration than a psycho-analyst does, is not allowed to reply that poetry is poetry, and not science or religion—unless he or some of his mistaken friends produce a theory that Poetry is Pure Poetry, Pure Poetry turning out to be something else than poetry and thereby securing respect.

Both parties, the liberal theologian and the scientist, are deficient in humanism. But what is more serious, to my mind, is that the humanist is deficient in humanism too, and must take his responsibility with the others. What happens, in the general confusion, is not only that each party abdicates his proper part, but that he interferes with the proper part of the others. The theologian is terrified of science, and the scientist is becoming terrified of religion; whilst the humanist, endeavouring to pay proper, but not excessive due to both, reels from side to side. And the world reels with him.

On the following point I speak with diffidence, recognising my lack of qualification where qualification is severe and exact. Humanism has much to say of Discipline and Order and Control; and I have parroted these terms myself. I found no discipline in humanism; only a little intellectual discipline from a little study of philosophy. But the difficult discipline is the discipline and training of emotion; this the modern world has great need of; so great need that it hardly understands what the word means; and this I have found is only attainable through dogmatic religion. I do not say that dogmatic religion is justified because it supplies this need—that is just the psychologism and the anthropocentrism that I wish to avoid—but merely state my belief that in no other way can the need be supplied. There is much chatter about mysticism: for the modern world the word means some spattering indulgence of emotion, instead of the most terrible concentration and askesis. But it takes perhaps a lifetime merely to realise that men like the forest sages, and the desert sages, and finally the Victorines and John of the Cross and (in his fashion) Ignatius really *mean what they say*. Only those have the right to talk of discipline who have looked into the Abyss. The need of the modern world is the discipline and training of the emotions; which neither the intellectual training of philosophy or science, nor the wisdom of humanism, nor the negative instruction of psychology can give.

In short, we can use the term Humanism in two ways. In the narrower sense, which tends always under emphasis to become narrower still, it is an important part in a larger whole; and humanists, by offering this part as a substitute for the whole, are lessening, instead of increasing, its importance; they offer an excuse to the modern theologian and the modern scientist (only too ready to grasp it) for *not* being humanistic themselves, and for leaving humanism to its own specialists. Humanism can offer neither the intellectual discipline of philosophy or of science (two different disciplines), nor the emotional discipline of religion. On the other hand, these other activities depend upon humanism to preserve their sanity. Without it, religion tends to become either a sentimental tune, or an emotional debauch; or in theology, a skeleton dance of fleshless dogmas, or in ecclesiasticism, a soulless political club. Without it, science can be merely a process of technical research, bursting out from time to time, and especially in our time, into sentimental monstrosities like the Life Force, or Professor Whitehead's God.

But in the full and complete sense of the word, Humanism is something quite different from a part trying to pretend to be a whole, and something quite different from a "parasite" of religion. It can only be quite actual in the full realisation and balance of the disciplined intellectual and emotional life of man. For, as I have said, without humanism both religion and science tend to become other than themselves, and without religion and science—without emotional and intellectual discipline—humanism tends to shrink into an atrophied caricature of itself. It is the spirit of humanism which has operated to reconcile the mystic and the ecclesiastic in one church; having done this in the past, humanism should not set itself up now as another sect, but strive to continue and enlarge its task, labouring to reconcile and unite all the parts into a whole. It is the humanist who could point out to the theologian the absurdities of his repudiation, acceptance, or exploitation of "science," and to the scientist the absurdities of his repudiation, acceptance, or exploitation of religion. For when I say "reconcile," I mean something very different from the dangerous and essentially anti-humanistic adventures of the Bishop of Birmingham or Professor Whitehead. And let us leave Einstein alone, who has his own business to attend to.

As I believe I am writing chiefly for those who know or think they know, what "humanism" means, I have not in this paper attempted any definition of it. I take it that the reader thinks he knows what it means, and that he will understand that I am putting before him the difference between what I think he thinks it means and what I think I think it means.

I have just one note to add, which is the preface to an extensive sequel. I believe that at the present time the problem of the unification of the world and the problem of the unification of the individual, are in the end one and the same problem; and that the solution of one is the solution of the other. Analytical psychology (even if accepted far more enthusiastically than I can accept it) can do little except produce monsters; for it is attempting to produce unified individuals in a world without unity; the social, political, and economic sciences can do little, for they are attempting to produce the great society with an aggregation of human beings who are not units but merely bundles of incoherent impulses and beliefs. The problem of nationalism and the problem of dissociated personalities may turn out to be the same. The relevance of this paragraph to what precedes it will, I hope, appear upon examination.

# The Plight of Our Arts

## FRANK JEWETT MATHER. Jr.

### I

Any expression of a humanistic society through the arts depends upon the acceptance by the artist of some sort of central authority. The authority is not that of official organisations or written codes; it is rather that of approved traditional ideals in which both the artist and the laity believe. In their application to the work of art, such ideals appear concretely as accredited conventions. In a humanistic society, these conventions assume no burdensome or arbitrarily authoritative form. They represent merely a body of successful experience—ways that have been tried and found good. The accepted convention tells the artist how he must begin; it does not tell him how he must end. It does, however, warn him off from any too abrupt breaking with tradition, and from any too urgent assertion of his individual taste save in so far as that taste finds sanction in precedent and in opinion other than his own. Right here is the stone of stumbling. The humanist artist willingly admits that his own genius is not his final authority. He checks its impulses by the practice and teaching of other geniuses, and by the degree of acceptance which its expression commands from competent criticism and patronage. It is not enough that he shall have expressed just himself; it matters quite as much that he shall have communicated himself to a fit public with whom he shares a confidence in the guiding conventions of his art and in ideals mutually honoured.

On the side of the artist, this relation will indicate a procedure of delicate adjustment. The accepted conventions of
his art and the ideals of the society for which he works, will
of course not fit him precisely any more than a ready-made
suit fits perfectly either the artist or layman. The practical
problem of the humanist artist, then, will be how far he
shall reshape himself to the expectations of his public; and
how far he may change these expectations in a sense favourable to his individual bent. And this implies chiefly a very
superior sort of judgment and common sense. The humanist artist will feel that it is a vain thing to have expressed
himself, however gorgeously, if nobody knows that he has
expressed himself, and he will also admit that the mere feel-
ingful and urgent self gains richness and value only when
it is measured by other selves in society.

On the side of society and patronage, a humanised art
would imply in practice a central authority lightly and genially imposed, a just offishness towards the artists who too
overtly repudiated the tradition, withal a somewhat sceptical
hopefulness towards experiment and innovation, a hospitable
desire to understand the artist even when his communication
is obscure, a wish to have its own ideals expressed through
the arts. In short a humanised society co-operates with the
artist to a degree difficult even to imagine to-day. It provides him with incentive, furnishes most of his æsthetic notions, helps him to realise himself through opportune criticism and companionship, thus taking an active part in what
is the essential thing—the formation of his spirit.

So far I have dealt in convenient abstractions which are in
part misleading. I have made the reciprocal relation between the artist and public too conscious, much more conscious than it has been in history. I shall presently try to
correct the error by appealing to precedents concretely in
given time and place. However, the over-emphasis on con-

sciousness as producing mutuality between artist and public may well be pragmatically justified. It seems unlikely that our society will simply gravitate towards humanism. On the contrary, if we are to achieve a humanistic social balance, it will apparently be done only through much taking of thought, on the part of both the enlightened laity and the intelligent artist. So the analysis I have tried to make of the mutually helpful relation of artist and layman in a humanised world, though it overstresses the conscious element in this reciprocity in seeming disregard of past history, may for that very reason suggest a programme for history yet to be realised.

Programmes, however, are entirely valueless except as they rest soundly on dynamic states of mind. Our problem as humanists is to create a state of mind in which neither artist nor layman will exaggerate the worth of his idiosyncrasy, nor yet follow the general drift unthinkingly. We are trying to make a man who is a friendly critic both of himself and of the society in which he moves, a man who accepts the growing complexity of living as offering him fascinating and profitable problems of adjustment. To maintain this hope in the face of the chicken-and-lobster-eating motorist, the radio fan, the devotee of the "talkies," the sycophant artist who bows to base authority, and the behaviourist artist who admits none but that of his own glands —to keep the hope of making humanists in the face of the daily American spectacle requires an audacity which even the Expressionist might envy. But we contributors to this symposium have actually seen a few humanists made, have helped a little to make them perhaps; and we are dealing with spiritual values which transcend ordinary statistics. A few thousand genuine humanists in America would make our society humanistic; a hundred humanist painters, sculptors, architects, musicians, and men of letters would make our art solidly humanistic. In this hope we keep our tiny banner up beside the hoardings that promise to beautify our teeth, remove our corns, clothe our bodies appealingly, or incase the relentlessly exposed legs of our women in silk as durable as filmy.

## II

That adjustment between artist and layman which seems so difficult to-day, until the seventeenth century and the beginning of modern times came of itself and in some such fashion as this—it hardly matters whether the scene be Italy, Spain, France, England, China, Japan, India, or Persia: in every case the basis was fine craftsmanship. Pretty much all objects of common use were delicately conceived and carefully made. The amateur of to-day gladly pays great prices for the ordinary grave figurines and temple vessels of China, for the horse trappings of the Scythians, for the common household gear and even the workman's tools of the European Middle Ages and Renaissance, for the comfit boxes and carved fobs of feudal Japan, for the peasant furniture of Brittany and Scandinavia. This general high level of craftsmanship depended chiefly on the fact that even the humblest craftsman was also a designer. To the joy of fit execution was joined that of successful invention.

A very few craftsmen became what we now call artists,—that is made finer inventions on a more impressive scale, designed a cathedral or a palace instead of a simple house, decorated an entire chapel instead of a bride chest or tournament shield, made a bronze statue instead of a chiselled ink stand. But the line between the craftsman and the artist was not a sharp one. At Florence a Donatello belonged to the Stonecutters Guild and officially was merely a very highly esteemed stonecutter. And every future artist entered upon his career as a simple apprentice in a craft. The tragedy and frustration so common in the artists' career to-day were absent. The apprentice with only a fine craftsman's endowment lived out his life contentedly as a craftsman. But he was free, had he the ability, to become an artist and to achieve the companionship of princes.

The step from craftsman to artist lay really in the artist's intelligent assimilation of greater subject matter or in his fuller expression of subject matter common to artist and craftsman alike. Such subject matter was furnished him by his ecclesiastical and temporal betters; he did not invent it. There was no hardship in this imposition, for the values of his betters were also his own. There was a like-mindedness and real co-operation between artist and patron. A romantic and sentimentally individualistic criticism has challenged this case. No person who knows either history or human nature, however, will hold that Giotto was hampered because he had to paint the legends of Saint Francis and those of the Virgin; that Raphael was great in spite of the fact that he had to find symbols for syncretic theology; that Hogarth is belittled by the fact that he so genially followed the literary, satirical current of his age. A humanistic criticism will hold, on the contrary, that an essential factor in the greatness of these artists was that, their themes coming almost ready made, they were spared the waste and perturbation of so-called original invention and were free to face in tranquillity their real problem of transformation and execution.

To recapitulate: the craftsman, until at most a couple of centuries ago, depended on a universal taste for the well-made thing, while the artist depended on the taste of a minority, the taste of an aristocracy with which he himself felt in harmony. The few remaining fine craftsmen of to-day find no general taste for the well-made thing upon which they may depend, while the myriad artists of to-day face no aristocracy whatever, no accepted body of taste whatever, but rather a congeries of pseudo-aristocracies each with its shifting preferences, which hardly deserve the name of tastes at all.

How the isolation of the artist with the virtual extinction of the craftsman has come about is a commonplace of history which need be recalled here only in its broad lines. The factory within a century has done away with the craftsman designer. Still earlier the crumbling of the old aristocracy of birth and religion at once put an end to community of taste at the top, and gave exaggerated scope to the already strongly rising ideal of originality and individuality as highest æsthetic values. A stable and spiritually profitable patronage ceased and was succeeded by a capricious and heavy handed patronage from a new wealth undisciplined either by tradition or by fine and broad personal experience. The artist's immemorial task of realising himself in society became almost impossibly difficult. If he were weak and clever, his resort was to sycophancy; if he were strong and wise, there was little for him but patience, resignation, and a tragic hopefulness; if he were strong and unwise, he became a rebel. And the rebel, in a manner perfectly familiar to the neurologist, built up his compensations, by which he extolled that isolation which was really his sore misfortune as his superiority and his advantage, until after three generations it has become a common conviction among artists that their proper task is self-expression in a void, that there should be no desire to communicate and, obviously, no need to be understood.

And just at the moment when the position of the artist was becoming barely tenable, the number of artists increased inordinately. The craftsman who didn't want to go into a factory but wanted to use his head and hands delicately, had to become an artist, while wholesale methods of education in the practice of art made the way to becoming an artist easy to any young person with a modicum of money and diligence. As if that were not enough, the false glamour thrown about the artist life by romantic poets and novelists brought new hordes of the unfit to join the bewildered survivors from the old régime.

### III

Now, any going back to the conditions of the Middle Ages or to those of the Renaissance is of course impossible; but if craftsmanship and art are again to become normal functions in a helpful social order, the old formulas, at least in principle, must hold. There will be no generally fine craftsmanship until most people want well-made things and get them from craftsmen who design; and the so-called fine arts will have no general importance until there are many patrons with a common bond of taste which is sympathetic to most artists. Is there anything which promises so desirable a reconstruction?

On the side of craftsmanship, I fear nothing is to be expected. The gallant counter-attacks of a John Ruskin and a William Morris against modern industrialism show just how much and how little can be gained from a militant reaction. A hundred passionate spinsters are printing batiks or glazing pottery in as many æsthetic last ditches, but they are mostly doing so at the expense of rich and generous eccentrics, in short are merely subsidised artists disguised as craftsmen. We are getting better designed things from the factory—the museums are working usefully to this end—but this reform only enlists a handful of professional designers, and does nothing to produce the old type of creative craftsman. In short we probably must say good-bye to the craftsman save as a picturesque survival, like the man who is skilful with the rapier or the long bow. All we can hope for is that some improvement in the general taste, which I think is reasonable to look for,—since for a century it could hardly have been lower,—may cause a discriminating demand for better designed factory goods. This of course leaves the problem of the artist and the craftsman just where it was, with the sole difference that the passing of the craftsman shuts off the possibility of any return of the artist to his traditionally best school, the shop of a good craftsman.

So if there is to be any useful rebuilding, I feel it must proceed after the very modern precedent of the skyscraper, from the top down. Much might conceivably be done to produce a more coherent and intelligent patronage for the fine arts, much is already being done by museums, art dealers, colleges and universities, and all manner of art societies. Indeed the increased activity of museums, collectors, and colleges in behalf of the acquisition and appreciation of fine works of art has persuaded Mr. R. C. Duffus that we are well launched on an American Renaissance, and to that effect he has published a very interesting book. Far be it from me to minimise the importance of activities in which I have been and am deeply engaged myself. One may gladly admit that to multiply our art treasures—and for a generation the multiplication has been astoundingly accelerated—is in itself an unqualified benefit. But the mere accumulation of great works of art and much talk about them does not imply understanding of them, and the question the humanist must raise is always—Are these masterpieces understood? And how are they understood? Mediæval Rome lay in full artistic decadence when much of the glory of her old art was visible on every hand. To understand any nobly conceived work of art, one must have lived nobly in deed, in imagination, or in both. To own a great work of art may be a mere counsel of personal vanity; to expound a work of art, a mere assertion of self-importance. A whole school of interpretation, which has its faculty, museum, and journal, tears the work of art from its human context and studies its forms as if these were ends in themselves. And this sort of teaching is popular. Along such lines one may make a generation of resolute pedants. For the humanist such teaching is not merely defective but positively harmful. On the other side, there is much sound and modest teaching, and the next generation of art patrons will be far better trained than that which is passing.

Yet all such useful activities are simply marginal. Without a predisposition in its visitors, the museum might just as well be unvisited, since it then has no more dignity or value than the peep show. It is a proper uneasiness before flattering statistics of attendance that has rightly induced our museums to inaugurate direct instruction in appreciation. It is a weakness and limitation of such teaching that it too often merely foments a diffused interest in art taken as an entity and not as related to human values generally. For appreciation really requires a right and balanced attitude towards life. It was really more important for Florence that her great citizens, while bowing to the glory that was Greece and the grandeur that was Rome, wanted a full and honourable life in Florence—it was really more important, I say, that they cared discriminatingly for the dignity of their ordinary activities and for the authority of their faith, than that they cared *specifically* for painting, sculpture, and architecture.

In short some aristocratic vision of the good life has always been the foundation on which great national art has been reared in the past. It behooves us then to ask what is in America our accepted vision of the good life? For upon it must rest our art. What do we all agree to (saving always negligible minorities of "knockers")? I fear it would come to these few articles of faith:—to make a lot of money by fair means; to spend it generously; to be friendly; to move fast; to die with one's boots on. This is a credo which has within its limitations positive merits, and it is by no means lightly to be decried, but it palpably offers little spiritual nourishment to the "art-artist," to quote a recent mayor of New York. A certain kind of art it feeds admirably. And it naturally gets the art it feeds—the immaculate bank clerk in campus clothes, the sylph-like apparition in the porcelain tub, the beach party in the classy car—the art of the advertisement generally. And this ideal also finds its authentic expression in the cheap heroics and shallow idealisms of the moving picture, and the potpourri of dubious music and eloquence over the radio. These are our representative arts, as sculpture was the representative art of Greece, or painting of Florence.

The prospect is more pleasing when we turn to architecture, really the only art that is perennial. Here there is at least a great progress, a far higher level of taste than that of a generation ago, a competent and audacious coping with unprecedented problems. Yet here as elsewhere the cult of haste works harm. No architect of a skyscraper is given time to think his building out. Perfection in the arts rests largely on trifles lovingly meditated, and what successful architect has time for meditation? We have in abundance such arts as we deserve, and we shall have better arts only as we deserve them through better ideals of life generally.

Painting and sculpture are kept alive by a sort of artificial respiration. It is to be hoped that the increasing public use of both in decoration may restore to these traditionally leading arts a fuller measure of vitality. As it is, these arts have joined fine craftsmanship as an elegant survival, like fencing or court tennis. Since painting and sculpture are the arts I most love, it would be pleasant indeed to come forward with a programme for their rehabilitation. But I have no such programme. I feel rather that we should at once accept the situation and emphasise it. The only remedy, and a partial one at that, is, I think, this: since painting and sculpture have become exotic, relatively unwanted, and subsidised arts, let us rebuild on their rarity value. If instead of making it ridiculously easy to learn painting and sculpture, we made it difficult, we should probably have better painting and sculpture. This could be done by withdrawing charitable support from the art schools, keeping open such as reasonably pay their way, and by suspending the artificially encouraged salesmanship of painting and sculpture. There would remain the human problem of what to do with the thousands of young men and women who legitimately wish to work delicately with their hands; but in a civilisation that is supplied from the factory, that problem seems insoluble. And withal there may be a satisfactory outlet in amateurism—this has happened notably in the art of the theatre at the very moment when the moving picture seemed to announce the end of the spoken play. In general I am not discouraging the support of survivals. Indeed I see in such support a singularly sympathetic act of patronage. But one should know what he is about. I have, for example, a predilection for the quill pen, but I should be very unwise to endow an institution for writing with the quill. And we are very unwise in America when, not really wanting their works, we artificially multiply painters and sculptors.

Whatever reform comes from within the arts, will probably not come from carefully fostered survivals nor yet from conscious revivals, but rather from the response of the wanted arts to a finer demand. The comic strip and the moving picture seem barometric to me, as does illustration for advertising. Whenever I see a marked improvement in these popular arts, I shall expect to find greater improvement in the traditional fine arts of sculpture, painting, and architecture. And while I am only a casual observer of these barometric arts, what I have observed of design for advertis-

ing and of the moving picture does not cause me either to
hope unduly nor yet to despair utterly. Certainly both have
improved much within my experience. There remains the
dilemma: can the democratic arts really acquire distinction,
that solicitude for perfecting trifles which we have already
remarked, or must they stop at a certain level simply because
they are democratic arts? It would be hazardous to answer
this question, but historically no democratic art, with the
possible exception of engraving, has as yet transcended fine
craftsmanship and successfully invaded the realm of great
ideas. That realm has without exception been occupied by
the arts that were frankly aristocratic.

## IV

Our desired rehabilitation of the traditional and also of
the new arts may in the last analysis depend upon the creation *within* our democracy of the right sort of an aristocracy.
Here we are back to the central problem of humanism—
how to produce a superiority that is generally accepted and
socially available. If we can make such an aristocracy, it
will foster the artist and the arts justly and generously; it
will provide a world in which the creative artist is no longer
a tolerated alien but solidly at home. Whenever such an
aristocracy has a clear and noble vision of the good life, it
will want symbols for its ideals, and will call upon the only
man who can provide such symbols—the artist.

One would like to think that the oncoming generation,
with unparalleled advantages in museums and in collegiate
instruction in art, endowed with a great open-mindedness,
audacity, and hopefulness—one would like to think, I say,
that this young generation will provide the needed humanistic support for art. But association with youth, delightful
as it is, gives me no very clear hope in any humanistic direc-

tion. The most typical and engaging youths and maidens of to-day illustrate merely the lovelier and more attractive traits of the barbarian. They have an unlimited confidence, very beautiful in its way, with the smallest background of lived or imagined experience. They think life is so simple that they may ignore all the traditional solutions for its manifold problems, trusting to their own instinct of the moment to meet emergencies that have engaged the best wits of generations of sages and saints. We have, characteristically tinged with humanitarianism, the mentality of the noble bandit sheik or the generous sea rover, who knows what he wants and asks nothing from tradition or authority. To make humanists of this generation of self-elected spiritual adventurers implies preliminary contrition and moral rebuilding. There was a better chance really of making humanists out of my own somewhat over-sophisticated and *fainéant* generation. At least we started from the sound postulate that life was complex, and the problem of living a problem of delicate adjustment in which one needed whatever help he might draw from any time or source. So I am really glad that I shall probably not see the young generation when it passes the forties. Bruised in its self-confidence, perplexed and baffled by a life envisaged too simply, it is all too likely to manifest a general revulsion to indiscriminately chosen formalisms—social, political, and religious—with the result that the middle-aged dull dog of to-day will be as nothing in view of his successor of twenty years hence. On the better side, a general return to formalism may be the opportunity for an intelligently aggressive humanism. It will be an advantage to find, what we to-day sadly lack, a basis of agreement on any traditional plane, however narrow. Thus the new generation may after all serve the ends of a future humanism, if only by living into entire discredit their barbarous programme of individualism.

In fine, the problem of a humanistic art is no discrete problem, but rather that of humanism generally. It has been my task merely to define the issue in a single aspect, and not at all to find a solution that could be adopted to-morrow. The deep gap that isolates the serious artist from a public content with the puerilities of the radio and the "talkie," will scarcely be bridged to-morrow or the day after. Many critics, indeed, hail the latter-day individualist as the finally liberated artist, and bid us joyously expect even more individualism than that which has already been so generously vouchsafed us. This may be a true prognosis. No one can safely deny the possibility that art may be permanently "on its own." If so, art will of course become merely an eccentric activity, an indulgence and luxury of coteries, hence of no more concern really to the humanist than the trade, say, of the perfume maker. On the other hand, no one can safely deny the possibility that art may once again be profoundly integrated with society. Every contributor to this volume is perforce thinking toward that reintegration, even if the theme be not in his mind nor the words on his pen. To my younger colleagues, then, in whom the hope of a new humanism lies, I leave the problem and the solution, with that chastened confidence which befits a humanist grown old in the most unpopular of faiths.

# The Dilemma of Modern Tragedy

ALAN REYNOLDS THOMPSON

## I

Most modern tragedy is depressing; classic tragedy is elevating. That the best tragic art of the past, in spite of the calamities it presents, elevates the spirit is obvious; but the cause of the "lift" it produces is obscure. If the cause were technical and formal beauty, *Ghosts* ought to be more inspiriting than *Macbeth*. If it were wholly the melody of verse—which most modern drama has foregone—no great classic tragedy could endure translation. But Greek tragedies can still powerfully exalt an audience, though presented in the English renderings of Campbell and Potter!

The problem seems particularly to have appealed to the German metaphysical mind. Hegel thought tragedy a transcendental reconciliation of opposites. Schopenhauer found in it resignation to loss of individuality and return to the universal Will. Nietzsche turned the latter's pessimism into the semblance of optimism by defining the spirit of Dionysus as an intoxicated joy in annihilation and union with nature.

But one hardly need resort to metaphysics, since the experience seems sufficiently explained by psychology. It is in my opinion chiefly the result of admiration. Every tragedy grows from a struggle of the individual against circumstance; but this emotional elevation we are discussing, as distinguished from more melodramatic thrills, seems to arise not from the mere struggle but from an impressive exhibition of

127

will. The spectator is inspirited because in tragedy he sees an exhibition of convincing heroism. The tragic hero achieves a spiritual victory in spite of a physical defeat. "To affect the soul, and excite the passions, and above all to move admiration," says Dryden, "is the delight of serious plays." [1]

In some respects the reverse of this view is the neo-classic doctrine of poetic justice, which is still held by some critics. According to poetic justice it is not the hero whom we are to admire, but the moral law which destroys him. Thus Mr. Ludwig Lewisohn writes: "Traditionally the serious drama deals with the transgressions of an immutable moral law by a self-originating will. . . . In each instance the destruction of the protagonist reconciles the spectator to a universe in which guilt is punished and justice is upheld." That some such view governed the *intentions* of religious dramatists like Æschylus or Racine we must admit; but for the modern sceptic at least their plays are inspiriting in proportion as the struggle exalts the endurance, if not the goodness of the hero. That such was even the intention of other dramatists, Shakespeare in particular, is more than doubtful.

Other critics like Mr. Joseph Wood Krutch foretell the extinction of tragedy because it is dependent on an anthropocentric view of the universe. It is the "tragic fallacy," says Mr. Krutch, to fancy that one's "passions are important throughout all time and all space." Though we may agree that they are not, to conclude from that rather obvious fact that tragedy is dead seems not wholly logical. Whatever the nature of the world, human greatness remains important for human beings; and Mr. Krutch would seem to give away

---

[1] I have considered the tragic emotions more fully in an article, "Melodrama and Tragedy," *Publications of the Modern Language Association*, September, 1928.

his case by so plainly admiring greatness in the very tragedies whose passing he deplores.

The ethical victory of the tragic hero is not a vindication of a moral order in the universe; neither is it a victory for an elaborated system such as religion fosters. Macbeth is wicked but admirable. Something primitive and universal in mankind responds to courage, fidelity, endurance, even for evil ends. Such admiration rises spontaneously from our strongest impulses, those toward survival and success. In the theatre to behold a man steadfast in his will even to death is to feel our own natures enhanced and to discover in ourselves unrealised powers. Such heroic manifestation of will is essential to tragedy of the great tradition, and is found in Sophocles, in Shakespeare, in Corneille alike.

Several influences have combined in destroying heroic tragedy. It was the tradition of the Renaissance to make the hero a prince, the mere semblance of nobility securing a deferential response from the audience. Modern democracy has changed all that. Industrialism, furthermore, has fostered the feeling that success is synonymous with getting rich. And science has not only helped destroy popular traditions that might have nourished a modern spirit of admiration, but has fostered a wintry air of scepticism, making man appear not an imperfect angel but a super-educated monkey. Psychology in particular has been industriously cutting at the root of heroism, the belief in free will, by exhibiting the mechanical causes for conduct.

The writer of tragedy who succumbs to these influences finds himself thus in a dilemma. Unable to believe in greatness, he cannot inspire others. If he would gain elevation, he must falsify his beliefs; if he would express his candid view of life, he must forego the tragic lift. Heroic tragedy was the outcome of a view perhaps pessimistic about things in general, but always optimistic about the human quality of individuals. The modern view is pessimistic about everything. As Hardy expressed it, the prospect most harmonious with the temper of the thinking modern would be a gaunt waste in Thule. As a result the dilemma of the naturalist poet is this: *He cannot be both honest and sublime.*[2]

## II

This statement will be more convincing when illustrated with examples drawn from various manifestations of the tragic spirit—in narrative poetry and the novel as well as in the drama.

I have emphasised the effect of science; and at first thought it might seem that the great romantics of a century ago, who preceded the scientific disillusionment, still kept the heroic tradition alive. It is true that they inherited the tradition, but in their hands it became not heroism but heroics. The romantic tendency was to seek thrills rather than truth, and to draw less from human nature than from a literary fashion.

*Hernani* and *Ruy Blas,* for example, are highly effective constructions of clap-trap, to which Hugo's beautiful and rhetorical verse gives a semblance of significance. But they can be taken seriously only by abandoning the intelligence. To-day they seem no more tragic than Dumas *père* or the *mélodrames* of the Boulevards from which Hugo learned his technic. As melodrama they are, to be sure, still entertaining.

[2] Since this paper was written my attention has been called to "Humanism and Tragedy," an admirable article by Mr. F. McEachran (*Nineteenth Century and After,* July, 1929). Based on Professor Babbitt's three levels of human conduct, naturalistic, human, and religious, Mr. McEachran's thesis is that tragedy, since it demands an assumption of human dignity, cannot develop in a naturalistic age like the present, and is difficult in a religious one. The age of Pericles, of Elizabeth, and of Louis XIV were humanistic; they were followed by naturalistic decadence in which man and nature were equated and tragedy became impossible. Mr. McEachran's "human dignity" and my "heroism" seem equivalent.

Such romantic literature of escape did not of course decrease in popularity with the development of science, but it distinctly lost literary prestige. After the fifties and sixties the romantic who would be taken seriously had to cope with scepticism and disillusionment. Thus Rostand, writing *Cyrano de Bergerac*, was careful to preserve the smile of sophistication; he delicately played with pathos, and even flirted with comedy. We can take the extravagances of the drama half in the spirit of play and enjoy them as a fairy tale. Its heroism is the heroism of fancy, not of life. It is in a similar spirit that we enjoy the thrillers and detective tales of to-day. We seek them for recreation only; and it is difficult to imagine that such romance can ever again be thought of as seriously tragic.

The romantic writer, however, can scarcely be expected to be content with the rôle of popular entertainer. Though for the past fifty years on the defensive, he has persisted in attempting the exaltation of tragic art. Maeterlinck, for example, sought to reconcile pessimism with romance by developing a fatalistic "static drama" and throwing over it a Pre-Raphaelite mist of romantic symbolism. With him a symbol became less a visible sign of another object than a stimulant to emotional intoxication; and if we look at the early plays with clear heads we see that they are rooted in a determinism fatal to the heroic tradition. Later Maeterlinck grew more optimistic, but in *Monna Vanna*, which was inspired by Browning, we get exaltation of passion rather than will.

Whereas Maeterlinck tried to preserve romantic values, if not heroism, by reconciling them with science, the great Russians, Tolstoi and Dostoevski, evaded scientific pessimism by escape into a romanticised Christianity. The result was no less fatal to heroism. As they saw it, the Christian paradox was that the worst persons achieve the greatest regeneration; and they presented it with extreme violence. Thus in Tolstoi's *The Power of Darkness* the leading character is not only a drunkard, a lecher, and a murderer of his own child, but he is hopelessly craven, stupid, and weak. Yet he wins salvation by public confession. Such a conversion seems more emotional than religious, since it is the result of no discipline of the will. But apart from such questions it would appear obvious that such a play as this is poles apart from heroic tragedy. It is Tolstoi's sentimentalised conception of Christian poetic justice which is exalted.

The exaltation which the romanticist failed to achieve, the scientific naturalist did not even attempt. Ibsen, apart from his great intrinsic importance, is interesting because he shows the transition from the one mode to the other. His early plays were modelled after Scribe and Schiller; and use of the sagas links him with the heroic tradition. Though sceptically, he exalted the will and prophesied the superman. But his mature work shows the effect of science: men are portrayed more as victims than shapers of events, and responsibility is shifted from the individual to society. His transition from romanticism to scientific naturalism was made easy by the fact that romanticism had already identified man with nature. Disillusion concerning the latter brought about degradation of the former.

Though the increasing use of symbolism gives Ibsen's later work a romantic tone, the plays are built on studies of mental abnormalities which seem almost intended to demonstrate the non-existence of heroism. The fall of the master builder is indeed a symbol of the falsity of what Shaw calls "ideals." But Ibsen's anti-heroic tendency is seen perhaps most forcefully in the famous tragedy of his middle period.

In *Ghosts* the formal resemblances to Greek tragedy and the element of human error obscure the essential differences. The animus vitalising the action is the attack upon a false code of morals—or "ideals"—of which the heroine is the victim. And, as is proper in a naturalist tragedy, the *Spirocheta pallida* is made the *deus ex machina*. The emotional effect, furthermore, is not elevation but horror. We can admire the author for honesty and daring, but not the characters. The best of them, Mrs. Alving, is admirable only in intention, and false to her convictions, as the author makes a point of showing. She is at the curtain so far from a "spiritual victory" that there remains for her a dilemma which is probably the cruelest in dramatic literature: killing her own son or letting him live an idiot.

The contrast between this play and, let us say, *Hamlet* is plain when we compare Oswald's cry, "The sun—the sun," and the final speech of Fortinbras:

> Bear Hamlet, like a soldier, to the stage;
> For he was likely, had he been put on,
> To have prov'd most royally; and for his passage,
> The soldiers' music and the rites of war
> Speak loudly for him.

The former is the bitter irony of disillusion, the very mockery of the romantic cliché, "Then came the dawn." The latter ends the play with eloquent praise.[3]

### III

The elevation which Ibsen gains in *Ghosts* through beauty of structure and atmospheric effect does not carry over to the theme; here the author frankly chooses honesty and foregoes sublimity. Few or no writers since have been at once as great and as honest. If we observe the literature of the

[3] It is to be noted, as further illustration of the anti-heroic tendency of modern thought, that critics have sought to explain Hamlet as not a hero but a psychopath. What Shakespeare wished his audience to feel, however, seems open to no doubt.

last quarter century to see how it has met the dilemma, we shall find perhaps an explanation of current anarchy and experimentation. Some take refuge in subtle evasions, disguised by the cleverness of novel technic or material. But those who do not evade the issue follow two roads: *the road of laughter*, which goes by way of irony and satire; and *the road of tears*, by way of pathos or cruelty.

The former path, since it leads away from the tragic emotions, need not detain us long. With effort the romantic can school himself into a detachment of head from heart in which he can smile at the contrast between his dreams and the reality. His laughter may be bitter, but it is laughter. Pirandello, aware of the flux and illusoriness of life, deliberately contrasts it with the permanence and significance of fiction; and extracts mirth from the grotesquerie and cleverness of his paradoxes, in spite of the disillusionment underlying them. Anatole France armoured his sensibility with detached artistry and the *esprit gaulois*. Aldous Huxley, too much the moralist to be wholly detached, solaces himself with savage satire. The whole work of Cabell is a series of repetitions of one bitter "jest" involving the night before and the morning after. Such writers, emotionally romantic but intellectually sceptical, choose to laugh at their predicament rather than weep.

The road of tears concerns us directly. It usually follows the way of pathos. Though Aristotle made pity and fear correlative emotions, it is a fact that we feel the former more for the weak victim like Ophelia than for the hero, and that the more we admire, the less we need weep. Pathos must be subordinate in heroic tragedy if the play is to elevate our spirits. Obviously, however, the modern who sees nothing to admire is left with pathos as his chief effect.

Pathos and horror we find in Hardy, little mitigated by any admiration except for the author's artistry. Rarely we find a heroism of sorts in characters like Michael Henchard; but it is significant that the author ended his novels with *Jude*. Galsworthy's habitual irony always borders on pathos if not sentiment. French "naturalism" is harsher and at times, as in *Madame Bovary*, finds expression in bitter irony. But pathos is none the less its most powerful effect. *The Old Wives' Tale* of Arnold Bennett is an English imitation; here we feel the pathos of mere mortality quite apart from anything the very ordinary characters do. In Theodore Dreiser, "naturalism," though sadly in need of pruning, still bears its bitter fruit. It is characteristic of its spirit that Dreiser uses the word "tragedy" with reference to the fate of a Clyde Griffiths.

But since pathos skirts the gulf of sentimentality, the "hard-boiled" generation since the war have turned from it. Those of the younger group who cannot laugh have as a result begun to explore another emotion, which lies even deeper in our nature, and which is also compatible with disillusionment. The savage in all of us finds a fierce and hard delight in torture. Significantly the word "sadism" has become fashionable. We may name the emotion "cruelty," though the word is perhaps inadequate.

In the drama an important forerunner of contemporary exploitations of cruelty and sex, as well as of expressionism, was Frank Wedekind. Cruelty is manifest in James Joyce. In D. H. Lawrence it accompanies a pathological exaltation of sexuality, and thus gives him greater hardness than his American parallel, Sherwood Anderson. A very interesting instance of it is the work of a contemporary American poet whose fame is still unequal to his remarkable achievements. I speak of Robinson Jeffers.

Jeffers' long narrative poems spread a more than Thyestian banquet of horrors. With surprise we learn that in private life the author is so unwilling to inflict pain that "he never picks a flower wantonly." But in his art he more than compensates for such sensibilities. *Roan Stallion*, for example, depicts the passion of a modern Pasiphaë. The unlucky husband is trampled by the stallion, and the woman shoots the animal. *Tamar* deals with incest between brother and sister, and ends with a fire which burns down the house and its more or less crazy inmates. *The Tower Beyond Tragedy*, though treating the Clytemnestra legend with great power, ends in the incest motive between Orestes and Electra.

The perversity of theme, however, is partly compensated by elevation of treatment, for Jeffers has a certain grandeur of style, drawing as he does upon Greek literature, the Bible, modern psychology, and physical science for thought, and the beauty of natural scenery for description. A passage which illustrates at once his power of style and his drift toward cruelty is found in preparation for the crucial scene of *Roan Stallion*.

> Humanity is the start of the race; I say
> Humanity is the mould to break away from, the crust to break
> through, the coal to break into fire,
> The atom to be split.
> Tragedy that breaks man's face
> and a white fire flies out of it; vision that fools him
> Out of his limits, desire that fools him out of his limits, unnatural
> crime, inhuman science,
> Slit eyes in the mask; wild loves that leap over the walls of nature,
> the wild fence-vaulter science,
> Useless intelligence of far stars, dim knowledge of the spinning
> demons that make an atom,
> These break, these pierce, these deify, praising their God shrilly
> with fierce voices: not in a man's shape
> He approves the praise, he that walks lightning-naked on the
> Pacific, that laces the suns with planets,
> The heart of the atom with electrons: what is humanity in this
> cosmos? For him, the last

Least taint of a trace in the dregs of the solution; for itself, the
  mould to break away from, the coal
To break into fire, the atom to be split.[4]

In interpretation of his thought Mr. Louis Adamic quotes
Mr. Jeffers as saying that civilisation tends inevitably toward
downfall through sexual introversion. Although to attempt
to "break out of humanity" after the fashion exalted in *Roan
Stallion* is, to be sure, dangerous, "misinterpreted in the
mind of a fool or a lunatic," nevertheless the fault of the
civilised person is that he "regards man exclusively," "founding his values, desires, his picture of the universe, all on his
own humanity." Mr. Jeffers thus levels his attack directly
at the foundation of humanism, and allies himself with the
naturalists who seek salvation in the physical.

He thus flies from normal humanity into cruelty and per-
version. But the end of these is death. And in poem after
poem is expressed the longing for the peace and endurance
of granite,—of the grave. The violent destruction of the
individual is the logical outcome of his creed, and the denial
of human values leads to the annihilation of humanity.

This tendency, the extreme development of which we find
in Jeffers, we find in less degree in our leading American
dramatist. But in Eugene O'Neill it is obscured by other
qualities; and generalisations are rendered difficult because
he is groping and experimental, not only in technic but in
philosophy. Because of this difficulty as well as for his intrinsic importance, O'Neill requires special consideration.

### IV

A writer's 'prentice work is likely to be revealing, and
O'Neill's is no exception. The one-act play *Thirst*, for
example, reveals an imaginative absorption in the violences

[4] From *Roan Stallion, Tamar, and Other Poems*, Boni & Liveright, 1925.

137

and brutalities of life. Most of the one-acts in the volume with *The Moon of the Caribbees* have more normal and convincing characterisation, but about half are built upon abnormal situations involving incipient insanities or morbid passions.

This interest in mental abnormality has not diminished. O'Neill's plays are studies in psychopathology. *Beyond the Horizon* deals with a weak romantic who takes refuge from harsh reality in dreams, and finally dies of consumption. *Gold* is a melodrama growing out of an insane delusion. *Diff'rent* is the horrible case-history of a victim of sex-repression. *The Hairy Ape* describes a character who, if he is not a mere symbol, develops from incipient to raving madness. A play with a normal beginning, "*The First Man,*" turns out to be a study of an emotional fixation. *Welded* depicts two egotistical introverts in whom goes on the torturing conflict between passionate love and uncontrolled temperament. The flames of lust and greed, fanned into madness—these are the materials of *Desire Under the Elms*. *The Great God Brown*, viewed apart from its symbolism, portrays split personality and madness. *The Fountain*, beneath its exotic romanticism, is the story of an *idée fixe*. The plot of *Strange Interlude* might have come from the case-book of Freud. If we cannot judge the chief character of *Lazarus Laughed* by human standards, we can recognise in Caligula and Tiberius realistic studies of psychic abnormalities born of lust, cruelty, and fear. And the author's latest play, *Dynamo*, is a study of religious mania.

The blighting effects of our industrial and social life seem hardly adequate to explain this persistent interest in the pathological. To follow the method of the new psychology which O'Neill uses so largely, we are likely to be correct if we seek an emotional frustration; but American life is hardly the chief cause. Similar interests are seen, for example, in Ibsen, Strindberg, and Wedekind, all of whom must have had their effect on the younger dramatist. My suggestion is that O'Neill has found his highly romantic temperament incompatible with the teachings of science, and has sought to evade the dilemma of modern tragedy by the road of tears, exploiting both pathos and cruelty.

That his temperament is highly romantic is obvious. His early work is almost Conradian in atmosphere; and his great vigour of imagination is strikingly displayed in the gorgeous settings and strange situations of plays like *Marco Millions* and *The Fountain*. Indeed, in the melodrama of fear and horror he is a genius, fertile in themes to startle and amaze, and skilful in adapting them effectively to the stage. Such a play as *Ile*, moreover, is not only horrible but poetically true. *The Emperor Jones* is in my opinion his masterpiece, perfectly constructed and artistically inevitable. The settings and plot contribute with as inexorable an art as that of Poe to a single emotional effect, which is furthermore bound up with a clear and convincing problem in character. The theme of *The Emperor Jones* is the regression of a negro to savagery; and as we watch the succession of weird visions, and feel the emotional crescendo of the tom-toms, at the same time we see the disintegration of the negro's mind. The parallel progress of outer and inner effects is beautifully executed; and behind the individual we become aware of the dark tragedy of his race.

But with so luxuriant a fancy, O'Neill has never been content to construct a dream-world of his own, out of despair of the real one. He has never abandoned the search for his dreams in actual life, and as a consequence in his later plays his visions of beauty are forever being distorted by the lurid light of disillusion. Thus he has seldom written pure romance. *Marco Millions* becomes heavy satire; and *The Fountain* leaves a bitter taste. For the most part he seeks to deal realistically with contemporary life.

To see men as mere parts of a mechanistic and soulless universe, and at the same time to long passionately for the beautiful visions of imagination, is to find those visions a torture unless they can in some way be reconciled with reality. Lesser writers have often been diverted into a seeming reconciliation of them by becoming ardent propagandists; by adopting programmes of reform, and writing problem or thesis plays. But while O'Neill shows the romantic's characteristic hatred of tradition and restraint, he is not content to do less than face the fundamental problem. And if he hates "puritanism" and sympathises with its victim, he by no means blindly admires the libertine. Indeed, he seems to find no man whom he can whole-heartedly admire; he can exalt no character or cause, and thus does not gain the elevation of heroic tragedy. He finds life a muddle; he leaves it a muddle.

Too often, indeed, the muddlement gets into the construction as well as the themes of his plays. *Desire Under the Elms*, one of the most nearly tragic of his plays, starts as a study of greed, with old Cabot as the central character. Cabot, in fact, has heroic qualities, for he is a man of will. But half way through, the play turns off into the more alluring theme of sexual lust; old Cabot is thrust into the background; and the ending is, surprisingly, the traditional one of crime and retribution. The play lacks artistic unity; it falls in two.

The lack of unity is felt, again, in *Anna Christie*, which in spite of the author's expressed intention has for the audience simply a conventional happy ending. It is strikingly manifest in *Strange Interlude*. The central character of this alone knits together the various situations and themes of the nine acts. Of the situations three or four distinct plays might have been built. Of the themes there are at least eight; and it is impossible to say which the author considered central. Much, for example, is said about "happiness" as the end of life. Again, the doubtful value of self-sacrifice is illustrated. From Darrell's point of view, love, that blind biological urge, seems to be a modern variety of Fate. More than once Nina expresses the notion that God is a woman. The most powerful scene of the play is where Nina exults over her "three men": are we to look for possessiveness in love as a theme? Or a woman's need of several sorts of love? Or is the play a study in relativity with reference to insanity? Certainly the character with the insane inheritance is actually the most normal person. Or perhaps we have a study in the results of meddling with other people's lives. The popular success of this play is hardly an indication of unification. That success seems to be attained in spite of lack of unity, and to rest chiefly on the novelty of the nine acts and of the technic of spoken thought, on the frank treatment of sex, and on the great power of characterisation and of separate situations.

Here is a writer with a genius for the theatre, a powerful imagination, and great emotional force, who except in shorter studies of melodramatic horror seems unable to canalise his energies into rounded and unified works of art. He suffers the conflict he symbolises in "Dion Anthony," between his inborn longing for goodness and beauty, and an acquired frustration, cynicism, and despair. Often the despair conquers; but we must honour him for the fact that, having no faith, he persists in seeking one. Unlike lesser writers he is no compromiser with truth as he sees it; but in one play at least he has persuaded himself into a positive affirmation. The play is *Lazarus Laughed*.

The symbolist technic of this play forces attention upon

the underlying theme. Only Lazarus is unmasked, and he is thus shown freed from the illusions of mortality. The rhythmical repetitions and symmetrical groups of the choruses materialise ethical sympathies and antagonisms. And the theme is stated repeatedly: there is no death.

But when we try to understand this affirmation we are repeatedly baffled. It cannot be the Christian belief in personal immortality. The resurrection of Lazarus would give ground for such a view were it not obvious that the author has taken over a Christian legend merely as starting point for his non-Christian allegory. Not only is Christian immortality not preached, but Christian morality is not expounded. The hero displays not humility but arrogance. For him men are not evil until redeemed by the grace of God; they are innately good but perverted by fear. He thus incites them not to love one another because children of a loving God, but to live passionately and instinctively. To be freed from the fear of death means for those who come under his spell not to live on earth after the Golden Rule, in meekness to forgive and suffer wrong; but to drown all human interests in a mad delight in death. And they laugh with exultation at the prospect of annihilation. The paradox seems essentially irrational.

Cries Lazarus: "Once as squirming specks we crept from the tides of the sea! Once as quivering flecks of rhythm we beat down the sun. Now we re-enter the sun! Cast aside is our pitiable pretence, our immortal egohood, the holy lantern behind which cringed our Fear of the Dark. . . . We will to die!" In a manner strikingly similar to that of Jeffers, O'Neill exalts pan-evolutionary nature; having passed beyond horror at the scientific demonstration of an inhuman universe, he attempts to pull himself out of humanity into a rapturous acceptance of Nature. But Jeffers finds no source for laughter in his god "that laces the suns with planets, the heart of the atom with electrons." Whence does O'Neill derive his mirth?

He may well have got his inspiration from Nietzsche. I have summed up Nietzsche's idea in *The Birth of Tragedy* as "an intoxicated joy in annihilation and union with nature." Significantly it is just following an attack on Christianity that he exalts the laughing mood. We must fear the "romantic," he says, because the romantic tends to end comforted like a Christian. "No! ye should first of all learn the art of earthly comfort, ye should learn to *laugh*, my young friends, if ye are at all determined to remain pessimists: if so, you will perhaps, as laughing ones, eventually send all metaphysical comfortism to the devil—and metaphysics first of all! Or, to say it in the language of that Dionysian ogre, called Zarathustra:

" 'Lift up your hearts, my brethren, high, higher! And do not forget your legs! Lift up also your legs, ye good dancers—and better still if ye stand also on your heads! . . .

" 'This crown of the laughter, this rose-garland crown—to you, my brethren, do I cast this crown! Laughing have I consecrated: ye higher men, *learn*, I pray you—to laugh!' "

It needs intoxication—of one Dionysian sort or another—to find such incitements mirth-provoking. It is necessary to abandon all reasonable grounds for comfort except the rather chilly one that we are physically made of stardust, and therefore should rejoice to dissolve our living complexity back into it. *Lazarus Laughed* indeed arouses a fair measure of the necessary intoxication, so imaginative and emotional is it. But its comfort can last, I fear, only while we actually hear the laughter of Lazarus.

## V

Thus our most gifted American dramatist, together with other finer spirits of to-day, is unable to accept traditional modes or satisfy the desire for admiration and worship. Romanticism, in identifying man with nature, hastened the decay of a heroic tradition which it at first attempted to foster; and under scientific naturalism the decay ended in dissolution. Whether the author uses a so-called "naturalistic" technique after Ibsen or Maupassant; or whether, like Wedekind or Jeffers or Cabell, he seeks other modes of expression, so long as he thinks of man as in no way superior to the outer world or different from it, he is none the less subject to the naturalistic point of view.[5]

Recently, to be sure, certain developments of science have given rise to hopes of mysticism within a naturalistic monism. The argument, so far as an unscientific reader understands it, seems to run thus: Einstein has offered proof that time and space form a continuum and that events are "relative." Studies of the atom have upset orthodox conceptions of physics, and physicists themselves are beginning to talk about matter in terms that sound for all the world like Bishop Berkeley. Science admits a mysterious enveloping Unknown.

The new hypotheses, of course, merely re-enforce the acknowledgment of ultimate mystery which thoughtful people have always made. The novelty of the new mysticism is that it builds not on theology or metaphysics but mathematics and laboratory experiment. The next step in its argument is the dubious one.

If science grants an enveloping Unknown, the man who

[5] Should I remind the reader that in thus generalising I admit exceptions? One such, whom I have discussed elsewhere (*Sewanee Review*, April, 1929) is, in my opinion, Joseph Conrad.

144

would explain that Unknown in terms of his desires is as likely to be right as one who explains it in inhuman terms. And if there is a chance that one's desires may be true, it needs no psychologist to assure us that plenty of people will immediately assume that they are true. For them science seems to justify mysticism and open the door for the hosts of dreams, so long shut out of a rationalistic universe. But the weakness of such wishful thinking seems obvious; and to the humanist the whole argument is beside the point because it would vindicate human values by naturalistic data.

If some scientists are nowadays growing mystical, it is not therefore logical to deny the facts that their controlled experiments have demonstrated. The dilemma of modern tragedy remains very real. There is no refuge in obscurantism through return to illusions which science has shattered. Reason denies the objective reality of our dreams; and so long as the honest man accepts a monism which identifies man with nature, he can find no justification for tragic exaltation.

The humanist, however, denies the necessity for this identification. Without in the slightest degree disparaging the truth or worth of physical knowledge he maintains that the realm of value has significant validity when taken as distinct from the realm of fact. The realm of value belongs to man; that of fact, to outer nature. One depends on the other, but the two are different.

Value depends on the operation of physical laws, but it remains value. The fallacy of the naturalist has been the assumption that to explain the cause of a thing is to explain away its value. Human emotions may be caused on the naturalistic plane by the secretion of endocrine glands or what not; on the human plane they remain what they were to Homer or Shakespeare. It is interesting to know about

145

chromosomes and Mendelian laws, about biochemistry and vital machinery; but human values remain the same. Whatever the findings of science, man humanly speaking is still what he always was: comic, pitiful, despicable—now and then sublime.

The humanist is concerned with the realm of values, and thus is concerned with ethical laws. The lives of all men progress under these laws; and the endeavours of great men have been to discover and formulate them. To the humanist it seems evident that literary art, dealing as it does with human actions, must deal with ethical laws, which are the foundation of conduct. And it would seem obvious folly to attempt to divorce literature from them.

Romantic art as recreation is a blessing to jaded mortals; and naturalistic art at its best is, within its limits, penetrating. But to the humanist it seems that both types of art have failed in dealing with ethical laws. The romantic is always an extremist, demanding perfection, or denying the existence of goodness. The naturalist has become so absorbed in the mechanism of the instrument that he has become deaf to its music. The humanist desires emotional satisfaction; he desires to face the truth. But he also wishes to preserve a normal humanity in which human values are central. Though hearing the revelations of science, he keeps his ear attuned to the music of humanity. Though enjoying the thrills of liberated feeling, he is unwilling to purchase them at the expense of moderation or proportion. He believes not in prohibition but in temperance.

Ethical laws are what make man human, and it is these that the artist must ponder. And to find guidance he cannot do better than follow Arnold's advice—not less sound for being tiresomely familiar—to know the best that has been thought and said in the world. He must break with the contemporary tradition of romantic scorn for tradition; he must seek to become a part of the great tradition, by knowing the best. To become a part of it does not mean to attempt mere imitation; it means that the artist will be forevermore dissatisfied with pettiness or insincerity in himself, and will have a lofty but possible standard by which to measure his work.

Those who work in the "modern temper" are unable to discover a worthy heroism to exalt. But if one turns to the records of classic art, he will find a nobility of spirit no less admirable to-day than in the past. His response will be an evidence of the existence of heroism, a proof of its reality in human nature. It will be a proof of its reality, of course, not in perfection but in aspiration. And if one looks about him he will find the same aspiration in living men and women. He will find it even expressed in deeds—imperfectly, humanly. If he should be artist enough to give adequate expression to what he feels and sees, he could rise above the dilemma against which naturalism has forced our modern literature.

Cynicism will, to be sure, urge that every man finds what he looks for, and to look for greatness will lead to a denial of evident imperfections. The humanist professes himself not unaware of the latter. Long before naturalist novelists pictured the *bête humaine,* Christianity declared man innately evil; but unlike naturalism, Christianity believed man capable of redemption by Grace. The humanist as such is not concerned with theology, and is content to believe that Grace, however it comes, is sometimes found. He is inclined to doubt that it comes only to those who have joined a church; he is inclined to believe that nobility is found now and again in all sorts and conditions of men. But the main thing is that it exists; and no artist who does not see the good with the evil sees life steadily and whole.

To follow the narrow path between cynicism and romantic

idealisation; to recognise the imperfections in man and the inevitable domination of physical force over the individual, and yet to preserve admiration for the indomitable spirit which drives the individual to will and to do nobly; and finally to find adequate means of artistic expression—that is the task of one who would write great tragedy. Though hard, it is still possible. Only when the artist follows lofty standards can he hope to control and guide his own efforts toward sublimity. While humanism offers him no magic key to success, it offers him hope, and a discipline.

# An American Tragedy

### ROBERT SHAFER

## I

Mr. Theodore Dreiser's critical friends have always been ready to admit his deficiencies as a literary artist, and these deficiencies are really extraordinary. Nevertheless, by universal consent Mr. Dreiser stands at the head of the realistic movement in American fiction, not merely because he is its pioneer, and has endured obloquy and even persecution for the Cause, but primarily on account of his seriousness and singleness of purpose, his depth of keen feeling, and his earnest reflectiveness. His work also anticipates in important respects the efforts of the post-realists and super-realists, so-called, and altogether has a present salience which insistently demands consideration.

The work, however, cannot be assessed—cannot indeed be understood—apart from the man; and fortunately Mr. Dreiser has written much about himself.[1] He was born in 1871 in Terre Haute, Indiana, of German Catholic parents who struggled vainly against poverty. In the schools of another Indiana town he received the elements of an education, but apparently learned little of value to him beyond reading and writing. In boyhood and youth, in school or out, he became acquainted with a number of the better-known writers, chiefly of fiction, of the nineteenth century,

---

[1] In that which follows I draw chiefly upon *A Book About Myself* (1922), but also make use of *A Hoosier Holiday* (1916), *Twelve Men* (1919), and *Hey Rub-A-Dub-Dub* (1920). *A Traveler at Forty* (1913) is also a revealing book.

but without gaining from them more than momentary entertainment. He has said that as a boy he "had no slightest opportunity to get a correct or even partially correct estimate of what might be called the mental A B abs of life."

If the truth is to be told, one reason for this lay clearly within himself. For he was, as his records show him, a stupid boy and young man, lapped in vague reverie and hazy dreams of enjoyment, and roused slowly to puzzled observation and thought. "No common man am I," he used to tell himself when he was scarcely out of his 'teens, with no evident reason save that with adolescence came an intense craving for freedom from the shackles of common life—freedom to indulge fully his temperamental longing for sensuous and materialised delight. This self-conceit helped to prevent him from learning what could have been learned during his boyhood, and, as he grew older, aroused in him bitter resentment against the limitations of his early environment.

Those limitations, at the same time, were extreme. The Dreiser household was one combining almost unrelieved ignorance with perfect tastelessness, presided over by a father whose consuming interest was a Catholicism degraded into mere ceremonies and prohibitions. Mr. Dreiser explicitly denotes the quality of the purifying influence dominant in the home and community of his youth: "One should read only good books . . . from which any reference to sex had been eliminated, and what followed . . . was that all intelligent interpretation of character and human nature was immediately discounted. A picture of a nude or partially nude woman was sinful. . . . The dance in our home and our town was taboo. The theatre was an institution which led to crime, the saloon a centre of low, even bestial vices. . . . It was considered good business, if you please, to be connected with some religious organisation. . . . We were taught persistently to shun most human experiences as either dangerous or degrading or destructive. The less you knew about life the better; the more you knew about the fictional heaven and hell ditto. . . . In my day there were apparently no really bad men who were not known as such to all the world, . . . and few if any good men who were not sufficiently rewarded by the glorious fruits of their good deeds here and now! . . . Positively, and I stake my solemn word on this, until I was between seventeen and eighteen I had scarcely begun to suspect any other human being of harbouring the erratic and sinful thoughts which occasionally flashed through my own mind."

By the time Mr. Dreiser had fairly formed the suspicion that, despite appearances, other people might not be much better than himself, his family had begun to break up, following the death of his mother, and he himself had been thrust into the world—or rather into Chicago, where the Dreisers by now lived—to earn his way. He did manage to spend one year at Indiana University, to the great improvement of his health, but with no positive intellectual benefit, so that he refused to waste a second year, which he might have had there. He confesses this, it should be said, in no boastful spirit. He was in fact made to realise at Bloomington that there were elements of knowledge which it would be useful to him to acquire—but he found the effort hopeless. His mind could not be constrained, and, besides, the deficiencies of his earlier schooling stood in his way. Hence he returned to Chicago, to become a collector for an easy-payment furniture shop.

It was at this time that his feelings—scarcely yet his imagination or his reason—were awakened by the spectacle of "America on the make." He found that spectacle intensely vital. At the same time, too, he was doing the first reading that really came home to him:—he was reading a daily column of Eugene Field's in a Chicago newspaper. It gave him the notion of doing something like that himself, and sent him hunting for a post on a news-sheet. This he finally obtained, and at the reporter's desk achieved his real education, one not beyond his grasp. His first instructor promptly informed him that "life was a God-damned stinking, treacherous game, and that nine hundred and ninety-nine men out of every thousand were bastards." The truth of this generalisation Mr. Dreiser proceeded to establish for himself, by observation of those of life's realities which constitute news, and by intercourse with fellow-journalists. He discovered that practically all men, high or low, were lying hypocrites, outwardly professing a fine morality, but privately violating this without hesitation whenever it would serve their turn in the pursuit of gain or in the satisfaction of lust.

This was the reality, at any rate, which the young reporter saw, and which, as he says, broadened considerably his viewpoint, finally liberating him "from moralistic and religionistic qualms." So liberated was he, indeed, that he came to judge men "thoroughly sound intellectually" in proportion as he found them "quite free from the narrow, cramping conventions of their day." So liberated was he that he came to see the "religionist" for what he was: "a swallower of romance or a masquerader looking to profit and preferment." He came also to see behind "the blatherings of thin-minded, thin-blooded, thin-experienced religionists" only "a brainless theory." Nor was this the limit of his discoveries. He came further to see that life was not simply a ruthless struggle for material advantages, because, howsoever ruthless and intelligent one's struggle, still, one might be defrauded by sheer accident. Chance seemed, at times, the final ruler of all things—many of the reporter's assignments combining "to prove that life is haphazard and casual and cruel; to some lavish, to others niggardly."

152

Mr. Dreiser, it is fair to say, was the more ready to learn these lessons of experience because, as he plainly tells his readers, he himself was lustful and passionately eager for the material satisfactions of life. He longed to join in the antics of the rich, who alone, as he judged, were bathed in happiness. He felt, as he gazed enviously upon the gilded sons and daughters of earth, that, from no fault of his, life was tragically cheating him. And this sense of grievance, feeding upon itself, passed easily through a sentimental phase into bitterness, as his reminiscences show: "Whenever I returned to any place in which I had once lived and found things changed, as they always were, I was fairly transfixed by the oppressive sense of the evanescence of everything; a mood so hurtful and dark and yet with so rich if sullen a lustre that I was left wordless with pain. I was all but crucified at realising how unimportant I was, how nothing stayed but all changed. . . . Life was so brief, . . . and so soon, whatever its miserable amount or character, it would be gone. . . . But I, poor waif, with no definite or arresting skill of any kind, not even that of commerce, must go fumbling about looking in upon life from the outside, as it were. Beautiful women, or so I argued, were drawn to any but me. . . . I should never have a fraction of the means to do as I wished or to share in the life that I most craved. I was an Ishmael."

Not always, of course, was Mr. Dreiser sunk in a bitterness induced by self-pity and sentimental regret. Often in moments of successful work or of flattering companionship he was quickly lifted up into a mood of expansive self-satisfaction, equally unbalanced. Then he would say to himself: "I must be an exceptional man. . . . Life itself was not so bad; it was just higgledy-piggledy, catch-as-catch-can, that was all. If one were clever, like myself, it was all right." It was indeed magnificent, so long as the slave of temperament could dream of his heroic future as something assured. But dreams, like life, were unstable, and the fever for self-advancement, becoming intolerable from its intensity, would transmute itself—not every time into frank self-pity—but sometimes into tearful "sympathy for the woes of others, life in all its helpless degradation and poverty, the unsatisfied dreams of people." And from the downtrodden for whom he wept he also drew a lesson. The hideous inequalities both of fortune and of capacity which he saw, proved to him that democracy, like morality, was a sham, a hollow convention, irrelevant, indeed opposed, to the facts of life and practice.

Mr. Dreiser's journalistic career took him from Chicago to St. Louis, and thence, with several stops on the way, to Pittsburgh, during a period of rather more than three years. In these years, he says, speaking of his "blood-moods or so-called spiritual aspirations," he was "what might be called a poetic melancholiac, crossed with a vivid materialistic lust of life." His body, he adds, "was blazing with sex, as well as with a desire for material and social supremacy." It is not surprising, consequently, that he found himself able to entertain carnal desires for several women at the same time—though this at first surprised him, and troubled him also, until his day of liberation from "moralistic qualms." It is not surprising either that he presently was captivated by a charming country girl, several years older than himself, who had no single idea and only one desire in common with him. He had welcomed his liberation from "moralistic and religionistic qualms" the more complacently because of the simplification of thought and conduct to which it pointed. From this time the conduct of life was to be straightforward as well as simple, in accordance with the brutish yet vital law of following your dominant impulse regardlessly, ruthlessly, slavishly. But now this liberation itself was mainly instrumental in plunging him into a new, long-continued, and grievous difficulty. For his simple country maiden, though she was drawn to him as he was drawn to her, was nevertheless rigidly conventional, immovably "moralistic," one of the predestined pillars of an ordered society and a stable family. She steadfastly refused to yield him her body without marriage, and he, alas, was not only unable to support her but deeply unwilling to marry her even if he could.

Clearly this pair did not understand all that divided them in spirit, but, still, Mr. Dreiser knew from the first some portion of the truth. For he knew what love really was: it was a mere "blood-mood"; it was a vivid lust crossed with poetic fires; it was irresistible, of course, but it was like everything else, transient, shifting, evanescent. He already suspected, as he later concluded, that monogamy—marriage indeed of any kind—was a debasing institution which not only killed the love that brought men to it, but also deformed and dwarfed their personalities. It might not harm stupid and lethargic men, but the man of individuality, at least, the highest type of citizen, required utter freedom to follow his vital impulses—required the joys of the sexual act "without any of the hindrances or binding chains of convention." He knew, in fine, that "the tug of his immense physical desire for his beloved" might easily have been satisfied, despite his poverty, without compromising the future, and without doing a hurt to society, had there only been "any such thing as sanity in life," outside of himself. He even knew, after the first raptures of idyllic feeling had passed, that any other beautiful woman would have served his need as well; but, nevertheless, he clung to this one, because in fact no beautiful woman whom he found accessible did keep alive in him the same fever of desire. Yet his beloved remained immovable, and so drew him on, through several years of miserably divided feeling, into a marriage finally accomplished after his carnal fires had cooled, owing to the passage of time and the casual ministrations of certain other fair creatures, more pliant, but unsatisfying.

I dwell upon this painful episode, following Mr. Dreiser's own example, because it tells so much. It was the crucial event of his early life, and it left an ineffaceable scar. The fact is, indeed, that without definite knowledge of this miserable union, it would not be easy to understand how Mr. Dreiser became so obstinately fixed in those notions of life which journalism and its associations gave him and which he was eager to accept. Without definite knowledge of this marriage, further, it would be impossible fully to understand his novels; for none of them could have been written quite as it stands save in the light of this afflictive experience of his, and several, it is extremely likely, could not otherwise have been written at all.[2]

Some knowledge of another side of Mr. Dreiser's life, however, during his years of work for the news-sheets, is also necessary for those who would understand his novels. He has told us that in St. Louis the great literary idol of his associates was Zola, and after Zola, Balzac. These novelists, and especially the former, were constantly held up to him as models by one of his assignment-editors, who made it abundantly clear what Zola stood for. Mr. Dreiser read none of the Frenchman's books at this time, but he did read an unpublished novel by two St. Louis newspaper men which made a deep and lasting impression upon him and which, as he later discovered, was wholly inspired by Zola and Balzac. This was "the opening wedge for him into the realm of realism," and, too, "it fixed his mind definitely on this matter of writing," firing him with a desire to create

[2] I refer particularly to *Jennie Gerhardt* and *The "Genius."* Limitations of space unfortunately prevent me from considering here any save Mr. Dreiser's latest novel, *An American Tragedy*.

something of the sort himself. He thought the novel "intensely beautiful," "with its frank pictures of raw, greedy, sensual human nature, and its open pictures of self-indulgence and vice." In these indirect ways, evidently, Zola exerted upon the young reporter an influence real and significant. It was, indeed, probably much more important than the direct influence exerted by Balzac not long thereafter; though the accident which brought Mr. Dreiser to a fevered and ecstatic reading of many of Balzac's novels, while he was in Pittsburgh, marked what was for him "a literary revolution."

The crowning stage of Mr. Dreiser's education, however, was now to come, while he was still in Pittsburgh, with his discovery of certain of the writings of Huxley, Tyndall, and Herbert Spencer. Huxley, Mr. Dreiser credits with finally dispelling the "lingering filaments" of Christianity still trailing about him; and Huxley's work of dispersion was completed by Spencer's *First Principles*. This book wholly "threw him down in his conceptions or non-conceptions of life" by its "questioning or dissolving into other and less understandable things" all that he had deemed substantial. "Up to this time," he says, "there had been in me a blazing and unchecked desire to get on and the feeling that in doing so we did get somewhere; now in its place was the definite conviction that spiritually one got nowhere, that there was no hereafter, that one lived and had his being because one had to, and that it was of no importance. Of one's ideals, struggles, deprivations, sorrows and joys, it could only be said that they were chemic compulsions. . . . Man was a mechanism, undevised and uncreated, and a badly and carelessly driven one at that."

The seeming ill logic of some of these remarks—the sudden concern over spiritual things felt by one who had hitherto devoted himself whole-heartedly to the world by sensuous appearances—is not unimportant. Clearly Spencer's book left an abiding mark on Mr. Dreiser because it represented in a general way the abstract conclusion towards which his own observations had been pointing. Without knowing it, and without any attempt to set his intellectual house in order, he had himself been drifting towards a mechanistic naturalism. Spencer made him aware of this, and if, as he thought, that awareness left him crushed and hopeless, it at least seemed to clear his mind of rubbish, and to give his view-point self-consistency and finality. Nevertheless, he did not come forth a Spencerian; and, indeed, his debt to the *Synthetic Philosophy* may easily be exaggerated—the more easily because it really is important.

Mr. Dreiser emphasises the fact that his reading of the *First Principles* was followed by an emotional revulsion—a revulsion which the Synthetic Philosopher can scarcely alone have caused. And in truth just at the time when he stumbled upon Spencer his feelings were strained to the breaking-point. He had just returned from a last desperate, yet unsuccessful, effort to seduce his country maiden, which left him crushed, not only by that defeat itself, but by the consciousness that the gratification he was bound to secure was now driving him towards a marriage for which he had no capacity, no desire, and no prospect of sufficient means. Moreover, immediately after his Western visit he had gone, for the first time, to New York, where he had received an extraordinarily vivid impression of all the glories and delights of that worldly success, with its attendant wealth, which he so intensely craved. The sight had fired him to renew his efforts after so grand a reward, but, at the same time, had made him gloomily feel his distance from it, lodging in his mind a stubborn doubt if it could, after all, ever be attained by him. The combined weight of these experiences had intensified his already bitter sense of the world's

158

indifference to his desires and aims, of the world's unconscious cruelty, and of its brutal injustice. He had eagerly embraced the world at his earliest opportunity, had reviled those who opposed themselves to it—and what was the world doing for him, what was it not blindly and carelessly doing against him? He was brought to the point of sheer despair, and was ready to turn upon the world—yet not ready to turn his back upon it. For he had not the slightest conception of any other than sensuous and worldly values, of any other than material gratifications which might bring to him fulness of life. Years ago he had defiantly closed *that* door, without in the least knowing what he was doing, and it was never to be opened to him. He was miserably exasperated by defeat, but the world's appeal was still insistent and compelling, and would be heard and obeyed for many a year, whether or not it became suspect for a siren's call.

In these circumstances the *First Principles* came really as a god-send. The book had the impressive appearance of being the voice of science itself uttering at last the Truth. Yet its weight and authority left undisturbed Mr. Dreiser's worldliness and some of his dear prejudices. It left, indeed, everything as it was with him; but it did appear to rob everything of value, and so, as he thought, left him crushed and hopeless. Actually, however, it offered him a species of consolation for the crushed and hopeless state into which he had already been plunged by his efforts after a "realistic" way of life. A species of consolation;—because, though the dehumanised conception of the world and life presented by naturalism was "cold comfort," still, it did enable one who felt badly used to turn upon the universe and *say*, if not feel, that life was a meaningless and unimportant phenomenon anyhow.

The *Synthetic Philosophy*, Mr. Dreiser tells the world, "eternally verified" his "gravest fears as to the unsolvable

disorder and brutality of life." Precisely; as these turns of
phrase show, it left his feelings what they had been, likewise
his desires and aims, and his sentimental humanitarianism
and more. What Spencer gave him was something to fall
back upon and *say* in hopeless or disillusioned moments, but
something which, leaving him otherwise where he was, even
helped to preserve him inviolate from self-criticism or self-
discipline. Following the guidance of temperament and
mood, he took from Spencer what he wanted, and nothing
else; and it so happened that this included little or nothing
specifically characteristic of Spencer as against various other
naturalistic thinkers. The tone, indeed, of Mr. Dreiser's
naturalism, as well as its emphasis upon accident and chaotic
disorder, is not only more sophisticated than that of
Spencer's, but abruptly contradictory of the Synthetic gentleman's grandiose fancy of one eternal, universal law infallibly
working to bring about perfection in all things earthly.

His dark emotional naturalism—and, it may be added,
several of the contradictions it has involved him in—bring
Mr. Dreiser, as some of his readers have perceived, close
to Thomas Hardy, in proportion as he is far from Spencer.
He does not mention Hardy in the record of his development which I have been following, but he is said to have
confessed to "an enchanted discovery" of that novelist in
1896, and his delight is what was to be expected. As far as
one can see, however, his indebtedness to Hardy, though
real, is not important.

## II

This, in summary form, is the story of Mr. Dreiser's
preparation for a novelist's career. His first novel was published in 1900, and his sixth in 1925. Though from an
early time he has had warm friends amongst the critics, still,
even the most devoted of these have harshly condemned

some of his books; and, in general, critical opinion, when not predominantly hostile, has been sharply divided. Nevertheless, in the face of whatever difficulties, Mr. Dreiser has slowly won a leading position in the world of fiction, for reasons which I began by mentioning. And his sixth novel, *An American Tragedy*, was, upon its appearance, widely proclaimed a masterpiece.

Certainly, moreover, *An American Tragedy* is by all odds the best of Mr. Dreiser's novels, though perhaps not the most *interesting*. In it his language is still faulty, as in his earlier books; the quality of his style is mediocre, when not worse; his narrative is badly proportioned;—but, nevertheless, the novel also has excellences which its author had not previously achieved, and which are seldom to be found save in works of a serious and mature artistry. It has a sombre inevitableness, a self-contained adequacy, a restraint, dignity, and detachment which bespeak not merely the experienced craftsman, but also the workman's sure grasp of his theme united with a deeply emotional confidence in its truth and importance. A far higher intelligence is exhibited in its execution than in Mr. Dreiser's play, *The Hand of the Potter* (1918), whose theme is similar in several respects. If one should name a single change indicative of the intelligent masterliness of *An American Tragedy*, perhaps the most significant is the fact that in this book, for the first time, Mr. Dreiser has permitted his characters and events to speak entirely for themselves.

But though *An American Tragedy* marks a really notable advance in technique, and a heightened plausibility thus attained, partly through restraint, still, it exhibits Mr. Dreiser's thought and the essential quality of his realism entirely unchanged. How Mr. Dreiser reached a mechanistic naturalism has above been shown, and how he became conscious of the fact. The appropriate result was that all his novels became tales of human irresponsibility, constructed to illustrate life's contradiction of the hollow conventions of society, and life's obedience to blind laws which make the individual's experience a chaos with an end unrelated to desert. This is the theme of *An American Tragedy,* as of the earlier novels. It is a tale of human irresponsibility, supported by youthful prejudices never relinquished, built up on false antitheses, and capped by a merely circumstantial realism calculated to give the narrative a deceptive air of importance.

Youthful prejudice, for example, transparently dictates the important part played by religion in this novel. Religion is represented as an illusion capable of deceiving only those blind to life's realities—the hopelessly incompetent and unintelligent, those whose advocacy would itself discredit any doctrine. Religion's illusory nature is said to be self-evident, indeed, since it has much to say of Providence, yet manifestly bestows on the convert no worldly rewards, in satisfaction of the real needs and desires with which he is endowed, not by his own design or wish. Convention, too, is represented as a force which sways only the stupid and lethargic, which makes no demands entitling it to respect, and which the intelligent disregard deliberately, the temperamental wilfully. Intelligence itself is pictured as merely an instrument useful for devising methods of self-advancement;—in other words, as the servant of inborn temperament. And temperament is the one irresistible, compelling force in life, to which all else is ultimately obedient. Hence no one is really responsible for anything;—save, perhaps, the novelist who sees this important truth, at length, and by careful selection of appropriate matter is able to picture it for us.

Not even Mr. Dreiser's expert care and long practice, however, are sufficient to enable him to evade a difficulty inherent in the nature of his theme. For the predicament of

Roberta Alden is infinitely sad, and her creator narrates her history and murder with an exemplary truthfulness which emphasises that sadness to the full. Nevertheless, the reader's sympathy is not invoked. The girl, on the contrary, is presented as the inevitable resultant of inheritance, environment, and sex, and she lives as an embodied energy rather than as a person. Extraordinary pains are taken, with all the multitudinous details of her story, to balance causes against effects, and she emerges a plausible creature. There is nothing incredible in her being just conventional enough and unwary enough and love-sick enough to suit the story's purpose; but, too, there is nothing in her nature or her history to render either important. Indeed, her grievous distress, leading up to her murder, takes on, under Mr. Dreiser's hand, the same significance as the squirming of an angleworm, impaled by some mischievous boy—no less, but certainly no more.

"Chemic compulsion" draws Roberta Alden as it draws other substances. "Chemic compulsion" epitomises the book. It "just happens"—and this is all—that "chemic compulsion" entangles Roberta with the squid—Clyde Griffiths, the defeated squid. For readers of Mr. Dreiser's "epic" tale, *The Financier*, who recall the apologue of the lobster and the squid cannot fail to recognise Clyde Griffiths as the embodiment of the latter—and his cousin Gilbert as the patient, triumphant lobster. The squid, it need scarcely be said, commands no more sympathy than Roberta;—indeed, most readers inevitably must sympathise with the spirit of the "irate woodsman's" brutal question during the trial. This undefiled son of the forest asked: "Why don't they kill the God-damned bastard and be done with him?" But, just for this reason, it has to be remembered that Mr. Dreiser exhausts every possible means so to account for Clyde as to preserve him from all blame. The squid is the complete plaything of "chemic compulsion," the paragon of irresponsibility, the perfect exemplar of the truth as the truth has been revealed to his creator.

This being so, it is little less than a miracle that Mr. Dreiser has contrived—through the infinite detail of a merely circumstantial realism—to save Clyde Griffiths' humanity sufficiently to maintain the reader's "suspension of disbelief" until the end of the book. Undoubtedly he has done so, though he has not succeeded in making all readers feel that patience has been adequately rewarded. They have been impressed, as is fitting before so monumental a composition; they have been troubled; they have not been recompensed. Eight hundred and forty pages devoted to the unconscionable prolongation of a mere sensational newspaper story! Remarks to this effect I have heard more than once; and they roughly indicate the real difficulty—the inevitably self-destroying effect of such an effort as Mr. Dreiser's, in proportion as it is successful.

This difficulty, however, does not actually lie in the plot of *An American Tragedy*, as the remark just cited implies. The bare plot of the *Agamemnon* of Æschylus might equally well form the basis of a mere sensational newspaper story, and Clytæmnestra in that play and in the *Choephori* makes for herself, not without seeming justice, the plea that is made for Clyde Griffiths. Not she, but Destiny, she says, through her its helpless instrument slew Agamemnon; and she also pleads that she did not make herself, yet can only act out her inborn nature. But it is not for his plots, nor because he was well acquainted with Mr. Dreiser's view of life, that Æschylus lives on still amongst us. His dramas have a perennial and deep value for mankind because, rejecting the plausible notion of "chemic compulsion," he struggled with profound conviction to convey a very different meaning through their form, characters, and action. Without evading any of its difficulty, he asserted his faith that Moral Law uncompromisingly governs the life of man, making for an order which is divine, in the face of a chaos intrinsically evil, and that men are fully, if tragically, responsible for the consequences of their acts, whatever their motives or compulsions, so that ignorance and self-conceit are equally as criminal as violence.

This is not to say all, of course, but it may suffice to show how Æschylus and, more clear-sightedly, Sophocles cut straight through to the centre of the human problem and propounded a solution which, if not the only one, nor by itself a complete one, is still, strictly speaking, irrefutable, being founded directly upon facts of experience which have not changed with the passing generations;—an unassailable solution, moreover, which gives weight and meaning to every individual and to all of his acts. And hence it is that the bloody and sensational fables of Æschylus and Sophocles, triumphantly formed in full harmony with their meaning, have an interest and value for men which time does not exhaust.

Mr. Dreiser's difficulty is not that he has different facts of experience to interpret;—he has precisely the same facts concerning an essentially unchanged human nature. His difficulty is that his mechanistic naturalism compels him so to select and manipulate facts of experience as to deny, through his narrative, that human life has any meaning or value. The attempt is suicidal, and the more consistently it is carried out the more completely is Mr. Dreiser forced to divest his creatures and their actions of any distinctively human quality and meaning. The more successful he is the more insignificant his work becomes. *An American Tragedy*, as I have said, is more skilfully, faithfully, and consistently executed on the naturalistic level than any of its author's earlier novels, and precisely for this reason it contains no single element of tragedy in any legitimate sense of the word, and it impresses thoughtful readers as a mere sensational newspaper story long drawn out. In other words, in proportion as Mr. Dreiser contrives to accomplish his self-imposed task he has nothing to tell us except that there is nothing to tell about life until it can be reduced even below the apparent level of animal existence, to the point where it becomes a meaningless chaos of blind energies.

Whether or not any real sense of the self-destroying character of this effort, to create a literature as valueless and insignificant as possible, will ever strike Mr. Dreiser's consciousness, I should not venture to guess. But only an obstinate self-conceit, or an invincible stupidity, one imagines, could have kept him from seeing the absurdities into which he was forced, in the course of half-a-dozen sentences, when he recently attempted to draw up a brief statement of his present belief. He wrote: "I can make no comment on my work or my life that holds either interest or import for me. Nor can I imagine any explanation or interpretation of any life, my own included, that would be either true—or important, if true. Life is to me too much a welter and play of inscrutable forces to permit, in my case at least, any significant comment. One may paint for one's own entertainment, and that of others—perhaps. As I see him the utterly infinitesimal individual weaves among the mysteries a floss-like and wholly meaningless course—if course it be. In short I catch no meaning from all I have seen, and pass quite as I came, confused and dismayed." [3]

To this point has Mr. Dreiser's naturalism driven him. If the general sense of this awkward yet mannered statement comprised the truth about him and his work, he would, of course, never have been asked to make it. He would, in all probability, have been confined long ago to an asylum; and

[3] From the *Bookman*, September, 1928 (Vol. 68, p. 25).

he would certainly never have written any of his books. Those books, moreover, have manifestly not been written just for his own entertainment. They have been written because he felt he had something to say—because of his certainty that he had come to know the truth, as men in general knew it not. And with singular faithfulness of purpose and of industry, involving what for him must have been almost superhuman effort, because of his defects of mind and training, he has devoted himself to the struggle to express the truth as he conceived it—that is, to reduce it to consistency and give it coherent form. He has also neglected nothing, within his limits, to make it impressive. He has thus lived a rationally purposive life, reducing at least to symptoms of order the welter of his impressions and impulses, controlling at least fitfully his rebellious temperament, and mastering (or "sublimating") at least partially his almost pathological obsession by sex. For the sake of self-expression—or, as I shall presently suggest, of self-justification—he has thus achieved an appreciably disciplined life, and so has in his own person, against his own literary aim, furnished a convincing refutation of his philosophy. He has effectively proved that *An American Tragedy* gives form to a view of life as gratuitous as it is unmeaning.

Fortunately it is now realised by an increasing number of people that naturalistic philosophies are merely speculative ventures, which derive no valid support from "modern science." And it has, besides, been shown above how little "science" had to do with the formation of Mr. Dreiser's naturalistic prejudice. Mr. Dreiser, on his own showing, was first awakened to a sense of life as a problem to be solved by his discovery of the radical contrast between the ethical standards of his father and his church (as he understood its teaching), and his own spontaneous impulses and desires. His haphazard, undirected education gave him an

167

unexcelled opportunity to learn that there were many others like himself, that they seemed to be the most vigorous members of their communities, and that they never hesitated to transgress every ethical standard, when they could get away with it, in their struggle for self-advancement and self-gratification. He treasured every impression which seemed to be on his side against ethical standards by which he stood condemned. His self-esteem had been gravely shocked by the discordance he had discovered, and he now found the means to restore it and, indeed, to strengthen it, by appeal from home and church to the larger world. Not he was in the wrong of it, but the "senseless," "impossible" theories which would have convicted him of shameful tendencies. "In shame there is no comfort, but to be beyond all bounds of shame," says one of Sidney's Arcadians, and this Mr. Dreiser might thenceforth have taken for his motto.

Governed by this apolaustic prejudice, he has since continued his transparent course of seeing only what he has desired to see, or rather of admitting the reality of only what has suited him, while setting down all else as either hypocrisy or delusion. And while it is true that no one escapes the necessity of bringing only a selective attention to bear upon the outer world, it by no means follows that we are all alike cut off from "reality." On the contrary, it does mean that the basis of our selective attention, the interests and purposes served by it, are of fundamental importance. And the disastrous effect of Mr. Dreiser's apolaustic prejudice is that it encouraged him in slavery to mere temperament, in helpless surrender to the chaotic flow of "natural" impulses, while it brought to his attention from the outer world only what fed itself, the antics of complicated beasts with strange illusions. The trouble with what he thus saw is not that it was non-existent, some gross trick of the fevered imagination;—it was there to be seen—it is there, in grievous plenty.

168

No, the trouble is that none of it has positive significance. The naturalism which it fathers lights up the animal in man, but tells man nothing of that which positively distinguishes him from the beast—more, it vindictively denies that anything save hypocrisy and delusion does so distinguish him. And while it seeks to dissolve our humanity, it ends, as it ends in Mr. Dreiser, in a bottomless morass of misrepresentation and despair. This is the American tragedy of our confused age which constitutes the real import of Mr. Dreiser's masterpiece.

NOTE—For permission to quote from the writings of Mr. Dreiser, I am indebted both to him and to his publisher, Mr. Horace Liveright.

# Pandora's Box in American Fiction .

## HARRY HAYDEN CLARK

America, Carlyle wrote Emerson, "is verily the Door of Hope to distracted Europe; which otherwise I should see crumbling down into blackness of darkness."

The Door of Hope! It is perhaps time now to ask down what corridors this door has led, to scrutinise the precise quality of American hope. Is it a new hope, or a disguised form of the European hope which has led "to blackness of darkness"? What, for example, have our fiction writers, reflecting the American mind, past and present, reported regarding the success of their quest for happiness? If they have reported that certain sorts of hope have led to despair, what evidence is there that other sorts lead to joy? For "the desire for happiness," says Arnold, "is the root and ground of man's being. Tell him and show him that he places his happiness wrong, that he seeks for delight where delight will never really be found; then you illumine and further him." Let us sketch the quality, first, of the hope of a paradise of supernal beauty; second, the hope of an American paradise of nature; and finally, the hope of "A Paradise *within* thee, happier far."

## I

If we consider the European background of the hope to escape to a paradise of supernal beauty and bliss, we find that in the classical legends of the Golden Age, in such Renaissance writers as Lyly, Sidney, and Spenser, and in such later work as Thomson's *Castle of Indolence*, this idyllic Arcadianism was either frankly recreational and non-philosophic or else a cloak for allegory. Not until the middle of the eighteenth century was the idyllic dream taken seriously. Revolting from earlier and contemporary restriction of the imagination, Akenside advocated refusing to "restrain" one's "soaring fancy," Joseph Warton glorified the "creative and glowing imagination," and Edward Young sought to escape "this pestilential earth" by the "creative power" of the imagination to call forth paradisiacal beauties, "shadowy beings and unknown worlds," in the "vast void beyond real existence." He exalted a genius which was to "wander wild" in "the fairy land of fancy," "reign arbitrarily over its own empire of chimeras," and "sport with its infinite objects uncontrolled." Thus in *Vathek* Beckford created a sensuous and erotic paradise with its five palaces which he destined "for the particular gratification of each of the five senses." "The light that never was, on sea or land," enthralled the youthful Wordsworth, but he soon questioned it as a "fond illusion." Keats sought to escape on "the viewless wings of Poesy" from the "weariness" of actuality to the "charmed magic casements." Shelley, the high priest of this ceaseless and aimless quest for the unattainable, tells us that only his "fearful and monstrous" story of *The Cenci* is "a sad reality"; otherwise he "dreams of what ought to be, or what may be." For him the Spirit of Beauty leaves "This dim vast vale of tears, vacant and desolate." His is a longing indeterminate, a

> "devotion to something afar
> From the sphere of our sorrow."

> "I loved I know not what—but this low sphere,
> And all that it contains, contains not thee."

*Alastor* and *Epipsychidion* are matchless records of his fruitless quest for the phantom of desire. DeQuincey's fantasies are "filled with perishing dreams, and the wrecks of forgotten deliriums." *The Lady of Shalott* and *The Palace of Art* testify to Tennyson's reluctant renunciation of the life of illusion. Swinburne characterised himself in *A Nympholept*, while his friend, the author of *The Earthly Paradise*, strove to

> "build a shadowy isle of bliss
> Midmost the beating of the steely sea."

With this background in mind, let us see to what extent the American story-tellers' hope for a paradise of supernal beauty coincides with the idyllic, indeterminate hope of the English romanticists. In *The Author's Account of Himself*, Irving, our first master of the short story, states his Old World longing "to escape, in short, from the common-place realities of the present," to "the shadowy grandeurs of the past," the "earthly paradise" of "Bellissima Granada" and the legend-haunted Alhambra. *The Legend of Prince Ahmed al Kamel*, dealing with the quest for the phantom of desire, illustrates the idyllic quality of his imagination. The Prince, called the "Perfect" on account of his "super-excellence," receives from a dove tidings of a fair princess —"no flower of the field could compare with her for loveliness." In the Spanish spring-time the Prince, a "pilgrim of love," resolves to "seek this unknown princess throughout the world." Guided by a parrot and an owl, he eventually finds her in the court of her hostile father. The lover produces his "silken carpet of the throne of Solomon," and after confessing his devotion, "the carpet rose in the air, bearing off the prince and princess . . . and then disappeared in the blue vault of heaven." Irving, however, sought "escape . . . from the common-place" not only in the picturesque fantasies of Old Spain but also in the glamorous aspects of the American past, as illustrated in *The Legend of Sleepy*

*Hollow.* In "a remote period of American history," among "some of the goodliest scenes of the mighty Hudson," Ichabod rides on a "fine autumnal day" through the "rich and golden livery" of a natural paradise to win the "peerless," "ripe and melting and rosy-cheeked Katrina" and her "unimaginable luxury." Introduced by lines from *The Castle of Indolence, The Legend* illustrates Irving's somewhat sentimental and humorous continuation of the merely recreational Arcadianism of earlier days. And the ruse of the Headless Horseman, in connection with the "twilight superstitions" of one who was "a perfect master of Cotton Mather's *History of New England Witchcraft,*" suggests the interesting tendency of the native Puritan interest in things unearthly, with the waning of faith, to become a subject for the æsthetic imagination as in the case of Hawthorne and Poe.

Unlike Irving, Poe takes the idyllic dream seriously. He defines the Poetic Principle as "simply the Human Aspiration for Supernal Beauty," manifested "in an elevating excitement of the Soul." Of course, as every one knows, his vigorous reason controlled the decadent imagination and emotion of the earlier Gothic school and made him perhaps our greatest master of the short story technique. But let us illustrate and define the content of his "aspiration," his "elevating excitement of the Soul." Where does he seek happiness? One thinks of the "delirious bliss" of "the Valley of the Many-Coloured Grass" in *Eleanora*. We might better, however, turn to *The Domain of Arnheim,* where Ellison, with "*a fortune of four hundred and fifty million dollars,*" seeks to satisfy his passion for an exclusively "physical loveliness," his "four elementary conditions of bliss," which are "free exercise," "the love of woman," "contempt of ambition," and "an object of unceasing pursuit." After a four year quest he finds in the "luxuriant nature of the Pacific Islands" "an elevated table-land of wonderful fertility and beauty"; it was the "Paradise of Arnheim," combining everything rich and voluptuous. Ellison, however, sought to gratify the "one passion of his soul, the thirst for beauty," "above all . . . in the sympathy of a woman, not unwomanly, whose loveliness and love enveloped his existence in the pure atmosphere of Paradise." Thus the content of Poe's aspiration, as well as his references here to the "chimera of the perfectionists" "Turgot, Price, Priestley and Condorcet," to "Fonthill," the birthplace of *Vathek,* and to the "rapt day-dreams of De Staël," suggest that his aspiration is essentially one with that ceaseless and aimless sensuous longing already illustrated in the English romanticists. Or take *The Island of the Fay,* which deals with the contemplation of "the glory of God" in "natural scenery"—"all within the Spirit Divine"—in a "rivulet and island," "all one radiant harem of garden beauties." Shelley-like, he sees approach the "enchanted" island a gentle Fay in a "fragile canoe" with a "phantom of an oar." This vision of loveliness, however, passed "disconsolately with her boat into the region of the ebony flood," and "darkness fell over all things and I beheld her magical figure no more." Thus, as Professor Foerster has so finely said, Poe gives us only "shuddering harmonies of the murky subconscious, and roseate harmonies of sensuous longing posing as spirituality. . . . His vision oscillated not between the earthly and the supernal, but between the infernal and the Arcadian." But what did Poe report regarding the success of his aspiration for supernal beauty? "To be thoroughly conversant with Man's heart," he concludes, "is to take our final lesson in the iron-clasped volume of Despair." Thinking of writing a book on his life, he said: "No man will ever dare write it. No man could write it, even if he dared. The paper would shrivel and blaze at every touch of the fiery pen."

Perhaps the most vigorous and passionate Arcadian in American literature is Herman Melville, mariner and mystic. Descended from Dutch and New England parents proud and conservative, Melville was driven to "the water world," he tells us, by "sad disappointments . . . united with a naturally roving disposition." He deserted his ship and found in the valley of the Typees "perpetual hilarity. Surrounded by all the luxurious provisions of nature," the innocent natives enjoy the idyllic bliss "that springs principally from that all-pervading sensation which Rousseau told us he at one time experienced: the mere buoyant sense of healthful, physical existence." This was before the missionaries and "the worst attendances of civilisation" drove "all peace and happiness from the valley." In *Mardi,* frankly idyllic and nympholeptic, devoted to the savages "as they are not," Melville's nostalgic idealism and his hatred of reality become intensified. Here he creates a dream-girl, Yillah, "the earthly semblance of that sweet vision, that haunted my earliest thought," and the book is a record of the allegorical quest for her through all the nations of the earth. It follows Unitarianism and Transcendentalism, with their hope for the infinite perfectibility of men; it is the quest of *Alastor* and *Epipsychidion,* the quest of Novalis for the Blue Flower. "But fiery yearnings their own phantom-future make, and deem it present. So, if after all these fearful, fainting trances, the verdict be, the golden haven was not gained;—yet, in bold quest thereof better to sink in boundless deeps than float on vulgar shoals; and give me, ye gods, an utter wreck, if wreck I do." If Melville fled, however, "not so much bound to any haven ahead as rushing from all havens astern"—such as the "Babylonish brick-kiln of New

York," "Commonness and Conventionalism," "mines and marts," and Democracy, "the harlot on horseback"—his first-hand experience with the reality of a sea red in tooth and claw as well as "the mystery of iniquity" tended to clash with his dreams of Utopia. *Moby-Dick* was born of this clash between the hope of a paradise of supernal beauty and the sight of a malignant reality from the deck of a whaler. We have his own commentary on the final results of nympholeptic longing:

> "Explain this darkness, exorcise this devil, ye cannot. . . . The truest of men was the Man of Sorrows, and the truest of all books is Solomon's, and the Ecclesiastes is the fine hammered steel of woe. All is vanity. All. . . . He who . . . calls Cowper, Young, Pascal, Rousseau, poor devils all of sick men. . . . And your only Mardian happiness is but exemption from great woes—no more. . . . Sadness makes the silence throughout the realms of space; Sadness is universal and eternal."

Let us skip the realism of the later nineteenth century, most of which is essentially arid, and approach such a figure as Floyd Dell. Born of autobiographical revery, *Moon-Calf* is the history of a "lonely, unhappy, desperately desiring and bewildered child" in various Middle Western towns as he sought refuge in dreams from "the mysterious and troublesome real world which he feared and disliked." The avenues of escape are two: the "gorgeous fantasies which were unrolled for him in the pages of books," and the quest of the dream-girl. Lured by the hope of "freedom, of happiness, of a world altogether new and beautiful," Felix becomes a Socialist, only to find later that "that garret Utopia had somehow lost its savour." He becomes a factory worker —in the chaste language of his boss, "the messiest, absentmindedest, God-damn carelessest person he had ever seen around a factory." And then he tries newspaper work, and is again discharged. Then "he wanted, with a kind of

176

nostalgia, to write that novel." Like Shelley, he sought refuge from a world to which he refused to adjust himself by turning "his gaze inward upon a world of ideas and dreams." As Wheels says, "The world itself is hideous. You can't do anything with it. But you can dream beautiful dreams. . . . There is no other beauty." An "incorrigible Utopian," a member of the Agnostic Society, Felix escaped to poetry—an "enchanted land"—loving the "drug-like beauty" of "words, which were like a perfumed breeze out of nowhere, or out of some strange life lived before, affecting him with a strange nostalgia."

> "Nay, I was sent a wanderer
> On Beauty's desperate quest—
> To go forever seeking Her,
> Nor, ere I find her, rest."

And then there is the quest for the dream-girl. First there is Rose, the gardener's daughter, whom he meets in the attic and to whom he reads Rousseau's *Confessions*. One night they stay in the woods, watching the stars, and "awakened chill and stiff, a little before dawn." In "the innermost caves of fantasy" she was the "Virgin Queen" of Atlantis, and he her Harper. . . . "She was . . . hope that turns to despair." And then there was Margaret, Helen Raymond, Daisy Fisher, Emily, Mrs. Miller, Lucy, and finally Joyce, with whom he spent the nights in the cabin. He explains to Joyce that he seeks "something better than just ordinary, everyday happiness," that he doesn't believe in private property, God, the home, or the support of one's wife. He wants a companionship "at once light and gracious, irresponsible and sincere, generous and self-respecting!" Finally he felt "a discrepancy between her and a not very distinct ideal of his imagination." He "clung to the memory of his shadow-land of ideas" in preference to the "world of desperate reality," and when his beloved Joyce tells him she is to work out her human destiny with another the "world of his dreams fell shattering about him." Obviously, *Moon-Calf* is the creation of the sort of hope which robbed Shelley of "peace within."

Let us turn to Willa Cather, whose main theme is the struggle for æsthetic or emotional self-realisation amid the sordid environment of either the frontier or an industrial society. In *O Pioneers!* most piteous is the fate of the fair Marie Tovesky, murdered in the arms of her lover. In *The Song of the Lark* Thea Kronsburg develops her rare voice in spite of a gossipy Colorado town. "There is only one big thing—desire." In *My Ántonia* the heroine says, "That is happiness—to be dissolved in something complete and great." Her lust for richness of experience leads to her becoming an unmarried mother and finally the mother of a large family. In *Youth and the Bright Medusa* a typical story is that of Paul, whose longing for an æsthetic paradise in a flatly stolid industrial town led him to robbery and to suicide after a week's fulfilment of his hopes. Most instructive, perhaps, is *The Professor's House*, based on the fruitless struggle of the romantic spirit against materialism and convention. The Professor does not "think much of science as a phase of human development"; he resisted the new "commercialism" in education; he preferred his old dingy study to the one in the pretentious house which his worldly wife and daughters had planned; he loathes the petty quarrels of his daughters over fashions; and his wife accuses him of "shutting yourself away from everybody." In place of materialism and convention, however, he seeks to substitute not a central interest in what is most richly and typically human but rather a refuge in the romantic past: in the pomp of the Middle Ages when man was "a principal in a gorgeous drama with God"; in the bygone glories of the Spanish ad-

178

venturers; in reliving in revery his youth, "the realest of his lives"; in the loving study of many a quaint and curious volume of forgotten lore; and in his interest in his former student's worship of the ancient Cliff-dwellers. The seemingly irrelevant interpolation of Tom Outland's story of his inability to interest official Washington, "so petty, so slavish," in his "religious emotion" regarding his discovery of the relics of the Cliff-dwellers is explained by its paralleling and under-scoring the Professor's own struggle—the romantic spirit struggling in vain against materialism and convention. Finally, when the Professor's family departed for Europe, he "thought of eternal solitude with gratefulness," and "wanted to run away from everything he had intensely cared for." One night while he is resting in his old study a storm blows out his gas stove and slams his window shut: he awakens to find himself "nearly asphyxiated"; he wished to die. "He hadn't lifted his hand against himself—was he required to lift it for himself?" He cannot bear the thought of his wife's return and the continuation of their way of life. Finally an old friend revives him, but he found that "he had let something go—and it was gone: something very precious." He reflects that "his apathy" will not trouble a family "preoccupied with their own affairs." No, the merely romantic devotion to what is picturesque in the storied past will never avail in the quest for peace in a conventional and materialistic environment.

Like Poe, Joseph Hergesheimer strives to escape "the dreary and impertinent duty of improving the world" in his worship of an unattainable beauty. His friend Mr. Cabell finds "in all the Hergesheimer novels" "men labouring toward the unattainable, and a high questing foiled." For example, in *Linda Condon*, based on this theme, Peyton, a sculptor, seeks in vain to win the beautiful Linda, who marries another. The sculptor endeavours to sublimate his passion in the creation of a great statue, which is destroyed by a mob, and he dies in forlorn desolation.

"Love was the supreme force, and its greatest expression a desire beyond the body. . . . The endless service of beauty. Of course, a woman—but never the animal; the spirit always. Born in the spirit, served in the spirit, ending in the spirit. A direct contradiction, you see, to nature and common sense, frugality and the sacred symbol of the dollar. . . . The old gesture toward the stars, the bridge of perfection, the escape from the fatality of the flesh. Yet it was a service of the body made incredibly lovely in actuality and still never to be grasped. Never to be won."

This spiritualised beauty, however, is of course dependent upon sensuousness, and Mr. Hergesheimer asserts that "the whole discharge of my responsibility was contained in the imperative obligation to . . . put down the colours and scents and emotions of existence." And, like Keats, like all who found life on a merely sensuous beauty, he is haunted by the dread of transience, by "that sharp sense of beauty which came from a firm, delicate consciousness of certain high pretensions, valours, maintained in the face of imminent destruction . . . in the category none was sharper than the charm of a woman, soon to perish in a vanity of array as momentary and iridescent as a May-fly." He tells us that he creates ideal beauty as a result of "the assault of a persuasive discontent." Nothing matters but an unattainable sensuous beauty; and this merely impresses him with its evanescence. This transient beauty can be arrested only by art, and he begins a later essay on art with the words, "I am getting damned tired of art. . . ."

Perhaps the endless and aimless longing for the unattainable has received most elaborate treatment at the hands of Mr. Hergesheimer's friend, James Branch Cabell. In *Beyond Life*, a series of essays, he outlines his literary creed, his hostility to realism. Holding that "veracity is the one unpardonable sin," he "perceives this race . . . to be beyond all wording petty and ineffectual," and he follows the "instinct of any hurt animal to seek revenge . . . in the field of imagination" by retreating to Poictesme, "that fair country . . . which is bounded by Avalon and Phæacia and Sea-coast Bohemia, and the contiguous forests of Arden and Broceliande, and on the west of course by the Hesperides." Let us examine the quality and success of Mr. Cabell's aspiration as embodied in *The Cream of the Jest.* Felix Kennaston, the hero, is actually a conventional novelist, a conservative property-owner, a Presbyterian, and a good husband. Inwardly, however, he is a dreamer who seeks to escape from the thralldom of actuality in his quest of "Ettarre, who embodied all Kennaston was ever able to conceive of beauty and fearlessness and strange purity, all perfections, all the attributes of divinity, in a word, such as his slender human faculties were competent to understand." "It is the cream of a vile jest," he says, "that I am forbidden ever to win quite to you, ever to touch you." These magic dreams of Ettarre are induced by a sigil—a broken disc which Felix found on one of his walks. Finally, near his death, it is discovered that this magic sigil is only "the metal top of a cold cream jar," and his dreams become a tale told by an idiot, signifying nothing. This is perhaps the blackest pessimism in American literature—the conviction that reality is a "dragging nightmare," and the discovery that the illusion which alone makes life bearable is founded on nothing more sacred than the broken "top of a cold cream jar." And it should be noted that, all Mr. Cabell's books being parts of a "Biography," Felix is nothing less than a symbol of "humanity." "His history was, in essentials, the history of our race thus far. All I advanced for or against him, was true of all men that have ever lived."

*Jurgen* may be said to deal mainly with the poignancy of

the realisation of the contrast between the veiled loveliness of youthful illusions and a cold and ugly sensuous reality; relief is sought through an escape from this reality in dreaming of these illusions now shattered, or in dreaming of new illusions. In actuality, Jurgen is only a dirty little pot-bellied pawn-broker of the Middle Ages married to a shrewish, cowardly wife. Through magic, however, he is enabled to pack into one year "the follies of a quarter of a century," to seek through a land of fabulous loveliness the phantom of desire. There he meets Dorothy la Désirée, "in all things perfect," as he had loved her in the "garden between Dawn and Sunrise"; in reality she was a "horrible lascivious woman." And there in her robe of flaming silk is the young Guenevere, "the fairest of mortal women"; there is the Queen Sylvia Tereu of pallid charm who vanishes at dawn; there is Anaitis, the personification of a nature myth, with her ecstatic rites and sensual orgies; there is the plump Chloris, loveliest of Hamadryads; there is Queen Helen, for whose fabulous beauty he hungered even in childhood; there is the proud Dolores, "lovely as a hawk is lovely"; there is Florimel who dwelt by the Sea of Blood; and there is Phyllis, Satan's wife, "the loveliest little slip of devilishness." Of one and all Jurgen tires. His remark that his "tender heart and tolerably keen eyes" force him "to jeer out of season" to avoid "far more untimely tears" reminds us of the Bohemian Byron who finally confesses with infinite sadness:

"If I laugh at any mortal thing,
    'Tis that I may not weep; and if I weep,
'Tis that our nature cannot always bring
    Itself to apathy."

And in the end we have Jurgen's Shelley-like admission of the futility and hopelessness of his aimless longing:

"Oh, nothing can help me, for I do not know what thing it is that I desire! . . . For I am Jurgen who seeks he knows not what. . . . I have gone romancing through the world, . . . nowhere have I found what I desired. . . . I am compact of weariness and apprehension, for I no longer discern what thing is I, nor what is my desire, and I fear that I am already dead."

It is evident, then, that in the hope for a paradise of supernal beauty Americans have been lured as by a Siren to an abyss of despair of which the English romanticists, who experimented with this idyllic hope, warned us over a century ago. The Edward Young who sported in his paradisiacal "empire of chimeras" "cast the total" of his life as "despair." Keats reported that in the romantic "Temple of Delight"

"Veiled Melancholy has her sovran shrine."

And Shelley of the iridescent dreams, who would

"Hope till Hope creates
From its own wreck the thing it contemplates,"

confessed in the end:

"Alas! I have nor hope nor health,
Nor peace within nor calm around."

Very beautiful are these rainbow visions—but they are conjured out of night.

## II

Let us turn to a second sort of hope—the hope of an American paradise of nature. Although the paradise of nature appears in Vergil, in Renaissance pastorals by Lyly, Sidney, and Spenser, in Perdita's shepherd home and in the sylvan cave of Cymbeline's sons, its use was mainly either decorative or allegorical until the eighteenth century. In 1711 Shaftesbury proclaimed the natural man benevolent, compassionate, and altruistic; and as such he appears in *Ossian*. Pope said, "The state of Nature was the reign of God." Rousseau broadcast the doctrine that civilisation had tended to corrupt the morals of mankind, while he described the enchanting life of man in a natural paradise. Cowper united literary simplicity, religious emotionalism, and the naturalistic humanitarianism of Rousseau. Burns glorified the simple peasant close to nature. And Coleridge and Southey dreamed fondly of an American Pantisocracy— "A Dell of Peace and Equality"—on the banks of the Susquehanna. In 1771, Philip Freneau, our first man of letters, deriving his radical democracy and his devotion to the indigenous scene from naturalism, envisaged "The Rising Glory of America":

> "A new Jerusalem, sent down from heaven,
>  Shall grace our happy earth, . . .
>  Thence called *Millennium*. Paradise anew
>  Shall flourish, by no second Adam lost . . .
>  No tempting serpent to allure the soul
>  From native innocence."

Indeed, it is interesting to speculate upon the extent to which this English romantic faith in the "native innocence" of mankind, transplanted to the inexhaustible resources of the American frontier, has under these unique conditions furnished philosophic sanction for an unbridled materialism which has become so characteristically national. Frontier isolation tended to breed self-confidence, equality, self-reliance, optimism, contempt for artificial distinctions and a dependence upon the material world. Crèvecœur in 1782 defined "an American" as a "new man who acts upon new principles."

"We have no princes, for whom we toil, starve, and bleed: we are the most perfect society now existing in the world. Here man is free as he ought to be."

Our first novelist who sought a paradise of American nature was James Fenimore Cooper. Revolting against both the feudalism of aristocratic Europe and the crude democracy of Jacksonian America, Cooper sought refuge in projecting his ideals in the character of Leatherstocking and also in such a Utopian paradise as in *The Crater*. Whatever one may think of Cooper's Indians, his "females," his woodcraft, or his rhetoric, Leatherstocking remains a great contribution to the fiction of the world, "perhaps," according to Professor Paine, "the greatest embodiment of native character in American literature." He is strangely compounded of Cooper's memories of his old hunter-friend Shipman, of the heroic saga of the early frontiersman as synthesised in Daniel Boone, of the Rousseauistic-Wordsworthian myth of the natural man spiritualised by contact with forest and stream, and of the idealism of American manhood. According to Cooper's summary,

". . . His feelings appeared to possess the freshness and nature of the forest in which he passed so much of his time, and no casuist could have made clearer decisions in matters relating to right and wrong. . . . In short . . . he was a fair example of what a just-minded and pure man might be, while untempted by unruly or ambitious desires, and left to follow the bias of his feelings, amid the solitary grandeur and ennobling influences of a sublime nature."

In 1828, however, we find Cooper disillusioned: "All attempts to blend history and romance in America have been comparative failures. . . . The baldness of American life is in deadly hostility to scenic representation." And in *The Crater* (1847) we find him creating a Utopia in a fabulous mid-Pacific island in order to furnish a contrast to the wretchedness of contemporary American life. This is a story of how some folk, shipwrecked on a reef which is the crater of a volcano, succeed in causing vegetation to grow, of how they create a "settlement surrounded with a sort of earthly paradise" which is finally "buried beneath the ocean." The story, as Cooper conceives it, is a parable: "Of such is the world and its much-coveted advantages. For a time our efforts seem to create, and to adorn, and to perfect, until we forget our origin and destination, substituting self for that divine hand . . ." Already, in *The Monikins* (1835), born of bitter disenchantment, Cooper the former idealist had presented the world as a country ruled by a race of monkeys who laughed to scorn the Yahoo race of mankind. The hope of an American paradise of nature ended for Cooper in disillusionment; natural goodness, democracy, human ideals are revealed here as sounding brass and tinkling cymbals. Professor Pattee compares Cooper's final pessimism with that of Mark Twain: "Both began as border-minded individualists, parochial-minded, intoxicated with American idealism; both by travel and by wide contacts with urban pessimism were educated into blasé cosmopolitanism . . . and both went out at last in utter misanthropy. . . . It is an American evolution!"

The most significant history of our national quest for a material happiness is perhaps embodied in the work of Mark Twain, whose much-discussed pessimism may be explained mainly by the fact that, as the spokesman of frontier America living exclusively "in the present," he served as the faithful mirror to a whole nation in which an Industrial Revolution, philosophic mechanistic determinism, and the collapse of illusions led to despair. His stories illustrate the changing importance of the two planes of consciousness in the frontier mind—the consciousness of a hopeful and radiant illusion, and the consciousness of a hopeless and sordid reality. Take three stories, representing three different periods. *The Jumping Frog* (1865), dealing with the winning of a bet by roguery, embodies in a humorous way the reckless exuberance and joyousness of the dawning West after the Gold Rush. To this type belong also the books which glorify the "natural man" and the free-born American—*Roughing It* (1873), *Tom Sawyer* (1876), *Life on the Mississippi* (1883), and *Huck Finn* (1884). In contrast, his first book, *Innocents Abroad* (1869), represents the frontiersman's life-long contempt for European tradition and Europe, "one vast museum of magnificence and misery," groping "in the midnight of priestly superstition for sixteen hundred years." A story of a second period, *The Million Pound Bank Note* (1893) mirrors a materialistic "gilded age" in which, lured on by a fabulous hope, men bowed to the Golden Calf while the spectre of reality haunted their thoughts. In this story the two planes of consciousness are in equipoise until the end, when the plane of illusion prevails. It is the tale, briefly, of how a poor tramp masquerades as the owner of a million pound bank note; grim poverty stalks behind him, but every one worships the illusion of his wealth, and he finally wins the girl of his heart as well as the million pounds. The story is a parable of the West: these were the days of illusory fortunes in transcontinental railroads, in iron and steel, the days of the Morgans and Carnegies and Fricks and Goulds. "I am," said Mark Twain, "frightened at the proportion of my prosperity . . . Whatever I touch turns to gold." In 1895 he was bankrupt. But take a story representative of the third period—*The $30,000 Bequest* (1907). A poor book-keeper and his wife, learning of a promised fortune at the death of a relative, each night "put the plodding world away, and lived in another and a fairer, reading romances to each other, dreaming dreams, comrading with kings and princes." They increasingly neglect realities and scorn their associates. "The castle-building habit, the day-dreaming habit—how it grows! What a luxury it becomes; how we revel in them, steep our souls in them, intoxicate ourselves with their beguiling fantasies—oh, yes, and how soon and how easily our dream life and our material life become so immingled and so fused together that we can't tell which is which, any more." Just as the Golden West was unable to keep its "dream life," its illusions, triumphant over its "material life," its stark reality, so with the brutal news that the "town had to bury" the deceitful relative, the poverty-stricken book-keeper and his wife "lived yet two years, in mental night, always brooding, steeped in vague regrets and melancholy dreams"—like the modern realists!

What did Mark Twain report regarding his early hope for a material paradise? In *The Mysterious Stranger* (1916) he recorded his final despair, his conviction that life is cruel and meaningless—a "wandering forlorn among the empty eternities"—and in that nightmare of the fancy cowardice, hypocrisy and slavery are all that man can hope for. After the death of his daughter the master of comedy said, "My life is a bitterness, but I am content; for she has been enriched with the most precious of all gifts—the gift that makes all other gifts mean and poor—death." His *What Is Man?* and *To a Person Sitting in Darkness* express the same vein. "There is, of course, a Master Mind, but it cares nothing for our happiness or our unhappiness . . . As to the hereafter, we have not the slightest evidence that there is any . . ." To him man became "a poor joke—the poorest that was ever contrived!"

Although Hamlin Garland came to believe that "truth was a higher quality than beauty" and set himself down as "an unflinching realist," one must recall that he comes of a race of "potential poets, bards, and dreamers," that he traces in general the disillusionment resulting from an idyllic hope based upon an idealistic quest for an American paradise of nature. He records the "deep vein of poetry," the illusion, through which the pioneer viewed a sordid reality, "the place of the rainbow, and the pot of gold." "Beneath the sunset lay the enchanted land of opportunity."

> "When we've wood and prairie land,
>     Won by our toil,
> We'll reign like kings in fairy land,
>     Lords of the soil!"

Here is Pater's "Sangreal of an endless pilgrimage" transferred to prairie-land. Later he confesses, "I had idealised all the figures and scenes of my boyhood." "This land of my childhood," "its charm, its strange dominion," he has to admit, "did not in truth exist—it was a magical world, born of the vibrant union of youth and firelight, of music and the voice of moaning winds." Like Wordsworth's early "light that never was, on sea or land," Garland's illusion "has all the quality of a vision, something experienced in another world," covered with "a poetic glamour."

However, if the Son of the Middle Border sought a pot of gold at the foot of the rainbow which did not exist, if he is pursuing fancifully a phantom of hope, he is honest enough to record the results of such a quest. As he grew up he noted a "growing bitterness"—"disillusionment had begun." The Shelleyan rainbow of hope faded into the light of common day. What had been the "marvel of a golden earth before a crimson sky" became merely "Uncle Sam's domain, bleak, semi-arid, and wind-swept." "I perceived little that was poetic, little that was idyllic."

"What purpose does a man serve by toiling like that for sixty years with no increase in leisure, with no growth in mental grace? . . . At the moment nothing glozed the essential tragic futility of their existence. . . . The essential tragedy and hopelessness of most human life under the conditions into which our society was swiftly hardening embittered me, called for expression, but even then I did not know that I had found my theme. . . . Now, suddenly I perceived the futility of our quest. . . ."

It is clear, also, that Garland is attempting a serious generalised study of the outcome of frontier hope. The young orator, meeting his father, is shocked at his sudden appearance of age and gloom: "He had come a long way from the buoyant faith of '66, and the change in him was typical of the change in the West—in America." "The almost universal disappointment and suffering of the West was typical." "All the gilding of farm life melted away. The hard and bitter realities came back upon me in a flood . . . Every house I visited had its individual message of sordid struggle and half-hidden despair." Garland, then, has given us a cross-section of our national history; he has faithfully recorded the "almost universal" despair which greets men who would "reign like kings in fairyland."

Rolvaag's *Giants in the Earth*, "A Saga of the Prairie," is another impressive record of the Odyssey "Toward the Sunset" of the frontiersman and the finding of despair instead of the pot of gold. Per Hansa and his religious wife Beret, Norwegians, journey "straight toward the west, straight toward the sky line," "deeper and deeper into a bluish-green infinity—on and on, . . . for Sunset Land." Finally they halt and raise a sod hut in "the endless solitude," the "eternal, unbroken wilderness"; they plant crops, and winter sets in; Beret has a child. Here again we meet the two planes of frontier consciousness—idyllic hope built on illusion and the dread of a sordid and terrifying reality.

"That summer Per Hansa was transported, was carried farther and ever farther away on the wings of a wonderful fairy tale—a romance in which he was both prince and king, the sole possessor of countless treasures.  In this, as in all other fairy tales, the story grew ever more fascinating and dear to the heart, the farther it advanced. . . . Ever more beautiful grew the tale; ever more dazzlingly shone the sunlight over the fairy castle."

On one side there is the "divine restlessness," the "enchanting joyousness" of Per Hansa; on the other, Beret's poignant yearning for human companionship and inner spiritual peace which her dread of the stark reality cannot satisfy. "Bleak, grey, God-forsaken, the empty desolation stretched on every hand . . . How could one lift up one's voice against such silence!" As winter came on Beret saw only the snow, and for her the day "died in a pitch-black night that weighed down the heart." Her reflections give the key to the book:

"The country did not at all come up to her expectations; here, too, she saw enough of poverty and grinding toil. What did it avail, that the rich soil lay in endless stretches?  More than ever did she realise that 'man liveth not by bread alone.' . . . Even the bread was none too plentiful at times. . . .

"But no sooner had they reached America than the west-fever had smitten the old settlements like a plague.  Such a thing had never happened before in the history of mankind; people were intoxicated by bewildering visions; they spoke dazedly, as though under the force of a spell. . . . 'Go west! . . . Go west, folks! . . . The farther west, the better the land!'  Men beheld in feverish dreams the endless plains, teeming with fruitfulness, glowing, out there where day sank into night—a Beulah Land of corn and wine! . . . Ever westward led the course, to where the sun glowed in matchless glory as it sank at night; people drifted about in a sort of delirium, like birds in mating time; then they flew toward the sunset, in small flocks and large—always toward Sunset Land. . . . Now she saw it clearly: here on the trackless plains, the thousand-year-old hunger of the poor after human happiness had been unloosed!"

As she expects to die in childbirth, she pleads with Per Hansa to take the other children back to civilisation: "Human beings cannot exist here! . . . They grow into beasts!" And the magic of a fairy tale turns out to be simply nature red in tooth and claw. In the last section of the book, entitled "The Great Plain Drinks the Blood of Christian Men and is Satisfied," the story is told of how Per Hansa the faithful, the hopeful, the loving husband and father, is frozen to death while going for a doctor to help a neighbour.

"There was the Red Son of the Great Prairie, who hated the Palefaces with a hot hatred; stealthily he swooped down upon them, tore up and laid waste the little settlements. Great was the terror he spread; bloody the saga concerning him.

"But more to be dreaded than this tribulation was the strange spell of sadness which the unbroken solitude cast upon the minds of some. Many took their own lives; asylum after asylum was filled with disordered beings who had once been human. . . . Then, too, there were years of pestilence—toil and travail, famine and disease."

The frontier is exhausted, but it should be carefully noted that the quest for a physical, external paradise lives on in the American machine-age, in the dream of an industrial Utopia. To take but one illustration recorded in our fiction, Sherwood Anderson's *Poor White*—paralleling the frontier stories—traces the transition from the optimism born of untapped resources to the despair of a standardised industrialism. It is the tale of a stolid boy, Hugh McVey, who manages to invent machines from which every one hopes great things; it is supposed to be typical, to present a cross-section of American life.

"In every mind the future was bright with promise. Throughout the whole Mid-American country . . . a hopeful spirit prevailed. . . . The youth and optimistic spirit of the country led it to take hold of the hand of the giant, industrialism, and lead him laughing into the land. . . . The thing that was happening in Bidwell happened in towns all over the Middle West. Out

192

through the coal and iron regions of Pennsylvania, into Ohio and Indiana, and on westward into the States bordering on the Mississippi River, industry crept. Gas and oil were discovered in Ohio and Indiana. Over night towns grew into cities. A madness took hold of the minds of the people. . . . Wealth seemed to be spurting out of the very earth. . . . Farmers owning oil-producing land went to bed in the evening poor and owing money at the bank, and awoke in the morning rich."

But Hugh McVey, "the poor white, son of the defeated dreamer by the river," finds mere money and the satisfaction of physical needs insufficient. "He was unfilled by the life he led." Conscious of "some indefinable, inner struggle," "he fought to accept himself, to understand himself, to relate himself with the life about him." For the sanctity of the individual personality America had substituted the worship of mass production, of material gain.

"It was a time of hideous architecture, a time when thought and learning paused. Without music, without poetry, without beauty in their lives or impulses, a whole people, full of the native energy and strength of lives lived in a new land, rushed pell-mell into a new age."

In place of the free workman, joyously expressing with his own hands the dream of his own mind, came the factory-hand, blindly bitter from the machine-standardisation which thwarted the self-expression which even the farmer enjoyed. In the town of Bidwell, Jim Gibson exults in selling machine-made harnesses and ruining Joe Wainsworth, the old harness maker. Finally, in a fit of rage Wainsworth kills his tormentor. Clara, the wife of Hugh McVey, points the moral:

"In her mind the harness maker had come to stand for all the men and women who were in secret revolt against the absorption of the age in machines and the products of machines. He had stood as a protesting figure against what her father had become and what she thought her husband had become. . . . As a child she had gone often to Wainsworth's shop with her father or some farm hand, and she now remembered sharply the peace and quiet of the place. . . . Everything worth while is very far away. . . . The machines men are so intent on making have carried them very far from the old sweet things."

And we have Anderson's summary indictment of industrialism:

"Modern men and women who live in industrial cities are like mice that have come out of the fields to live in houses that do not belong to them. They live within the dark walls of the houses where only a dim light penetrates, and so many have come that they grow thin and haggard with the constant toil of getting food and warmth."

Thus those who have sought an American paradise of nature, a physical paradise, have reported finding only despair. In essentials this hope is identical with the primitivistic and industrial hope which Europe found inadequate over a century ago. Wordsworth, the high priest of naturalism, confessed he had "too blindly reposed" his trust, and he had the wisdom to seek the support of the classical and the Christian traditions. And Ruskin and Carlyle exposed the criminal fallacies involved in setting material gain above the sanctity of the individual personality. But when this outworn, exploded philosophy, based upon primitivism, faith in natural goodness, absolute liberty, *laissez faire*, and reliance upon nature and material things, was transplanted to the vast material resources of a frontier land, it was given a new, hysterical lease of life. Now, a century and a quarter later, a disenchanted America agrees with the English naturalist who testified of his infinite "dejection" and his conviction that man

"may not hope from outward forms to win
The passion and the life, whose fountains are within."

194

## III

If those who have entered the American Door of Hope in quest of happiness have reported that it is to be found neither in the Land of the Blue Flower nor in the Land of Sensuous Desire, let us inquire what those have reported who have sought the happiness of self-perfection, of an exalted personal life, of "A Paradise within thee, happier far." This quest involves a definitely focused aspiration toward, and a disciplined imitation of what is most richly and deeply human, of what is most balanced and poised and complete, of what has in the past been reported to yield lasting contentment and peace. This sort of quest is very old. To Plato and Aristotle, justice, the crown of life, consisted of the ideal balance of all the desires. Behind the Horatian doctrine of the golden mean—*auream mediocritatem*—and Cicero's praise of *mediocritatem illam quae est inter nimium et parum* is the ideal of mediation and centrality. The Christian tradition, according to Mr. G. K. Chesterton, is peculiar in its reconciling of opposites, in its synthetic balance. At any rate, the worldly classical and the other-worldly Christian traditions have united in upholding the doctrines of imitation, restraint, of a dualistic conflict in man between appetite and aspiration, and of a definitely focused aspiration which culminates in inner peace. In the Middle Ages the "law for measure" was allied to the theory of the four humours, the balance of which caused health, the excess of any one of which caused "one-sidedness" and disease. In the Renaissance the author of *Everyman in His Humour* used satire to render eccentricity ridiculous, and the Hamlet who allowed all to be "sicklied o'er with the pale cast of thought" recognised that "by the o'ergrowth of some complexion," by "one defect," men "take corruption." He honoured Horatio, his "soul's choice," because in him "blood

and judgment are so well commingl'd." The Elizabethans
recognised that a great man, like a tall tower, must be balanced at all points, or be drawn down to ruin by his own
strength. If space permitted, one might trace through the
impetus given scientific specialisation and material progress
by Bacon and the Royal Society, through such figures as
Congreve and Pope and Edward Young and Rousseau, the
gradual evolution of the theory of humours into the theory
of the master-passion and the "original genius" of being
idiosyncratic. But let us remember that Milton, uniting the
Renaissance passion for sensuous delight and the Puritan
passion for saintliness, kept his sublime balance, his vision
of centrality, his ideal of self-mastery. His exhortation to
Adam as he leaves the physical paradise of Eden is his exhortation to us:

> "Only add
> Deeds to thy knowledge answerable; add faith;
> Add virtue, patience, temperance; add love
> By name to come called Charity, the soul
> Of all the rest: then wilt thou not be loth
> To leave this Paradise, but shalt possess
> A Paradise within thee, happier far."

Mindful of the dark impulses of the natural man, the great
liberal distinguished sharply between anarchy and the true
liberty resulting from the substitution of inner for outer
control: "License they mean when they cry Liberty," he remarks of the Cavaliers, "For who loves that must first be
wise and good." "He who reigns within himself . . . is
more than a king. . . . Real and substantial liberty is rather
from within than from without."

Americans may well be proud that this noble hope partially lives on in Emerson, our greatest man of letters, who
found Milton "foremost of all men . . . to inspire," to
communicate "the vibration of hope, of self-reverence, of

piety, of delight in beauty." Out of materialistic America has come this "friend and aider of those who would live in the spirit," who strove above all to celebrate "the Ideal and Holy Life, the life within life, . . . the spiritual powers in their infinite contrast to the mechanical powers and the mechanical philosophy of this time." It is true, of course, that Emerson did not altogether escape the contagion of his romantic age; that in his apparent praise of the unique and the individual, in his most un-Miltonic faith in natural goodness, in his belittling of logic, of tradition, and of the aid which culture can give as a guide to conduct, Emerson has a certain kinship with Rousseau. Let us grant it—and guard against it! One must recall, however, that part of his dubious influence has resulted from a superficial and piece-meal reading of Emerson, encouraged by his characteristic oracular device of presenting two conflicting statements rather than a balanced and qualified generalisation. If one reads all of Emerson, however, in an endeavour to relate and define his thought, it is apparent, as Professor Harrison and Professor Foerster have found, that his stronger affinities are not with Rousseau but with Plato and the humanists. His central doctrine of self-reliance turns out to be a reliance on a self which is not unique but common to all men, "a reliance upon man's share of divinity," upon his higher, universal self. "We become divine," he says, not by eccentricity, by revolt, but by "obedience," by conformity to "the common heart," to what is normally, typically, and nobly human. In fact he strictly warns us against the "rudeness" of failing to "distinguish between the private and the universal consciousness." He perceived the unity of man, the need of spiritual concentration; his occasional assumption of good intentions is balanced by his own Spartan virtue and his confession that "because the temptations are so manifold and so subtle," he agrees with Socrates and the

Hindoos in denominating the Supreme Being the "Internal Check." In common with the Christian tradition, he sharply severs the "law for man" from the "law for thing." He is aware of "the eternal distinction between the soul and the world," aware that too great a preoccupation with the out-ward, sensuous, mundane life about us (the "work" rather than the "workman") at the expense of "the integrity of your own mind" and deeper spiritual needs, breeds a dread of transience and hence "uneasiness" and despair. Behind the fleeting scenes of daily life he perceived "that which changes not," permanent human elements common to every one, the cultivation of which gave him that sweet serenity, that "cheerfulness and courage" which Arnold pronounced the outcome of his philosophy, "his abiding word for us." "Happiness in labour, righteousness, and veracity; in all the life of the spirit; happiness and eternal hope;—that was Emerson's gospel."

Here, then, in our own native tradition is a sort of hope which led to happiness. Can such a hope, however, be recon-ciled with the artist's devotion to beauty? To Emerson, as to the æsthetes, art is simply "the creation of beauty," "beauty is its own excuse for being," and "the Beautiful is the highest." But, unlike the æsthetes, he proclaims the unity and parity of beauty, truth, and goodness—"different faces of the same All." Beauty has "its source in perfect goodness"; it is "the mark God sets upon virtue." In other words, the rarest beauty is a by-product of that perfect har-mony by which a man realises his complete humanity, his complete happiness. This ideal of beauty was given the support of a literary creed by James Russell Lowell, who never feared to expose the weakness of a romanticism whose ultimate fruit was a "melancholy liver-complaint." He urged the study and creation of a literature which should be an ideal representation of life, "stripped of all unessential

particulars" by an imagination which found "the true ideal"
not by escape but by a purposeful selection of the real.  For
Lowell as for Emerson the "first duty" of the artist "is to
be delightful."  He distinguishes, however, between a
merely recreational "literature as holiday" and a literature
which, ideally "representing life, . . . teaches, like life, by
indirection."  Such a literature, ministering to all the higher
needs of the mind and spirit, yields the greatest delight and
the greatest beauty.

Aspiration and art of this quality, however, are rare in
American fiction.  We looked for them in vain in the seekers
for a paradise of supernal beauty, and in the seekers for an
American paradise of nature.  Great as is Hawthorne as an
artist, in my judgment he falls short of an aspiration of the
Emersonian quality on account of his penchant for the eccentric, the fanciful, and the morbid.  One seeks it in vain in
the realists' transcripts from life, which lack the selection and
focusing that distinguish art from experience.  There is
evidence, nevertheless, that the novel is no longer hostile
to the specifically human destiny of normal humanity, no
longer oblivious to that rare beauty which is the by-product
of the struggle by which a noble character imposes order on
the chaos of natural desire and approaches the imaginative
ideal of a life richly varied, finely poised, and of exalted
happiness.

I have space for but one example in modern fiction—
Dorothy Canfield's *The Brimming Cup*.  This deals with
the "eternal triangle" in a little Vermont town.  Marise
Chittenden, whose children have gradually taken her interest from Neale, her husband, becomes lonely when her children all go to school and she senses that "the days of her
physical flowering are numbered."  She is loved by Marsh,
a wealthy man visiting her elderly neighbour Mr. Wells;
Marsh tries to convince her that she is sacrificing "a world

of impassioned living" for "an outworn ideal" of "the traditional thing to do." The characters, not always vividly humanised, symbolise man's universe. Marise, the "brimming cup," "filled with some emotion . . . gushing up in a great flooding rush," typifies the surge of impulse. Marsh, a "swirly brook," to whom life is but a moment's "blind sensual groping and grabbing" before the "big final smash-up," typifies unbridled lust and greed. The "steady, visible light" of Neale's life, Neale who had found true freedom by conquering his "great, fierce, unguessed appetite, the longing for wandering, lawless freedom," typifies centrality. Mr. Wells, who surrenders "the happiness that comes of living as suits his nature" to help make the world more courteous to negroes, typifies humanitarian sympathy. The much-travelled Eugenia typifies "sophisticated cosmopolitanism," æsthetic escape: to her "everything's so commonplace"; she cultivates her fading beauty by "breathing in and out through one nostril, and thinking of the Infinite!" Cousin Hetty symbolises tradition; the Indian Touclé, mysticism. Marise sees her conflict as one not between "routine, traditional, narrow domestic life and the mightiness and richness of mature passion," but as a conflict between the lure of sensuousness and "what is deepest and most living in you." It is a psychological novel, a novel of introspection: it is based on the quest, not for what is conventionally moral, but for what in the end gives the richest human satisfaction. It presents a struggle based on self-reliance and self-conquest. Neale "wanted her to be herself, to be all that Marise could ever grow to be, he wanted her to attain her full stature." "Nothing is your own, if you haven't made it so." Marise wonders if her mother-love is what Marsh calls "inverted sensuality"; Neale says, "Look into your own heart and see for yourself." He "longed for her sake to have her strike out into the deep," he knew that peace could only come from

"Marise's acting with her own strength on her own decision."
He urges not outer but inner control—"as few umpires as
possible." In her conflict Marise sought "what was deepest
and most living in her . . . ; that was what the voices were
trying to cry her down from finding." She longed to be
"one with the great current"—Emerson's "stream of power."
She discovers that she is being lured by "the conventional
pose of revolt," that separation from her children would
not be true "growth and freedom, and generous expansion
of the soul." Like Milton and Emerson, she finally becomes free by discovering and obeying what is deepest
within:

> "She was a free woman, free from something in her heart that
> was afraid. For the moment she could think of nothing else be-
> yond the richness of that freedom. Why, here was the total ful-
> filment she had longed for. Here was the life more abundant,
> within, within her own heart, waiting for her!"

Joyous in her centrality, poise and freedom, she sees Marsh
as an "undeveloped and tyrannical soul, the cramped mind
without experience or conception of breadth and freedom."
"How narrow and cramped," and "blinded to the bigness
and variety of life" seemed people who thought that "a
woman of beauty and intelligence" was wasting her life
"unless she was engaged in . . . stimulating . . . sexual
desire." Marise had the serene joy of her home, her beloved children and her understanding husband; she had the
marvel of her music; and she had the surpassing wisdom
to seek her happiness not in the miraculous but in the common—in the symbolic neighbourly gathering on the night
of the blooming of the Cereus, that rite of beauty; in the
calm strength of simple folk whom experience has made
wise. And this woman, living out her "heritage, alive and
rooted deep," with her "vivid charm like an aureole of
golden mist," "felt slowly coming into her, like a tide of

a great ocean," the ineffable peace which comes from self-mastery, from the quest of what is most universally and nobly human. Calm and free, she was lifted "high, high above the smallness of life, up to a rich realm of security in joy."

## IV

What are we to conclude from this cursory sketch of the quality of three different sorts of American hope represented in our fiction? To the hope for a paradise of supernal beauty we owe much delicate artistry of a high order; one may maintain, however, as Emerson and Lowell did, that other things being equal, the truthful representation of typical humanity alone produces that harmony which yields the highest beauty. To this hope we owe much which, when read for recreation, can give delight; one takes issue only with those, like Poe and Cabell, who take Arcadianism seriously as a universal way of life and would substitute it for a literary ideal which resolutely confronts life and seeks to solve its meaning. To the hope for a paradise of American nature, a physical paradise, we owe the imposing of order upon the natural chaos of the wilderness; we owe the physical "improvements," the miracles of the machinery and science of a great nation. Of what ultimate avail, however, are material resources, physical comfort, time-saving machinery, and science unless the time and energy conserved are used for higher intellectual or spiritual ends, for the attainment of happiness? To those who have recorded this hope in fiction we owe the faithful preservation of an important aspect of the social history of America; but literature is greater than social history: it aspires to embody the meaning of life in terms at once timeless and universal and beautiful. Our frontier lands are exhausted, and those who have sought the physical paradise of a standardized industrialism have found nothing but boredom and despair. In place of this dead level of repression and standardisation let us develop a new respect for personality—for personality richly varied and healthily individual. Let us re-direct the joy-giving passion for creation through the matchless resources of the realm of the spirit. If both the rarest happiness and the rarest beauty are the fruit only of the hope of a paradise within, it would appear that American fiction would in the future be wise in dealing not with escape or with externalities but with the infinite variety and eternal mystery of the human soul's conflict between appetite and aspiration on its quest for an exalted inward happiness. Before we can expect American fiction to do this, however, the way must be prepared by the development of an adequate social imagination. For great art has always been organic with and supported by the life and vision of a whole people. Shakespeare was the "Soul of the Age," Dante the "voice of ten silent centuries." A hope must have throbbed in the breasts of a whole age before a writer can body it forth with the concentration, the brooding intensity, and the unerring congruency to human nature demanded of great art. Such a hope, such a social imagination, such an agreement in aspiration, can be developed best, perhaps, through education—through our interpreters of literature in college and university. Mindful of the heritage of heroic pioneers, we must embark upon our intellectual pioneering with the same resolute courage, the same loyal devotion, the same consecration to a high cause. Although our scholars are still being lured aside either to the camp of the æsthetes or the camp of the philologists, America must hereafter strive to develop the "middle-of-the-road" scholar who shall be, as Emerson said, Man Thinking, the delegated mind of society, whose major aim shall be the purposeful and discriminating interpretation of the record man has left, in terms of beauty, regarding "the conduct of life" and the path to peace. When such scholar-critics have developed such a social imagination, such a popular unanimity of hope, we shall be ready to receive the artist of genius who is to write for us the great American novel.

NOTE—For copyrighted evidence used in the foregoing essay I am indebted as follows: Sherwood Anderson, *Poor White* (Modern Library, N. Y., 1925); Dorothy Canfield Fisher, *The Brimming Cup* (Grosset and Dunlap, N. Y., 1921); James Branch Cabell, *The Cream of the Jest* (Modern Library, N. Y., 1922); *Jurgen* (Grosset and Dunlap, N. Y., 1927); *Beyond Life* (Modern Library, N. Y., 1919); *Straws and Prayerbooks* (Robert M. McBride and Co., N. Y., 1925); Willa Cather, *The Professor's House* (Alfred A. Knopf, N. Y., 1925); Floyd Dell, *Moon-Calf* (Alfred A. Knopf, N. Y., 1921); R. W. Emerson, *Complete Works* (Houghton Mifflin Co., Boston, 1903); *Journals* (Houghton Mifflin Co., Boston, 1909-14); *The Correspondence of Emerson and Carlyle* (Houghton Mifflin Co., Boston, 1888); Norman Foerster, *American Criticism* (Houghton Mifflin Co., Boston, 1928); Hamlin Garland, *A Son of the Middle Border* (Grosset and Dunlap, N. Y., 1927); Joseph Hergesheimer, *Linda Condon* (Alfred A. Knopf, N. Y., 1919); Mark Twain, *Complete Works* (American Publishing Co., Hartford, 1903); A. B. Paine, *Mark Twain, A Biography* (Harper and Brothers, N. Y., 1912); F. L. Pattee, "James Fenimore Cooper" (*American Mercury*, Alfred A. Knopf, N. Y.); Gregory Paine, Introduction to *The Deerslayer* (Harcourt, Brace and Co., N. Y., 1927); O. E. Rolvaag, *Giants in the Earth* (Harper and Brothers, N. Y., 1929).

# Dionysus in Dismay

STANLEY P. CHASE

Twenty-five years ago, when my generation were beginning to find their way around in the world of print and paint, a group of us used to meet occasionally to share each other's discoveries in contemporary thought and literature. You may smile at the association of the date 1904 and contemporary literature, and confessedly some of the objects of our attention were fantastic enough—Elbert Hubbard, Edward Howard Griggs, and even "I, Mary MacLane." The more daring among us were delving in Haeckel and Henry George; our conservatives, according to their bents, delighted in Kipling and Barrie, or a group of alluring Celts, or became expert in discriminations between the earlier and the later manner of Henry James. We all read, of course, William James and Bernard Shaw and H. G. Wells and Chesterton. In poetry, to be sure, we had no such variegated menu as the contemporary road-house affords; I should say that our diet was easily digestible and a little saccharine. For the most part, as I recall, we followed along the vagabondia trail after Richard Hovey and Bliss Carman. In that old college town near the coast, we could still thrill to such verses as

> Three of us without a care
> In the red September
> Tramping down the roads of Maine,
> Making merry with the rain,
> With the fellow winds a-fare
> Where the winds remember.

Frost and Sandburg, Lindsay and Masefield, had not come into our world—much less Walter de la Mare or Aldous

Huxley or Robinson Jeffers. But we were not so entirely neglected by the contemporary muse as you may suppose. We knew the early work of Yeats, and "The Hound of Heaven" of Francis Thompson; we had discovered the sonnets of Santayana; we could repeat a large part of *A Shropshire Lad*; and of course for our more cosmic moods we had Walt Whitman. Hundreds of other such groups must have existed, like ours callow, inexperienced, bumptious, but very inquisitive, very receptive. Not against us did the "new poetry" (no longer such) have to hurl its bolts.

And even in that distant, unreal decade of the nineteen-hundreds, before President Roosevelt, by a few kindly pages in the *Outlook*, put Edwin Arlington Robinson's name into every one's mouth, we knew the poet of "Tilbury Town" (only thirty miles from our own). There was one poem of his whose meaning used to be a great subject of dispute,—for we were than naïve enough to think that a poem must be susceptible of some rational explanation. It was entitled "Cortège," and had appeared in the *Captain Craig* volume of 1902.[1]

> Four o'clock this afternoon,
> Fifteen hundred miles away:
> So it goes, the crazy tune,
> So it pounds and hums all day.
>
> Four o'clock this afternoon,
> Earth will hide them far away:
> Best they go to go so soon,
> Best for them the grave to-day.
>
> Had she gone but half so soon,
> Half the world had passed away.
> Four o'clock this afternoon,
> Best for them they go to-day.

[1] Reprinted by permission of The Macmillan Company, Publishers.

Four o'clock this afternoon
Love will hide them deep, they say;
Love that made the grave so soon,
Fifteen hundred miles away.

Four o'clock this afternoon—
Ah, but they go slow to-day:
Slow to suit my crazy tune,
Past the need of all we say.

Best it came to come so soon,
Best for them they go to-day:
Four o'clock this afternoon,
Fifteen hundred miles away.

The half-benumbing, half-intensifying effect of the "crazy tune," the curious way in which a mere pattern of words can usurp the mind, now stealing its attention from the very grief they point to, and now flashing upon it a new aspect of that grief—something like that, I suppose, accounts for the fascination the poem had for us. But a number of us were dissatisfied with an explanation so simple. No, we wanted to know, first, who and how many persons were being buried at four o'clock to-day, and their relationship to the poet (was it, for instance, a former sweetheart and her husband?), and whether "she" in the third stanza was one of the deceased, and in what sense it could be said that Love "made the grave so soon," and what "half so soon" meant— was it any different from "twice as soon"? We even calculated that the burial must be taking place some fifteen hundred miles to the *west*, since otherwise, all (Protestant) funerals being held commonly at two o'clock, the poet's time would be twelve noon instead of four afternoon. All, of course, very silly and irrelevant questions.

Only a few years ago, in a poetry course, I was recalling these old agitations of ours, as a warning, I feel sure, against such literalness of interpretation. But, as will happen with class-room instruction, my admonitions produced quite the opposite effect from that intended, for one member of the class was so intrigued by the problem, even as we had been twenty years before, that he evolved the staggering theory that the poem was not about a funeral at all, but about a marriage. This ingenious view having been communicated, in a circuitous way, to Mr. Robinson, he settled the matter quite simply with the following note to the inquirer:

"I have long given up attempting to interpret my own poetry, but in this instance, would go so far as to suggest a funeral rather than a marriage. I remember this poem chiefly as a more or less reprehensible experiment in sound and feeling—a performance more pardonable thirty years ago—perhaps—than it would be to-day."

Of course, it was not Mr. Robinson's performance, but ours, which was reprehensible. We were treating an "experiment in sound and feeling" as we might have treated a deposition in court or an application for the payment of life-insurance; we were bringing to a poem an attitude of mind alien to its character *as a poem*. It was as if one should read Mr. Frost's "The Thatch" and demand to know *why* he "would not go in till the light went out." For "Cortège" in essential matters is not cryptic in the least; it is only irrelevant, external details that are left unexplained. And ultimately, I suppose, what we call a taste for poetry, of any except a very elementary sort, depends upon the possession of tact or intelligence to perceive just such a distinction.

I have used this personal recollection because much more frequently to-day and to a greater degree a somewhat similar feeling of puzzlement assails the reader of contemporary poetry. This simple instance of an obscurity gratuitously created by readers may lead to the consideration of a problem of poetic form more comprehensive than any question of mere technique (though technical elements of poetry are involved in it too), I mean the question of those necessities which are laid on poetry from its being a form of communication between mind and mind. For, I believe, from misapprehension and confusion in this matter, on the part now of poets and now of their readers, springs, to some extent, the unsatisfactory state of poetry at the present time. On the one side, there is reported a feeling of exasperation, by readers competent enough in other kinds of literature or in the older poetry, who "can make nothing of this modernist stuff," and on the other side the modernists' rejoinder that such readers are precisely in the position of my group of twenty-five years ago—lacking the intelligence to grasp what is essential and to disregard non-essentials. Surely a consideration of the nature and limits of that community of mind which must be assumed to subsist between the poet and his readers is not foreign to the subject of this book.

# I

At the outset we encounter the Crocean view of all art, including poetry, as expression merely, and conversely of all expression as art. But leaving the confusions of Signor Croce to be dealt with by others,[2] we are warranted in assum-

---

[2] "If you disregard critical trivialities and didactic accessories, the entire æsthetic system of Croce amounts to a hunt for pseudonyms of the word 'art,' and may indeed be stated briefly and accurately in this formula: art= intuition=expression=feeling=imagination=fancy=lyricism=beauty. And you must be careful not to take these words with the shadings and distinctions which they have in ordinary or scientific language. Not a bit of it. Every word is merely a different series of syllables signifying absolutely and completely the same thing."—G. Papini, *Four and Twenty Minds,* quoted by I. A. Richards, *The Principles of Literary Criticism* (1924), p. 255, note 4.

Mr. Richards adds: "It is interesting to notice that Croce's appeal has

ing, I think, that, generally and typically, the poet desires communication with other persons,—conceivably only one other person, or persons of the future, but at any rate communication and not merely self-expression. Otherwise, he wouldn't publish or circulate or read his poems, as generally and typically poets do. The theory of Laura Riding and Robert Graves [3] that the poet publishes (or "externalises") only out of consideration for the rights of the poem, which, like physical offspring, has attained an independent status with a life of its own, is a naïve and superfluous bit of mystification, sufficiently answered by the query, "Why then sign one's name?"—and I have not remarked any unusually wide return to the practice of anonymity. And one is led to wonder, as one turns the pages of our more advanced periodicals, what possible readers some of these poets are addressing. After a moderate success in comprehending, let us say, such diverse productions as those of the mediæval mystics, the wits of the Roman Empire and the Restoration, the English metaphysical poets, and the symbolist group in France, and after a period of conscientious schooling in the pronouncements of this newest movement, it is disconcerting to find oneself completely balked by the innocent-appearing contents of the latest anthology of verse. Among the ten possible but improbable interpretations of some poem, it

been exclusively to those unfamiliar with the subject, to the man of letters and the dilettante. He has been ignored by serious students of the mind. . . . [Papini] has here rendered a notable service to those who have been depressed by the vogue of 'Expressionism.' "

*Cf.* also the following from Gilbert Murray's *The Classical Tradition in Poetry* (1927), p. 243: "Everything that a man does is self-expression. The way a man laces his boots, the way he writes, the way he says, 'Goodmorning,' is probably different from the way followed by any other man, and is thus expressive of his personality. But it need not be good art for that reason. Imagine a pompous and egotistic man in a state of personal irritation, having to make an after-dinner speech. It would probably express him only too well, but it might not be a good speech."

[3] *A Survey of Modernist Poetry*, by Laura Riding and Robert Graves, 1927, p. 125.

seems somehow less than a sporting chance that the one you finally choose as the least implausible will be what was intended.

Take, for instance, this poem of Mr. Wallace Stevens, which I select not as an example of that writer's often delightful connoisseurship in verse, but as fairly representative of this decline in what has been called "communicative efficacy."

### ANECDOTE OF THE JAR [4]

I placed a jar in Tennessee,
And round it was, upon a hill.
It made the slovenly wilderness
Surround that hill.

The wilderness rose up to it,
And sprawled around, no longer wild.
The jar was round upon the ground
And tall and of a port in air.

It took dominion everywhere.
The jar was grey and bare.
It did not give of bird or bush,
Like nothing else in Tennessee.

Now the elements of this experience—the jar, its shape, colour, and quality, the hill in Tennessee where it is placed, the behaviour or appearance of the wilderness, the bird, the bush—stand doubtless in some kind of relation with each other in the poet's mind, have possibly certain symbolic values. Since we have no clues to these relationships and values, our mind is free to do anything it pleases with the bare grey jar, the hill, and the wilderness. This freedom, however, and any pleasure we may take in the separate

[4] From *Harmonium*, by Wallace Stevens, 1923. Reprinted by and with permission of and special arrangement with Alfred A. Knopf, Inc., authorised publishers.

images, in the rhythms, or the placing of the words, are not sufficient compensation for the state of uncertainty and slight irritation in which we are left. Very likely the little poem is meant to suggest nothing more than the superiority, to an intensely civilised person, of the simplest bit of handicraft over any extent of unregulated "nature," but it has been seriously interpreted to me, by devotees of recent poetry, as, respectively, an *objet d'art*, a sex-symbol, and a burial-urn containing the remains of a valued friend. And so it must remain, for me, not only like nothing else in Tennessee but like nothing else in the universe.

Considerable damage was done to this shallow affectation of knowingness of the last few years by Max Eastman's witty article in the April (1929) *Harper's*. A young intellectual from one of our well-known private schools told me that members of his group were observed to discontinue their perusal of *transition* [5] upon the appearance of Mr. Eastman's "The Cult of Unintelligibility." But contemporary poetry is still afflicted by an acute attack of that extreme of Puritanism—separatism: it asserts the right not only of private judgment, but of a private symbolism,—which is, æsthetically, of much graver consequences. My point here, of course, has nothing to do with the values or qualities of the experience which the writer is presumably seeking to share. I am simply saying that, in the reading of the slightest as of the most profound poem, a sense of singleness or wholeness is the most essential part of the experience, and that this totality of effect cannot be achieved if all clues to the way the poem is organised are withheld or too casually indicated. The enigmatic character of Dr. William Carlos Williams's poems, we are told, is due in part to his habit of jotting down free-verse impressions in the intervals between his profes-

[5] For the sake of "communicative efficacy," as the editors remind me, I should explain that *transition* is "an international quarterly for creative experiment," edited in Paris by a group of young Americans and others.

sional visits to patients. I can only hope that in writing out his prescriptions he makes a greater allowance for the mental capacity of the pharmacist than he seems to make for mine. To speak bluntly, the difficulty of reading much "modernist" verse is due less to the superior sophistication or cleverness of these writers than to their essential lack of art.

By contrast, in the following lyric of Elinor Wylie, even though it is a repudiation of something accustomed, beautiful, and comforting, there is so clear and deft an employment of symbol, so perfect a fusion of mood with image, that the effect of totality is achieved; the peace denied to this orthodox landscape (or universe) is momentarily attained in the very denial of it, and thus one of the functions of poetry is discharged.

### INNOCENT LANDSCAPE [6]

Here is no peace, although the air has fainted,
    And footfalls die and are buried in deep grass,
And reverential trees are softly painted
    Like saints upon an oriel of glass.

The pattern of the atmosphere is spherical,
    A bubble in the silence of the sun,
Blown thinner by the very breath of miracle
    Around a core of loud confusion.

Here is no virtue; here is nothing blessèd
    Save this foredoomed suspension of the end;
Faith is the blossom, but the fruit is cursèd;
    Go hence, for it is useless to pretend.

"The transport . . . that the poet kindles in us," observes Professor De Selincourt in his Inaugural Lecture at Oxford, "springs from our instinctive recognition that his form, a term that includes both rhythm and diction, is an entirely

[6] From *Trivial Breath*, by Elinor Wylie, 1928. Reprinted by and with permission of and special arrangement with Alfred A. Knopf, Inc., authorised publishers.

faithful rendering of his experience, so that we gain from it a sudden clear sense of fulfilment, such as we can hardly hope to gain outside the ideal world of art." That may be a rather narrowly æsthetic interpretation of Longinus's doctrine of the poetic "transport," but certainly "a sudden clear sense of fulfilment" is an experience which it is easy to miss in the poetry of our contemporaries.

In fact, this "sense of fulfilment" is precisely what the typical modernist, experiencing nothing of the sort in life itself and disdaining an "ideal world" thus cut off from reality, avoids giving us. He would regard it as part of the old hocus-pocus of orthodoxy. Life being to him fragmentary, inchoate, he would say that his poetry, if it is to be "an entirely faithful rendering of his experience," must itself produce an effect of inchoateness, fragmentariness.

## THE END OF THE WORLD [7]

Quite unexpectedly as Vasserot
The armless ambidextrian was lighting
A match between his great and second toe
And Ralph the lion was engaged in biting
The neck of Madame Sossman while the drum
Pointed, and Teeny was about to cough
In waltz-time swinging Jocko by the thumb—
Quite unexpectedly the top blew off:

And there, there overhead, there, there, hung over
Those thousands of white faces, those dazed eyes,
There in the starless dark the poise, the hover,
There with vast wings across the cancelled skies,
There in the sudden blackness the black pall
Of nothing, nothing, nothing,—nothing at all.

Here Archibald MacLeish, who stands somewhere between the centre and the extreme left wing in poetry, employs a

[7] From *Streets in the Moon*, by Archibald MacLeish, 1926. Reprinted by permission of Houghton Mifflin Company, Publishers.

traditional verse-form in a poem the theme of which is the absurdity of the spectacle of human antics in a cosmos without intelligibility or significance. He guards against any specious effect of "fulfilment" by the unexpected reiteration of the word *nothing*. Yet there remains the regrettable necessity of rounding out the sestet and capping the rhyme; and, more important, the method of presentation has imposed an adventitious kind of order on a scene which, in the poet's apprehension of it, is an even wilder scramble and jumble of absurdities. And so the sonnet, thoroughly "modern" in spirit, is quite conservative in technique. The distinctiveness of this new poetry, indeed, is less a matter of measures, whether new or old, than of the principle of association by which it is governed. It aims at an organisation of images and a succession of rhythms which spring more immediately from the poet's stream of consciousness.

In attempting to divert this stream through the reader's mind, without spilling over or filtering, some recent poets have adopted startling innovations in typography, including punctuation, use of capitals and small letters, spacing, and line-division. The fashion is prompted in part by a spirit of mere impishness, but back of it also is a certain amount of genuine experimentation in the resources and the graphical representation of language, the object being to prod the reader out of the lethargy and complacency which, it is alleged, are fostered by the conventions of verse-form and page-arrangement. Undeniably, if one is willing to play this game and doesn't mind having the rules made up as one goes along, some of the results are amusing. You will understand most readily what it is all about if you first take one of these poems down from some one's dictation, then attempt to write it as you think the poet would do to bring out the subtler shadings and nuances, and finally compare your representation of the poem with his. Here, for instance, are the words (written as ordinary prose) of a poem by E. E. Cummings from a group called "Impressions."

"I was considering how, within night's loose sack, a star's nibbling infinitesimally devours darkness, the hungry star, which will eventually jiggle the bait of dawn and be jerked into eternity, when over my head a shooting-star burst into a stale shriek like an alarm-clock." [8]

On the chance that at this point the reader may wish to try the experiment which has been suggested, I postpone to a later page Mr. Cummings's original arrangement of the words. If you will compare his printing of the poem with that above, you will see how the tininess and the quick little repeated nibbles of the mouse at the grain-sack are suggested by the short, broken lines; how ingeniously the shooting-star is made to interrupt the poet's revery; how the effect of flare, streaking, and slower fading is conveyed in the printing of "bursts"; and how the new simile of the alarm-clock impinges upon the retinal image of the meteor.[9] But —"the pleasures of sudden wonder are soon exhausted." After scrambling up a hundred or so of these typographical escarpments, I found that there was seldom a view from the summit commensurate with the discomforts of the climb, and my interest in the new sport began to flag. It is hard to imagine a mature artist interesting himself for long in this sort of preciosity.

Though each individual's inner life is in a measure unique, the mere attempt to convey some fraction of it to others by written or printed words presupposes a certain shared and common ground of human experience. Freshness, piquancy,

[8] From *Tulips and Chimneys*. Reprinted by permission of Alfred & Charles Boni, Inc., Publishers.

[9] For a more elaborate analysis of such effects in Mr. Cummings's poetry, see Laura Riding and Robert Graves, *A Survey of Modernist Poetry*, Chapter I.

gusto, can be properly savoured only when they are delicately blended with "human nature's daily food." The
importance of a common understanding upon essentials is
clear in the sphere of our personal relationships, which become rich and satisfying only with the mutual recognition
of things that may be *taken for granted;* oddities and varie-
ties are most engaging in those with whom we already own a
fundamental bond. Now the forms and conventions of
poetry may be regarded as so many aids to the speedier establishment of such understanding between reader and poet,—
the indispensable means by which an original experience is
so shaped and clarified that it has significance for others.
No one of these conventions, naturally, is absolutely fixed
or static, and skilful manipulation of their elements is constantly yielding new and unsuspected possibilities of æsthetic
pleasure, and even of social comprehension. For this reason
we may look with a tolerant and not unfriendly eye upon
such experimentation by some of our younger poets as I have
described.[10] Nevertheless, it is imperative that persons who
wish to modify or to replace the accepted vehicles of poetic
expression should have a clear understanding of what con-

[10] E. E. Cummings's poem, previously referred to, is printed by him as
follows (*Tulips and Chimneys,* New York, 1924, p. 78):

> i was considering how
> within night's loose
> sack a star's
> nibbling in-
> fin
> -i-
> tes-
> i
> -mal-
> ly devours
>
> darkness the
> hungry star
> which
> will e

vention in literature or art is *for*. Adequate treatment of this subject would require a separate book, and here I must content myself with a mere statement of faith: that some set of assumptions as to the experiences most valuable and important for mankind—in other words, of universals in the Aristotelian sense—is as necessary in the establishment or the maintenance of an æsthetic convention as in any purely social or political activity. Indeed, the most promising development in American poetry at the present time, I believe, is to be found, not in these centrifugal and eccentric movements, but in the considerable amount of genuine if less spectacular work which is being done upon the lines of a firmly rooted literary tradition.[11]

## II

In the last few paragraphs, though concerned primarily with the aspect of communicability, I have been skirting the topic which lies at the centre of all movements of thought and feeling in our day, and with which I shall be concerned through the rest of this essay. I refer to the prevalent spirit of disillusionment, a state of mind which in America has

```
       -ven
       tu-
       al
       -ly jiggle
       the bait of
       dawn and be jerked

       into
       eternity.  when over my head a
       shooting
       star
       Bur    s
                  (t
                      into a stale shriek
       like an alarm-clock)
```

[11] Such, for instance, as the poetry of John Crowe Ransom and Donald Davidson in the South, and of Wilbert Snow and Robert P. Tristram Coffin in New England.

218

made itself felt, acutely and widely, only within the last three or four years.

Certainly the mood of the younger generation of poets (the men and women now in their twenties or early thirties) is very different from the poetic temper of fifteen years ago —those exciting, strained, exalted, painful years that witnessed, among other things, the rise of the "new poetry" in England and America and, somewhat later, the beginning of the war. Any comprehensive view of the stream of poetry warns us not to make too much of these twists and turns between one decade and the next; yet there is some reason to think that we have now reached or are approaching one of the major bends in the course. The "poetic renascence" of 1912-1917 was, it is true, in reaction against certain nineteenth-century attitudes,—against its Puritan code in morals and its tradition of gentility in belles-lettres; as some one has said, it delighted in hurling bricks at the silk hat of Hamilton W. Mabie; but to the most characteristic force of nineteenth-century thought and life—namely, an expansive philosophy of naturalism, embraced with enthusiasm and glorified by a romantic imagination—it merely gave a fresh impetus.

> The serene and humble mould
> Does in herself all selves enfold—
> Kingdoms, destinies, and creeds,
> Great dreams, and dauntless deeds,
> Science that metes the firmament,
> The high, inflexible intent
> Of one for many sacrificed—
> Plato's brain, the heart of Christ;
>
> .    .    .    .    .
>
> Out of the earth the poem grows
> Like the lily, or the rose;
> And all man is, or yet may be,
> Is but herself in agony

219

Toiling up the steep ascent
Toward the complete accomplishment
When all dust shall be, the whole
Universe, one conscious soul.[12]

These lines by John Hall Wheelock epitomise the thought
that had been the main inspiration of the nineteenth century.
Despite their regular metrical form, with its reminiscence of
Emerson, we recognise in them the ecstatic evolutionary
naturalism of Walt Whitman.

Indeed, it was the spirit of Whitman, more than any
other, that presided over our "poetic renascence." Not, of
course, that all the poets who made their appearance in those
years were akin to him. Frost, for instance, was hardly more
like Whitman than he was like Pope; consciously, in his
living and in his poetry, he was facing and he has continued
to move in just the opposite direction. Nor perhaps in the
work of Masters or of Robinson [13] is the relation to Whitman
at once apparent, for superficially neither the *Spoon River
Anthology*, that sardonic record of stunted human growths,
nor Robinson's sombre studies of the thwarted lives of his
New Englanders suggest the tolerance, the breadth and
human warmth of the older poet's sympathies. But the
analysis of these unfortunate victims of a repressive and un-
humane morality (for such is the way the poetry of both
writers was commonly described, and such, in one aspect, it
is) was really in line with Whitman's gospel of emotional
emancipation, as well as with the new direction given to
psychology by Freud and Jung. In the work of Lindsay
and Sandburg, and notably in that of the far less original

[12] From the poem "Earth," in *Dust and Light*, 1919, published by Charles
Scribner's Sons.
[13] Mr. Robinson, of course, had been publishing poetry for nearly twenty
years before the new movement got under way, but his work was regarded
as belonging to it in temper and outlook.

Oppenheim (whose disappearance from current collections is itself significant of the change that has taken place), the influence of Whitman was patent. All the spokesmen and contemporary critics of the movement, from Amy Lowell (1917) to Bruce Weirick (1924), with varying degrees of emphasis, stress Whitman's primacy in American literature. He had had his lovers and disciples before, but now for the first time a group of American poets could give him whole-hearted welcome with no inner abashment to overcome. Throughout the earlier productions of the movement, even in the poems of the Imagists, whose theory and practice of verse were so different from his own, is diffused the vibrant spirit of Walt Whitman. It is experienced as a certain buoyancy and expectancy of mood, and most characteristically as an underlying trust in a life-force which is felt to be working here in America to high, unforeseen ends.

It would be an over-simplification, but somewhere near the heart of the matter, to say that the presence we are most aware of in the poetry of to-day is not Walt Whitman, but Thomas Hardy—his desolating irony, at least, if not his artistic and personal elevation. These younger poets accept, but coldly and without enthusiasm, the account which contemporary science offers of the universe and of the human make-up, and they are as hostile to the glowing affirmations of the great romantics as they are to the evasions and tepidity of the Victorians. Perhaps this is but an inversion, a different guise, of that restless and changeable temper which we call romanticism, but to me at least its emergence seems to be more significant than were any of the varied energies released by the last poetic movement. This new spirit is not more characteristic of poetry, of course, than of other expressions of the age. To some extent, though less here than abroad, it is an after-effect of the war—the inability of nervous organisations overstrained by the excitements of those years to respond to normal stimuli. It may be briefly described as a despair of achieving any reading of life in its totality which will be tolerable in the light of all we know and feel. "In the course of a few centuries," writes Mr. Joseph Wood Krutch in *The Modern Temper*, "[man's] knowledge, and hence the universe of which he finds himself an inhabitant, has been completely revolutionised, but his instincts and his emotions have remained, relatively at least, unchanged. He is still, as he always was, adjusted to the orderly, purposeful, humanised world which all peoples unburdened by experience have figured to themselves, but that world no longer exists." This modern sense of frustration differs from states of disillusion or pessimism experienced in the past in two respects. It is, for one thing, more widespread, producing a considerable body of poetry of sheer negation, turning some writers to mere elaboration of surfaces and appearances, and making itself felt as an undercurrent, now cynical, now passionate, in much writing which seems superficially to be almost free of philosophical implications. And secondly, this spirit of denial is a more positive and uncompromising thing than we have known in the past. Not only is it unable to effect any synthesis of its intelligence and its emotional promptings; it has come to believe that such a synthesis is in the nature of things impossible. It grows "more and more likely," continues Mr. Krutch, "that [man] must remain an ethical animal in a universe which contains no ethical element." His dilemma is that he cannot either feel as his intelligence bids him or think as his emotions would have him. Even the highest of the personal emotions, love itself, which had somehow eluded the cold touch of nineteenth-century science, has not been able to withstand the psycho-analysis of the twentieth. "Have you not heard," asks the lady in *Cavender's House*,

"Have you not heard yet, anywhere, death-bells ringing
For Love and poor Romance?   Biologists
And bolshevists are ringing them like mad—
So loud that Love, we're told, will soon be lost
With dodos, dinosaurs, and pterodactyls."

Specifically, a feeling is abroad that poetry is at some kind of
crisis or turning-point, and there are even predictions that
poetry of a sort that the past would recognise as such cannot continue much longer to be produced.

The poetry of T. S. Eliot has been praised for its seizing
of just this aspect of the modern situation, the sense of
frustration, of insignificance.   "The passions which swept
through the once major poets," writes Mr. Krutch, "no
longer awaken any profound response, and only in the bleak,
tortuous complexities of a T. S. Eliot does [the present age]
find its moods given adequate expression."   Love-making
carried on with an accompanying sense of its futility and
ridiculousness, an acquaintance with art and poetry which
serves only to confirm misgivings as to their relevancy for
us to-day, the employment of religious symbols to arouse a
poor mirthless mockery—in such experiences our young intellectuals find mirrored the age and body of their time.
The cryptic character of the writing, the sometimes arbitrary
connection between one image and the next, the casual
allusions to one person's recondite reading, are all indications of the contemporary sense of the individual's isolation.
The broken rhythms, the fragmentariness of the scenes or
movements, the deliberate foregoing of any rational principle of organisation, reflect the feeling of the fragmentariness of life itself, the modern inability to effect any kind
of integration of experience.   And this, we are told by some,
is the only kind of poetry which an honest and sensitive
mind in an age like ours can be expected to produce.

Mr. Eliot, though no longer belonging even nominally

to American literature, is worth attention because of his present high reputation in intellectual circles. He has written literary criticism of a kind especially needed at the present time, based as it is on a wide knowledge of literature, informed by a delicate taste, and guided by severe yet humane standards. And in his poetry he has shown himself capable of finding a comedy of the mind in these hesitations and inhibitions of modernity,—as in the early "Love Song of J. Alfred Prufrock." By the haunting, individual rhythms of his poems alone, we are apprised of an exceptional poetic endowment. Yet Mr. Eliot's literary output, poetry and prose, constitutes, to my mind, one of the most arresting paradoxes of this paradoxical age: an advocate of the sterner disciplines of the past ("classicist in literature, royalist in politics, and anglo-catholic in religion"), who gives to these causes all the organising power of a firm intelligence, and is content to let his poetry express chiefly the states of confusion, doubt, faintness, with which the positive principles of his thought have had to wrestle.

> "We are the hollow men,
> We are the stuffed men."

In a recent essay Mr. Eliot has ventured the opinion that a great event in the intellectual world would be the conversion of Professor Irving Babbitt to Roman or Anglo-Catholicism, but, he concludes regretfully, such a consummation, though devoutly to be wished, is hardly likely, for Mr. Babbitt "knows too much." Perhaps an even more salutary conversion, in its immediate effects upon other poets, would be Mr. Eliot's compassing, in his creative work, of those genuinely classical values of which, in his critical writing, he shows such fine apprehension. For a transformation of that kind, one need not fear that any man of letters knows too much. One may at least entertain the hope that Mr. Eliot's permanent reputation as a poet is not going to lie in the fact that he has voiced, more completely than any one else in verse, the confusion and disillusionment of this post-war generation.

The humanist is aware that poetry, like mythology, possesses no power of conferring immediate revelation of truth; he knows that its scenes and personages, its thoughts and passions, from the earthiest to the most ethereal, belong to the world of unsubstantiality, of illusion—of dreams, if you will. He will go further: this element of illusion, this impassable gulf between reality and our comprehension or representation of reality, is not confined to poetry and mythology; it is part of all our conscious life; it baffles us even in our attempt to comprehend that nearest thing of all —ourself. ". . . beneath the surface of all we see and feel, beneath the very act of seeing and feeling, lies the unredeemed chaos of desires and impressions, unlimited, unmeaning, unfathomable, incalculable, formless, dark. Life is but appearance, and this personality we call by our name is but illusion within illusion." [14] But working within the illusion is also a power to control and order these impulses, to check them or to bring them into a harmonious co-operation, yielding a serenity and a sense of stability which, of all human experiences, seems freest of illusion. It was the characteristic error of much nineteenth-century poetry (of Browning's in England, of Whitman's in America) to limit personality to the mere welter of desires and feelings, to

[14] Paul Elmer More, "Definitions of Dualism," Section LXXIII, in *The Drift of Romanticism* (1913), p. 291. The next section is almost prophetic of what has happened in American poetry of the last few years:

"In some men, especially in an age of spiritual apathy, the sense of disillusion may spring up without the corresponding assurance of faith. To such men nothing is real; they walk in a place of shadows, and feel that life is continually slipping away from them into a bottomless abyss. All their labour is to re-create for themselves the illusion which has been shattered, or, by ceaseless occupation, to escape the dull horror of the void."

225

find there its central "urge" (the favourite word of romantic criticism), and to erect upon such foundations a philosophy of the "ideal." But the hollowness of *this* illusion (the philosophy which found an immediacy of truth in natural instincts, impulses, and feelings) has to-day become all too apparent; and when its former adherents ask where then certainty can be found, they are bidden to direct their gaze to the abstract world of the physicist and the mathematician. Here, in the words of Mr. I. A. Richards, "intellectual certainty is, almost for the first time, available, and on an unlimited scale." [15] But even if this were so,—and one hears of developments in these fields that appear to make the certainty considerably less than absolute,—it would still be a certainty about matters that have no particular relation to the behaviour and feelings of human beings, and that give no support for poetry. The beguiling mirage of an Absolute fostered by romantic poetry has disappeared, only to be replaced by the mirage of another Absolute, terrifying though incomprehensible. And so we have come to the *impasse* already described.

From the point of view of the humanist, what has so suddenly collapsed is the towering structure of nineteenth-century romanticism, not any dwelling necessary to the continued life of poetry. For he has long recognised those metaphysical limitations with which contemporary physics is so deeply entangled; and he has been unwilling to trust metaphysics, any more completely than natural science, with the whole determination of a philosophy of life. Instead of asserting that intellectual certainty in the field of science is available now almost for the first time on an unlimited scale, he would postulate a large degree of what amounts to *practical* certainty, in all that concerns us most nearly as ethical beings, available now, as it has been for centuries.

[15] I. A. Richards, *Science and Poetry*, 1926, p. 60.

This assurance is embodied, for him, in the dualism of the great historic religions, in the teachings of Socrates and of Jesus, and in the most persistent traditions of European literature. But its final sanctions are not found in any "great tradition," however imposing; they are arrived at empirically and experimentally by any one who, divesting his mind of shibboleths and catch-words, will honestly examine his own impulses and springs of action. In his own soul he will find the cleavage, the dualism, which runs through human nature. This opposition of forces, by whatever names he calls them, by whatever symbols he represents them, may never be resolved; but in his mysterious power of intervention in their unending conflict lies, for him, the ultimate reality within the illusion. To the reading of poetry, then, he will bring the same habit of discrimination that serves him in the conduct of life, mindful that it is still a world communicating with ours by the gate of horn and the gate of ivory, and that the phantasms which issue therefrom may light our way a few steps nearer truth, or may deepen for us the shadows of the dark, chaotic flux.

To the consciousness of intellectual defeat and spiritual dismay, evidenced so widely in contemporary literature, it is not to be expected that poetry will for the present make any very direct or explicit answer. For we do not look to poetry for polemics, for the formulation of ethical or metaphysical ideas; and when poetry tries to assume a burden that belongs rather to criticism and philosophy, the result may have literary interest and excellence, as does Pope's *Essay on Man*, but is more likely to be merely dull and forced, like the later work of Wordsworth or Browning. In either case some fulness of life belonging to poetry when confident in its own right is missing. No, what we look for in the poet is some more pervasive or implicit evidence of his scale of values, some intuitive, and for that reason more

227

certain, indication of the quality of his response to life, felt
as unmistakably in his imagery, his diction, and his rhythms
as in those more ponderable elements of style which the
eighteenth century called "fable" and "sentiments." Thus,
in two stanzas [16] of A. E. Housman—

> The year might age, and cloudy
> The lessening day might close,
> But air of other summers
> Breathed from beyond the snows,
> And I had hope of those.
>
> They came and were and are not
> And come no more anew;
> And all the years and seasons
> That ever can ensue
> Must now be worse and few.

—something that belongs to his deepest intuition (his
acceptance, without evasion and without reconciliation, of
life's transitoriness) is caught in the very movement of the
lines and the simplicity of the words:

> They came and were and are not.

This pervasive sense of things chiefly valued and most deeply
felt, which every great poet's work gives us, is surely not
determined altogether by forces external to him. The poet
is something more than a highly sensitised receiving-set for
remote, scattered goings-on in the world at large. What
we prize in every poet we come to know intimately is some
irreducible, *given* quality of the personality. We shall not
easily accept, therefore, the current argument that, in an
age like ours of dissolving faiths, the only genuine kind of
poetry must be one which has cut itself off from belief of

[16] From *Last Poems*, by A. E. Housman, 1922, published by Henry Holt
and Company.

228

any kind.[17]   The history of English literature is not lacking
in instances of poets who have withstood the pressure of their
age: to recall only the greatest, the poems of Milton, from
*Lycidas* to *Samson Agonistes*, are triumphant testimonies
against the idea that poetry need be so utterly subject to
contemporaneous disintegrating influences.   But if we claim
for poetry a certain power of immunity from such forces,
neither, by the same course of reasoning, should we expect
too much from the *direct* effect upon it of those forces which
we think salutary, such as humanism.

   I do not mean to suggest here the notion of poetry's having
a life of its own in any transcendental sense, or to imply that
poets possess mysterious astral powers.   My thought is simply that the new humanism, before it is given any large
imaginative expression in American poetry, must expect to
prove its worth by responding to broadly human, and not
alone specifically poetic needs.   It will do this by its power
of bringing harmony into lives which are ordered in accordance with its insight, of establishing in society "a current of
fresh and true ideas," and of creating thus "a quickening and
sustaining atmosphere" which poetry can breathe.   I feel no
need of apologising for my use of these well-worn phrases
of Matthew Arnold; not only was he the best representative
of the spirit of humanism in nineteenth-century England or
America, but also, in his realisation of the hopeless disparity
between natural processes and human aims, he anticipated the
very pattern of our own dilemma.   The paralysis which came
over Arnold's poetic powers in later life is sometimes
attributed to the steady growth of his humanistic interests,
requiring the ampler medium of prose.   However that may
be, I believe it certain that his humanism—his sense, that is,
of the worth and fruitfulness of human powers when wisely
exercised and his acceptance of the limitations which such a

[17] I. A. Richards, *Science and Poetry*, Chapter VII.

view imposes—gave to his poetry nearly all that power of invigoration and refreshment for which we chiefly value it. A contemporary critic, R. H. Hutton, observed how frequently Arnold closes a poem on the burdensomeness of existence by some seemingly unconnected figure or story, such as the simile of the Tyrian trader in "The Scholar Gipsy," instinct with the pride and buoyancy of old world enterprise. " 'The problem is insoluble,' he seems to say, 'but insoluble or not, let us recall the pristine strength of the human spirit, and not forget that we have access to great resources still.' " [18] In such ways to-day, indirectly and obliquely, humanism may make itself felt as one influence among many upon contemporary poetry: by rendering accessible and operative, for the poets as for the rest of us, some of these moral energies from times of more robust faith and higher intellectual vitality than our own.

[18] Richard Holt Hutton, *Essays on Some of the Modern Guides to English Thought in Matters of Faith*, 1891 (Second Ed., revised), p. 146.

# Our Critical Spokesmen

## GORHAM B. MUNSON

"Art," I thought I heard a voice say as I sat down to my table, "aims to *be* something; while criticism aims first to clarify and then to *value* something.  Criticism is talk *about* something with a view to passing judgment upon it.  It is an aspect of man the valuer, weighing the actions, impulses, passions, thoughts, and imaginings of his fellow-men. Study the criticism of a period and it will show you the state of the general intelligence and the kind of values professed and in vogue, and above all it will enable you to divine the amount of consciousness of life's processes and meanings which is current in this period."

"So," I remarked to the air, "the subject I have been thinking about has some importance?  It has to do with man in his most human rôle, that of valuing, and it assists in indicating the range and depth and intensity of his awareness of life."

But there was no reply to this, and perceiving that I must dig with my own mind, I scratched down what I had previously decided should be my opening sentence.  I had been dwelling on the subject of American literary criticism from 1915 to the present.  About 1915 a new phase in our national letters began to be manifest.  Europe was well drenched in blood and the *Lusitania* was torpedoed in 1915—events that were vitally to affect us.  Mr. Dreiser's *The "Genius"* came out, and the next year, 1916, it was suppressed by its publishers out of deference to the power of a narrow censoring body soon to be effectively challenged.  American lib-

231

erals in the wake of Bull Moose Progressivism had hopefully
established the *New Republic*. Mr. P. E. More in the year
previous to 1915 had resigned from the editorship of the
*Nation*.

Afterwards there came our participation in the war: the
crushing of liberalism: post-war disillusion. There came a
ferment of new magazines and new publishers, captivating
the sons and leaving the fathers cold. There came a tide of
naturalistic novels, a foam of *vers libre*, a roar of essays
attacking the genteel tradition. Since 1915 the reputations
have been made of Messrs. Sinclair Lewis, Sherwood Anderson, Carl Sandburg, Waldo Frank, H. L. Mencken, and
Eugene O'Neill—to name only enough to establish a contrast with the writers of the preceding period. Inevitably
it happened that some excitable journalists in the midst of the
uprising promptly called this decade and a half an American
literary renaissance.

To me, on reviewing these years, they seem more like a
tragi-comedy, almost a tragi-farce. So when I penned my
premeditated first sentence I spoke of the tragi-comedy of
American criticism. But even if our recent criticism has been
very often foolish, we are to take it seriously for reasons
outside itself,—if my voice out of the air is to be believed.
I must now try to develop the line of thought that moves
out from the opening sentence I wrote down when my aerial
counsellor deserted me.

# I

There have been no villains in the recent tragi-comedy
of American literary criticism.

The leading critics of our nation have not been villains—
that is, amazing men of initiative, strength, and will bent on
destruction—but rather they make us think of well-inten-

tioned bookish gentlemen gyrating in the fields of certain hidden sociological magnets and vociferating their reflexes to the magnetic attractions. On behalf of a potential human greatness, there are perhaps great errors in the present world of literary criticism to be opposed, but there are with us no great men, no geniuses, to be overthrown. In other words, our critics are not germinative but derivative.

I mean, of course, our professional critics. It is plain that I am not setting out to praise them—not even by calling them villains, for villains must, to satisfy my conception of the scale on which the intellectual drama of the race has been played, possess a certain epical character. There is another world of criticism, the academic world, whose faults have often been exposed scornfully and truthfully. Lying out of the eye of the reading public, it never bears any relation, according to the professional critics, with what is being currently written. Yet it has its virtues of course: there is a laudatory paper for some one to write on recent advances in American literary scholarship: within academic circles there has grown up the only critical movement in our land now worthy of international interest, and the leaders of this movement, Professors Irving Babbitt and Paul Elmer More, are —I have several times committed myself to the assertion— the best living critics America can show. It is not with the academic world nor with humanism, however, that I am here dealing, but with the critics of the past fifteen years who have enjoyed something like popularity. First, let us follow the figure of the late Stuart P. Sherman, once a successful university professor, as he flies away from the campus into the full light of public attention beating upon the world of professional criticism.

Stuart P. Sherman is of exceptional interest to us. He admired Matthew Arnold: he wrote a popular exposition of Arnold, and a course of his entirely devoted to Arnold is said to have been popular with the students at the University of Illinois. Let us then, noting this affinity, measure Sherman by Arnold. The difference in their prose is the difference between distinction and mere competence. Sherman's is democratic: it is as if written in shirt-sleeves or talked with the feet on the table, the writer or speaker deliberately putting on easy manners. Note the "It's-a-plain-man-speaking" effect in the following typical passage at the beginning of Sherman's essay, *Towards an American Type:* "When I was in college, I used to poke around in the library a good deal looking for books which would take me out of the shallow water of college life into the deep channel of experience, into the serious life of the world. And naturally enough the works of Tolstoy came into my hands. Now one knows what a typical Tolstoy novel is, etc." [1] Lucid writing, of course, but it is not charming: it has none of Arnold's aristocratic sweetness.

I am going to try to point out a fatal lack of austerity in Sherman, a certain ultimate slackness of mind and purpose. The prose, so lustreless beside Arnold's, shows that Sherman failed to achieve any of the rarer virtues of verbal deportment: just as clearly one realises that not so superficially, so mushily, could Arnold have defined religion as, in Sherman's words, "that which binds us and holds us. Religion is that which at heart we do earnestly believe in, whatever it is." Nor could Arnold, doughty wrestler with himself, so easily drop his hard questions and substitute gentler ones. In the essay quoted from above, Sherman went on to raise the question all great minds have most seriously confronted: "Is life worth living, and for what purpose?" But it did not take him long to say, "Assuming that life is worth living, what are its durable satisfactions?"—a serious enough question, but subtly veering the asker away from any tragic vision

[1] From *Points of View*, 1924, Charles Scribner's Sons, publisher.

234

of life and encouraging him to settle into a limited pattern of behaviour that happens to appeal to his temperament rather than to go forth and lead the great adventure of pursuing perfection.

In his growth Sherman was influenced by the books of three conservative critics, Mr. Paul Elmer More, Mr. Irving Babbitt, and the late W. C. Brownell; and here again his conduct was significant of some lack of desperation in him or of some softening influence on the fibres of his mind. For under the pressure of the ideas of Mr. More and Mr. Babbitt he was a little impatient. They were too austere for his taste, whereas he could not admire Brownell sufficiently. But of the three critics Brownell dealt least in the primary ideas of life: he elaborated with a great deal of fine sense secondary ideas about literature and society. He had, it appears to me, a mind more localised in the nineteenth century than the minds of his two colleagues. And nineteenth-century minded, rather than classical minded, was Stuart P. Sherman: his perennial enthusiasms were for Emerson, Whitman, and Stevenson.

Sherman conceived that he was a spokesman for the "average man," and the point is important in estimating him. It makes it fitting that his style should be passably good but inconspicuous in any pageant of fine styles, fitting that his thinking should constantly deflect from issues that require an unusual severity of discipline for meeting them to issues that are less agitating to the pulse, and most fitting that he should seem not out of joint with his time, like a Forest Philosopher discoursing with men who regard motor-cars as a convincing symbol of progress, but that he should seem to be a contemporary with a touch of conservatism, crying with other average men for Prohibition and vituperating with them our one-time Teutonic enemies. My reader, are you now chiding me for drawing an unsympathetic portrait? Recall then one of the pieces in *Americans* (1922) and then say, if you can, that in respect to Sherman's chief weakness I am wrong. The piece in evidence is *An Imaginary Conversation with Mr. P. E. More,* wherein, after paying his respects to Mr. More's gifts, Sherman complained: "But he has done too little to meet his poor living fellow-countrymen." In fact, he said, and this is the self-incriminating statement, "Mr. More has not attended to the technique of ingratiation by which a master of popularity plays upon an unready public with his personality, flattering, cajoling, seducing it to accept his shadow before his substance arrives." [2] It all depends! The genuine writer does seek to reduce his reader by a species of white magic, he labours to compel him to be his slave. But this is a more virile conception of the writer's rôle than Sherman's ingratiator embodies. If one puts the emphasis on ingratiation rather than on the skilful imposition of one's values, then as is well known something is likely to happen to one's values. Consider the following sad example: Said Sherman, would that Mr. More had loved the aristocratic Plato less and Socrates more. "If," he went on, "Socrates were among us to-day, I am convinced that he would be a leader of the Democrats in the House; but Plato, I suspect, would be a member of the Senate from Massachusetts." Quite apart from the fact, apparently forgotten by Sherman, that Socrates at his trial spoke of his brief experience in politics and explained scathingly why he had thereafter abstained from politics, I say that what has occurred here in Sherman's illustration is the domestication of two men so uncompromisingly at variance with ourselves, so deeply critical of us that if we really felt their presence to-day, we would be, to put it mildly, thoroughly uncomfortable. But Senators and Congressmen do not abash us, and Plato and Socrates transformed into them take on an

---

[2] From *Americans,* 1922, Charles Scribner's Sons, publisher.

236

undisturbing and familiar air. This, I say, is a vicious technique of ingratiation. But there is more and worse: in the same paper Sherman eulogises the average man and then lets himself go deep in the sin of cant. "If 'P. E. M.' had a bit more of that natural sympathy of which he is so distrustful, he would have perceived that what more than anything else to-day keeps the average man from lapsing into Yahooism is the *religion of democracy*, consisting of a little bundle of general principles which make him respect himself and his neighbour; a bundle of principles kindled in crucial times by an intense emotion, in which his self-interest, his petty vices, and his envy are consumed as with fire; etc." [3]

In the lexicon of contemporary humanism there is a damning phrase, "unselective sympathy." I think it applies to what Sherman meant when he said "religion of democracy," else why does he base so much of his message on the statistical average man? He could, like Mr. More, have appealed to the latent common sense of man, which is not a visible property of the average man to-day any more than it characterises his leaders, or he could, like M. Charles Maurras, have tried to conceive clearly of a perfect and normal man and argued for a closer approach to normality in human affairs; [4] but no—there was working in Sherman an element of "unselective sympathy" and it made his grasp relax on enterprises of perfection. It was no divine average man he espoused.

When in 1924 he became literary editor of the New York *Herald Tribune*, Sherman had his opportunity to establish what our milieu sorely lacks, a vigorous *conservative* literary

[3] The rest of the sentence is "and he sees the common weal as the mighty rock in the shadow of which his little life and personality are to be surrendered, if need be, as things negligible and transitory."

[4] Also he could have mastered the philosophy of Mr. John Dewey and made his "religion of democracy" more respectable.

review.  But what he organised was essentially not different from any intelligent liberal review with romantic tendencies: many of his regular reviewers were, for instance, already identified as reviewers for the *Nation*.  We have followed Sherman from the academic world to the professional literary world, and it would seem to a superficial glance that Sherman changed remarkably in his transit from one to the other. He had been an assailant of Mr. Dreiser's naturalism: he was to praise *An American Tragedy*.  He had sneered, and not very well, at the "moderns": he was to become their friendly counsellor.  He had learned, he said, that it was a certain "vitality," no matter under what guise, that he wanted in letters, and this platform enabled him to do a great deal of explaining away of his altered views.  He became less provincial.

But underneath there was no change.  He had not the stuff of leadership.  For what was this element of "unselective sympathy" in him which he called a "religion of democracy"?  It was a fear of distinction, a fear of standing away from the mass, a fear of striving far enough ahead to be a leader.  Was Sherman, I wonder, one of those numerous professors who are so anxious to be taken as in spirit "one of the boys" that they will compromise the dignity of their learning, that they will feel *defensive* about the life of the mind?  As a critic certainly he was on the defensive in presenting his values to the average audience.  Of no marked force in himself, on him the registry of environment would be speedily and plainly made.  In an academic environment he had fought the New York critics.  He came as an editor to New York and the environment quickly persuaded him to blend with it.[5]

[5] A perusal of the *Life and Letters of Stuart P. Sherman*, published after this essay was written, increases my confidence in the diagnosis above of Sherman's weaknesses.  Mr. P. E. More wondered many years ago whether his young reviewer did not have "an inclination to avoid the central prob-

When Sherman died, the professional literary world eulogised fulsomely the *émigré* from the academy. That already tells us a great deal about this world. Let us see more distinctly what it was with which Sherman assimilated.

## II

It was a tragi-comedy begun in high spirits and closing now in disillusion and pathos. Three representative players have been Mr. Joel Elias Spingarn, Mr. Van Wyck Brooks, and Mr. H. L. Mencken: a study of their rôles will instruct us in the mediocrity of contemporary American criticism. The influence of the first of these is a most curious phenomenon in our recent history.

In type Mr. J. E. Spingarn is the leisured gentleman and scholar who adorns all too rarely our national society. His interests are wide: for a number of years he was in politics and he has distinguished himself by his generous efforts in behalf of the Negro: he has been an army officer and has, one fancies, a spark of the old-time gallantry of the military man. For us, however, he is the wealthy amateur of the arts and philosophy; but what, one may still ask, are his claims to critical leadership?

Like Sherman, Mr. Spingarn spent a number of years teaching in an academic environment. He specialised in the history of literary criticism, producing the three-volume compilation, *Critical Essays of the Seventeenth Century* (1909) and the volume, *Literary Criticism in the Renaissance* (1899), which pleased certain Italian thinkers and began that friendship with them later to be cemented by his championship of Croce. Neither of these works is more than

lem." Later, he warned Sherman: "I do not like to see a man of your ability and insight deliberately taking up the job of whitewasher" for democracy. And finally Mr. More said: "Yours is but a sickly sort of democracy at bottom, and needs a doctor."

the usual competent product of academic industry and research: Mr. Spingarn himself revolted against the type of
sterile scholarship they represent. In 1910 he delivered his
famous lecture, *The New Criticism*. He declaimed it at the
climax of a spree, for he had intoxicated himself with the
æsthetic theory of Benedetto Croce: he was in full cry against
academic dry rot. Consequently his statements at the time
were more extreme than those he would probably make on
the same theme to-day.

Nevertheless, for the purposes of a record, we must write
down such pronunciamentos in this lecture, in the addenda
to it in *Creative Criticism* (1917), in his article, *The Seven
Arts and the Seven Confusions,* and in his contribution to
*Civilization in the United States* (1921) as bear on the following topics: the essence of art, the function of the artist,
the duty of the critic.

Literature, he said, pointing to the trend of nineteenth-
century criticism, "is an expression of something, of experience or emotion, of the external or internal, of the man himself or something outside the man; yet it is always conceived
of as an art of expression." As for the artist, he bade him
know that "madness and courage are the very life of art.
. . . For the madness of poets is nothing more or less than
unhampered freedom of self-expression. . . . To let one's
self go—that is what art is always aiming at, and American
art needs most of all." The duty of the critic? To ask and
answer these questions: "What has the poet tried to do, and
how has he fulfilled his intention? What is he striving
to express and how has he expressed it? What impression
does his work make on me, and how can I best express this
impression?" With the flourishes of a platform speaker
who knows instinctively that it is not straight hard thinking
which sways an audience so much as the verve with which
possibly dubious generalities are pronounced, Mr. Spingarn

exclaimed vehemently that the new critics have done with the whole question of standards, including genres, hierarchies, and moral judgments.

This is, of course, an unsubtilised outright statement of romantic æstheticism. Mr. Spingarn was positive that the critic's essential response to a work of art must be æsthetic, but he has always withheld what exactly he means by the æsthetic emotion or response or judgment. (It *is* hard to make concrete statements about the so-called æsthetic emotion.) But that did not in the least militate against the "æsthetic response" being used as a campaign catchword. For Mr. Spingarn had written the proclamations for a new generation of American writers. This is the curious phenomenon I spoke of. One is astonished not just at the slight quantity of Mr. Spingarn's writing in proportion to his reputation, but more astonished at the complete lack of originality in the documents of this apostle for originality. He added nothing to the Crocean doctrine: he clarified nothing or modified nothing in it. He did not even apply it, abstaining, then and since, from concrete criticism of individual works. He merely proclaimed it. And a widespread revolt against standards followed in American criticism. So hearty, and eventually so wilful and silly, was the revolt that in 1922 its opponents were entertained by the issuance from Mr. Spingarn of a restraining manifesto entitled *The Younger Generation*. This time, recoiling from the destructiveness of the young men, Mr. Spingarn would herd them back into an idealistic fold, back to "discipline, character, morals, imagination, beauty, freedom." Very often before, romantic expansiveness has run its course into disillusion: it is a soberer Crocean who said, "I, who once called upon young men for rebellion and doubt, now call upon them for thought and faith."

It is not Mr. J. E. Spingarn, enthusiastic amateur of

letters, trained scholar, man of feeling, who can detain us, for there is literally nothing in his writing for the mind to work on: as a thinker, he is thoroughly derivative and weak on definitions. But what Mr. Spingarn stands for, the theory of self-expression, still needs a scotching.

"Self-expression" is simply a magical catchword of the black variety. It is a good catchword in that it emphasises the self, but it is pernicious to the best interests of the self. For to express one's self means no more than just to manifest oneself, and if we say self-manifestation instead of self-expression, we see at once how paralysing the latter term has been. It has placed the emphasis, one sees, on the artist *as he is* and not on his possibilities of growth: thus it has a static effect. Think now: impulses, people say, arise in them or occur to them; no one claims to create his own impulses, to self-induce his inclinations; in a manner of speaking, our impulses come to us from the outside. Therefore, advice to be spontaneous, to let oneself go without check, to follow one's impulses is necessarily advice—to do what?—*to live as unconsciously and mechanically as possible*. The romantic may just as well hand himself over to the Behaviourist psychologist, saying, "Here am I, a creature of whim and impulse, the living proof of your thesis of automatism." But the romantic is not sternly logical. He has been proof against the question as to the value of the self that is being expressed, and not only proof against it: self-expression as a theory has encouraged his conceit and sometimes fostered megalomania, thus pitching him deeper into bondage to *external* conditions, for conceit makes one exaggeratedly sensitive to the environment.

To identify one's self with the mechanical temperamental flux of one's existence and call that freedom is surely strange, and it is no wonder that it is a strange "science" which has risen to support this identification. I am of course referring

242

to psycho-analysis, spoken of respectfully by Mr. Spingarn, utilised as a probing instrument in biography by Mr. Van Wyck Brooks, and championed by Mr. Mencken. It does not seem necessary here to make a serious attempt to discredit psycho-analysis, for that is being done rapidly enough by such critics of it as Dr. Trigant Burrow, by the Behaviourists, by the academic psychologists themselves. The facts have never been other than these: that psycho-analysis is admittedly experimental (and therefore speculative in its procedures, unsure of itself), that its central conception, the unconscious, not to speak of its many little metaphors like the "censor," has never been objectively established, and that it has no ideal of psychological health toward which to guide its adherents (in lieu of such an ideal, the analyst has either gone in for an excessive relativity or he has taken the "reality" of the statistical average to be the norm). These are the undeniable facts and one who would like to take pride in the sturdy commonsense of the literary profession must regret that they were not kept in mind. Literary men to-day, one must conclude, are no less gullible than any other group. Naïvely, they welcomed the psycho-analytical dramatising of inhibitions as the causes of ills, they agreed at once that thought was a sublimation of sex energy and somehow not quite a legitimate function of man, they wiseacred in jargon about <u>that bastard soul, the</u> unconscious. Ah, my highly suggestible writers, it is easy come, easy go with your ideas: within a decade you will be sneering at psycho-analysis as now you sneer at Christian Science.

Mr. Van Wyck Brooks in his social studies and biographical interpretations came to use psycho-analysis with tact: he is not the sort of critic whose errors will be glaring. A sensitive man but shy of æsthetic ideas: a sociological critic of letters in control of a persuasive and considerate prose style: a sentimental naturalist, to use the terminology of

243

Mr. Irving Babbitt, but far from extreme in his humanitarian socialism and, despite his psycho-analytic superstitions, temperate in his faith in emotional expansiveness.

Who would dispute Mr. Brooks's central idea, namely, that an acquisitive society provides unfavourable conditions for the development of the artistic life? Of course it does. It badly nourishes its men of genius, and Mr. Brooks became almost obsessed with literary failure or what he conceived to be literary failure, as witness his books on Symonds, Mark Twain, and Henry James. He was continually calling the attention of the new writers to the conditions in the history of America which had hampered and throttled their predecessors: he showed how frontier life had made the machinery of existence, the actual getting of a living, paramount and from this necessity had originated the contempt for the arts of enjoying existence, and how this split had perpetuated itself in the divorce between the world of practice ("lowbrow") and the world of theory ("highbrow"): but he failed at the very crux of his pleading. For struggling and unappreciated writers are too ready to believe that the hostile environment is responsible for their shortcomings. They are likely to wilt into self-pity and to feel victimised. That is precisely the effect that Mr. Brooks's writings produced, even though he casually said: "If our literature is to grow it can only be through the development of a sense of 'free will' on the part of our writers themselves. To be, to feel oneself, a 'victim' is in itself not to be an artist, for it is the nature of the artist to live, not in the world of which he is an effect, but in the world of which he is the cause, the world of his own creation." But Mr. Brooks has not grown eloquent on this theme. He seems rather to have the sweet wistfulness and yearning of one pledged to a lost cause. This mood of wistfulness and yearning, this image of oneself as an outcast, lonely and eager, has not revived and will never, it seems to me, revive the spirit of the American writer.

Was it fortuitous, as in the example of Mr. Spingarn, that Mr. Van Wyck Brooks should have held a certain leadership, should have put far more than most of his generation his impress upon American taste and thought in literary matters? It would seem that he has been a leader *faute de mieux*, for although a charming minor critic, he has never managed to awake an indomitable desire among his followers to master the odds. He voiced the sentiments of a wistfully rebellious generation but shed no light on the object of their rebellion, the achievement in a democracy of real individuality.

That is the problem Mr. H. L. Mencken has at least perceived, and his bold tone better fits a leader in our present straits than Mr. Brooks's gentle accents, but alas! He "solved" the problem of being an individual in a "democratic" nation simply by striking an attitude of swagger, and like Midas he is cursed with a touch that changes all objects into some one thing else. It is easy—and this is the secret of his influence—to adopt Mr. Mencken's attitude toward the current affairs of men. Let me quote his *Catechism* and you will have it in one simple lesson. "*Q.* If you find so much that is unworthy of reverence in the United States, then why do you live here? *A.* Why do men go to zoos?" But let us observe the man in the zoo, traipsing open-mouthed and superciliously from cage to cage, grinning in silly patronage at the imprisoned beasts who at least are true to the laws of their being, and shall we not mock at man's cheap sense of superiority based not on what he (poor lunatic!) has done for himself but only on what Nature has made of him? No, no, it is not by contempt for the inferior that man will grow but by dissatisfaction with himself. The net effect of Mr. Mencken's writings, however, is to produce self-satisfaction and a feeling of false superiority, and this naturally enough makes for personal passivity.

As for the Mencken touch! It turns everything to horse sense (not to be confused with the hard-won virtue of commonsense) and it is admirable when it is applied to current cant, as this: "Law Enforcement becomes the new state religion. A law is something that A wants and can hornswoggle B, C, D, E and F into giving him—by bribery, by lying, by bluff and bluster, by making faces. G and H are therefore bound to yield it respect—nay, to worship it. It is something sacred. To question it is to sin against the Holy Ghost."

But shrewdness is not enough when one is trying to cope with master-ideas, and in their realm Mr. Mencken is, as he might say, a clodhopper. One of the master-ideas in æsthetics and psychology, one that has engaged great minds and been pondered upon each century since the *Poetics* was introduced into European thought, is the Aristotelian conception of *katharsis*. Hear Mr. Mencken after the sages and the learned have spoken. He is saying that capital punishment affords *katharsis* to modern societies. "*Katharsis*, so used, means a salubrious discharge of emotions, a healthy letting off of steam. A schoolboy, disliking his teacher, deposits a tack upon the pedagogical chair; the teacher jumps and the boy laughs. This is *katharsis*. A bootlegger, paying off a Prohibition agent, gives him a counterfeit $10 bill; the agent, dropping it in the collection plate on Sunday, is arrested and jailed. This is also *katharsis*. A subscriber to a newspaper, observing his name spelled incorrectly in the report of a lodge meeting, spreads a report that the editor of the paper did not buy Liberty bonds. This again is *katharsis*." [6] And this again is cheap intellectual vaudeville

[6] From *Prejudices: Fourth Series*, Alfred A. Knopf, publisher.

or—it is clodhopperism. Something like this always happens when Mr. Mencken fingers the diamond ideas of the world; the process of degrading intellectual grandeur to horse sense began when he grossly misunderstood Nietzsche years ago.

By way of a last word on this idol of the emancipated Rotarian, do not forget that Mr. Mencken, destructive critic that he is, is also given to fulsome and extravagant praise of certain transient artists. Mr. Edgar Lee Masters' *Spoon River Anthology*, he says, is "the most eloquent, the most profound and the most thoroughly national volume of poetry published in America since *Leaves of Grass.*" Conceivably, it may be the third, but is it eloquent, is it profound? Such judgments are not uncommon when Mr. Mencken feels a praising mood come on.

## III

Into the critical pond presided over by Messrs. Spingarn, Brooks, and Mencken leapt Sherman. His academic values were in deliquescence, and he was greeted with cheers when he began to revise his former estimates and with eulogies when he died untimely. Much may be said for the three critics I have taken as big frogs in this puddle: do not forget the gusto of Mr. Spingarn's temperament, the historical consciousness and fine humanity of Mr. Brooks, the valuable scavenger-work of Mr. Mencken. But after all is said there is no seed, no fertility in the viewpoint of each. We must stress their failures: the failure of Mr. Spingarn to offer for application and development æsthetic ideas, the failure of Mr. Brooks to give the new American writers an image of themselves that would effectively inspire them against the crushing forces of their environment, the failure of Mr. Mencken to escape sophisticated superstitions as he escaped gross superstitions. Look at their disciples and behold clearly the limitations of the pond's masters.

Mr. Mencken has bred a score of little Menckens, men who imitate his style, who spend their time demonstrating, as Mr. Kenneth Burke said of Mr. Mencken, the stupidity of many a stupidity and invariably showing that it is stupid: they have no more capacity for realising great central ideas than Mr. Mencken. Mr. Brooks has inspired Mr. Lewis Mumford, who is a pleasing writer on architecture, a literary critic who seizes on the romantic elements of Emerson, Thoreau, and Whitman and repeats with spirit what his predecessor has said, a thinker whose general terms are vague, and who is impractical because of his credulity as to what modern letters can actually effect in modern society. His distinguishing trait, like Mr. Brooks's, is a certain fine, sensitive, generous humanity, but beware here! Without a corresponding growth of intellectual power, a corresponding stress on deeds, this fervour may degenerate into mere emotional bluff. And the followers of Mr. Spingarn? Are there any now? There is an æsthetic school of young critics, but they derive rather from Mr. Ezra Pound and the T. S. Eliot who wrote *The Sacred Wood*. For after all Mr. Spingarn only winded a horn and left the startled and delighted self-expressionists to hunt for themselves.

We have, it would seem, come to the end of a decade and a half of exuberance. Enter mournfully Mr. Joseph Wood Krutch to confess the disillusioned after-thoughts of the modern romanticist. It is a supine admission he makes, without blushes be it added, when he says in beginning his account of the modern temper or mood: "I have been compelled to make references to many facts or supposed facts in biology, psychology, and anthropology. Obviously no person is qualified to assert them all with authority and obviously I am much less qualified than many others, but when I state them I do so not as facts, but simply as commonplaces which we have been taught to believe. My subject is not any series of objective facts, but a state of mind, and in the effort to describe and account for it I am responsible not for Truth, but for the convictions, scientific or otherwise, which I and my contemporaries have been led to hold . . . if the tenets of Freudianism or the hypotheses of the Darwinian theory are false, they have at least been so accepted as to influence the modern temper quite as unmistakably as if they were true . . . these supposed facts have an emotional significance. That is as far as it is necessary to go if they are to be used as I use them, only in the effort to account for a mood." [7]

Shades of the heroes of the mind! Here is a critic who can entertain the possibility that much of our contemporary "knowledge" is untrue, and then merely wring his hands elegantly in the melancholy produced by *assuming* that it is true. In *The Modern Temper* (1929) romantic criticism in America culminates in weak despair.

As we should expect, there have been departures lately. There is Mr. Walter Lippmann,[8] as able a cartographer of the Kingdom of Whirl as Mr. Krutch. He sees clearly that the bell-tent of civilisation is in collapse because society has no common human aim, no hold, that is, on a center-pole capable of raising the whole structure. "The effect of modernity, then," he says in *A Preface to Morals* (1929), "is to specialise and to intensify our separated activities. Once all things were phases of a single destiny: the church, the state, the family, the school were means to the same end; the rights and duties of the individual in society, the rules

---

[7] From *The Modern Temper*, Harcourt, Brace & Co., publisher.

[8] Mr. Lippmann is not a literary critic but his views are pertinent to this discussion.

of morality, the themes of art, and the teachings of science were all of them ways of revealing, of celebrating, of applying the laws laid down in the divine constitution of the universe. In the modern world institutions are more or less independent, each serving its own proximate purpose, and our culture is really a collection of separate interests each sovereign within its own realm." [9]  And the remedy he proposes, who can quarrel with it? The "good life," he says, is an *acquired* disposition,—surely an advance over the implication of the other critics we have mentioned that somehow the "good life" would *naturally* come to pass, if one could only eliminate puritanic inhibitions and flow with one's desires. No, says Mr. Lippmann, we must develop "detachment, understanding, and disinterestedness in the presence of reality itself." We must enter into a new asceticism— who would have anticipated five years ago such a phrase from our new critics?—defined as "an effort to overcome immaturity."

This is excellent in that it perceives the problem and the goal of the clear-insighted modern man, but does not Mr. Lippmann underestimate the enormous psychological difficulties that block the passage from unregenerate to regenerate man? One has the feeling that his is a paper solution, and one is appalled to read of his hopes for psycho-analysis as a technique for achieving the re-education of desire. The aim of psycho-analysis is adjustment to reality, and Mr. Lippmann adopts the dangerous phrase. It is dangerous: for what does "adjustment" in practice mean but taking the position of maximum comfort, the following of the path of least resistance? Continual adjustments by beings to an environment progressively unfavourable mean the progressive deterioration of a species: ultimately adjustment means extinction. Perhaps the dinosaurs can give us a lesson in the fallacy of adjustment. It is farcical for this critic to patron-

[9] The Macmillan Company, publisher.

ise Pythagoras, for instance, who "could not have known any tested method either of equipping his followers to appreciate science or anything besides a crude asceticism as a means of moral discipline," as long as we can contrast the ancient perception of the human necessity of surmounting the environment with the contemporary belief in the value of adjusting (merely reacting) to it.

Nevertheless Mr. Lippmann among others has articulated what will probably be the fundamental position of American criticism in the next decade, namely, the conviction that we are thinking and acting chaotically and senselessly, and the deep surmise that man can "learn to desire the kind of happiness which is possible." The brilliant but eccentric Mr. Waldo Frank has dwelt for some time on the dissolution of the Mediæval Synthesis of Europe. America he announces is the grave of Europe and he hopes for a kind of miracle: a generation within the grave of a mystical revival. He too has had his thoughts turned to the all-important question of a method of realising Wholeness in fact as well as in concept. You will find his method outlined at the close of *The Re-discovery of America* (1929). It is, I fear, hastily constructed, and more than smacks of amateurishness and of the armchair. One wishes that he had not rushed in where sages fear to tread, but he has at least thrown the question of a method for the development of human potentialities into open discussion.[10]

The most impressive of the contemporary critics who offer

---

[10] Even in a footnote I mention Mr. Ludwig Lewisohn with some reluctance, and only because there are so few critics among us who have any interest in trying to plot a direction for the future. Pauline Christianity (grossly libelled by him as akin to the degenerate puritanism of our day) must be destroyed, he preaches. Salvation lies in a fusion of Hellenism (Science) and Judaism (which he interprets selectively and sentimentally). He is a suggestive writer: he is also a prig, a special pleader, and embarrassing in his frequent intervals of self-pity and in his intrusions of hearth-side intimacies (proper for telling only to his closest friends) into the public medium of print. One cannot take this muddled romanticist seriously.

us "a way out" is Mr. T. S. Eliot, but before examining him, it is proper to repeat here that I am excluding from this paper any consideration of the formidable opposition party to all that has been described thus far, the new humanists whom the romanticists have found raised up against them. In passing, I may say that I have before this dipped my freelance pen to the humanists in salutations of great respect mingled with a few misgivings, and I have not the least hesitation in volunteering to defend them against the oblique attack of Mr. T. S. Eliot.

This painstaking critic owes much to Professor Babbitt, far more than does Mr. Lippmann. There is in fact much overlapping between his views and modern humanism. Yet there is an issue between the new humanists and Mr. T. S. Eliot: it resolves itself into the question of Authority. Let us trace out the evolution of Mr. Eliot's ideas and we shall see the latent weakness of his position, and those who wish may compare it with the new humanists' position. In *The Sacred Wood* (1921) he began as an acute æsthetic critic, basing the exercise of criticism upon sensibility and intellect. He professed to be a classicist. Opposed to romantic excesses he was, in spite of an admiration for certain decadent poets, but was he a classicist? If so, what about the essay on *Tradition and the Individual Talent*, in which the idea of "creative imitation" is pushed to an extreme that makes one suspicious? Matters became explicit a few years later when he debated with Mr. J. Middleton Murry. In this debate Mr. Eliot admitted that such were the instabilities and insufficiencies of private judgment and private experience that a man should discipline himself in allegiance to some outside Authority, and for the literary critic this meant loyalty to the classical literary tradition. Something was here given away: the strict corroboration by personal experiment of classical wisdom was left out. Mr. Eliot was

252

revealed as by disposition a neo-classicist (with some romantic elements) thoroughly dependent upon literary authority.

The next step for him, as a man too intelligent and too
serious to evade the problems of social and moral chaos, was
to acknowledge that criticism in our age could not be so
limited as it was conceived to be in *The Sacred Wood*. On
the contrary, the critic he saw must become philosophic: he
must be a creator of values. But here again he was neo-
classical, for he searched for external Authority in politics
and in religion. In the former he is Royalist, in the latter
Anglo-Catholic.

Turn to his essays on style and order entitled *For Lancelot Andrewes*. They are the work of a fine judicial temperament, but not, not at all, the work of a general in the warfare of the mind. The distinction is worth making much of.
I have elsewhere [11] analysed the structure and procedures of
Mr. Eliot's prose to show its thoroughly judicial characteristics: its calmness and gravity, its balance and discriminatory
powers among precedents, its fulfilment in a final elucidation
arrived at by comparisons and analyses. It is not a full-
bodied prose, the weight of the whole man concentrated on
the pen, but the prose of a judge conscious of the weight of
authority *behind*, not in, him. Now observe that in *For
Lancelot Andrewes* Mr. Eliot, like a learned judge and with
an air of profundity, is continually pointing to the tradition
of a Church, set up as an authority external to himself. He
is at his best when he presents comparatively narrow ideas,
ideas about literary style for the most part, as in his exposition of the relevant intensity of Andrewes' prose. At
his most disappointing, he ventures upon a safe common-
place generality, as when he remarks, "The greatest tragedies
are occupied with great and permanent moral conflicts." The
last is true enough, but Mr. Eliot never talks very much or

[11] In *Style and Form in American Prose* (1929).

directly about this occupation, about the stuff itself of moral conflicts.

Likewise Mr. Eliot, apologist for religion, does not write about religion: he points to *a* Church and the intellectual riches of its history. "For us," he declares, "religion is of course Christianity; and Christianity implies, I think, the conception of a Church." And again, "And the spirit killeth, but the letter giveth life"—but we need both the letter and the spirit! Stress on the letter gives us legalism in religious thinking, and on the spirit gives us what Mr. Eliot calls "*Ersatz*-religion": the two, spirit and letter, must correspond. There we are! the last critical "leader" in this examination turns out to be merely sitting on a judge's bench and therefore necessarily inactive: he points out where Authority may be found, but one may doubt from the evidence of his writing whether Authority resides in him.

## IV

Following the course of Sherman, we entered the professional literary world and explored its criticism, coming finally to Mr. T. S. Eliot, whose latest departure turns our eyes outwards again to the academic world, to Professor Babbitt and humanism, or to the worlds of religion or philosophy. It appears to me that our purely literary critics have at one point or another all failed fundamentally: they are all leaders by default only and not by essence. Either they are bound to move towards the position of Mr. Joseph Wood Krutch, who realises that "all the bases upon which modern despair rests were laid joyously by people who were quite sure that they were serving humanity, and all the chains by which we are now bound so much more firmly to earth than we want to be were forged amidst shouts of triumph," or they are spying some loophole which on inspection seems not to exist. But in either case, and this is a hopeful sign, they are all converging toward a common realisation that King Whirl must, if possible, be deposed. The goal is seen: the reconstructed human spirit. But without adequate leadership how may we start to approach it?

Well, it is easy to exaggerate the power of literary criticism. If certain things in our culture have gone dead, criticism cannot revive them. The essential "about-ness" of the critical activity limits it to the guidance, stimulation, and judging of things in which there is still some life. But assuming that a funeral ceremony such as Mr. Krutch has conducted is still premature,—and it is premature so long as any doubt exists of final decay,—we may then try to conceive of what a genuine leader in critical thought would be like, and by this ideal measure ourselves.

Objectivity in judgment would be one of the principal marks of the leader. That requires a sufficient scale of values to stand outside not only the frame of one's century but outside the frames of all centuries. It means the ascertainment of *primary* laws in our field, which may be possible as it has been possible in physics to say that a few laws are true regardless of what frame of time and space one may be in. Objectively considered, literature may be found to have been in decline, not just for a century and a half or just for six hundred years but almost from its classical sources and from the Scriptures of ancient lands. Is this depressing? It is not depressing to contemplate a magnificent mountain from its base.

On the contrary, a real view of the heights of Parnassus and Olympus may inspire an uncommon elevation of aim— a second mark of the critical leader; it seems to me unnecessary to argue that the critics we have looked at do not realise how high man has ascended in the past or can conceivably ascend now. Their ideas of human greatness are small.

Really, *are* we practitioners of literary criticism distinguished by any grandeur in breadth and elevation of thought? No one can believe it.

Nor can I believe that we approximate the ideal critic in passion, in a burning unquenchable indomitable love of perfect things. This is the spirit that giveth life to standards that otherwise would seem too skeletal, too non-human to be glamorous and magical in their remoteness: this is the spirit that killeth despair and compromise. Infused with it, our imagined critic becomes single-minded and proof against deviations and resting-places.

Finally, he would, I conceive, be distinguished by an immense capacity for relating deeds to words. His interest would not cease with a beautiful formulation, but would continue until the formulation was embodied in experience. Not words alone, not deeds alone, but words *and* actions would be his great desideratum.

Of whom am I thinking? It is dangerous in calling attention to concepts or principles to cite examples until the concept or principle or, in our case, ideal has been thoroughly understood, and I dare not hope for that within the space of this paper. But with a caution not to debate the achievements of him but only to study his framework, I take the risk of nominating Matthew Arnold as having the build of a great critic. We need in our national letters a critic of the stamp and dimensions of Arnold.

## V

I append *The Prayer of a Young Critic.*

> But we have heard rumour of the Mistral.
> It is a cold wind that blows from the heights,
> Day after day it sweeps steadily down,

Cold and from above, changing the air
In the lowlands.
     We are dwellers in lowlands
And our air has been breathed before. It is
A sultry air: men talk to each other
In haze and their words are close and fevered.
A warm breeze crosses our little hillocks,
And then the dust settles down again.
Not near the Alps do we live.
         Great Genius,
Grant us an electric climate! Touch us
With snowy fire, send the Mistral to sweep
Bare our plain and proclaim the gaiety
Of altitudes, the glory of clear stars,
The exaltation of the sun burning
The rare air. Great Genius, send the Mistral!

# Behaviour and Continuity

BERNARD BANDLER II

## I

Until humanism and psychology are more suitably defined than they are at present the task of establishing their relations is hazardous. Psychology is still in a primitive state: its basic problems and principles are disputed, its relation to the other sciences is undetermined, and its method is loose and unsystematic. That it may be a science, however, is indubitable. The constitution of human nature is open to analysis: human behaviour no less than the stars and plants may be observed and hypothesis may be employed to order its seeming irregularities. But the common scientific ground of purpose which underlies the differences of psychological theories does not unite the humanists, and the problem of stating the nature and scope of humanism is correspondingly difficult. The absence of a common scientific ground, of an accepted subject matter and a technique, enables any man interested in human activities to call himself a humanist and to maintain his contention, whereas no man, unless technically trained, will consider himself a psychologist. He may observe society and deliver himself of apothegms and epigrams that characterise people truly— like the French moralists, La Rochefoucauld, La Bruyère, and Joubert. He may trace the influence of ideas on conduct, as Mr. Babbitt has done. But that is ethics and philosophy, not psychology. Psychology limits itself to studying how human beings behave and to reducing their most complex actions to primitive elements. Ethics evaluates their activities and judges them. So, however confusing the positions of contemporary psychologists and humanists, if we keep in mind the formal aspects of psychology and ethics, a study of the relations of the two may be instructive.

Upon psychology as a science, as upon physics and chemistry, humanism can have nothing to say. It may examine the logic of psychology and criticise its presuppositions, although that is properly the task of the cosmologist, like Mr. Whitehead. But towards the conclusion of psychology, the "laws" it may formulate, humanism's only possible attitude is one of interested acceptance. An ethics should not prescribe the limits of science, nor dictate the nature of its results. And if the science deals successfully with human actions, ethics, instead of criticising, should respect its results, that ideals may not be founded on ignorance and fancy but rather on knowledge.

Unfortunately, the amount of psychology which is scientific and relevant to human nature is small. Much of it reduces to physiology. The chemistry of the glands and blood, the nature of sensation, feeling, emotion, and of the thinking processes, and those predispositions of the body which we call instincts are ultimately problems of physiology and await the development of that science for their solution. What distinguishes psychology from physiology is the study of behaviour in society: the transmutation of the instincts and temperament into habits and sentiments. Of psychology proper we have, so far, elaborate programmes, a bewildering variety of theories,—part epistemology, part logic, part metaphysics, and part mythology,—a vast accumulation of data, some classifications, and hardly any science. Yet the studies of "types," "personality," "culture forms," and particularly the researches of psychiatrists contain many accurate descriptions of human behaviour. Their endeavour to ex-

plain the most sublimated actions, by reference to the constitution of the organism and to the determining factors of its
environment, approaches sound science.

But "behaviour in society" and "the determining factors
of environment" are vague phrases. If there is to be a science of behaviour and society two conditions are necessary:
first, that the organisms in spite of individual variations
should be essentially the same; and second, that the environment to which they react should be stable and limited. For
if each organism were essentially unique there would be no
basis for the science of psychology, and if the environment
were constantly changing there would be no conditions and
no control for studying the organism. But human environment, the totality of forces which affect us and help satisfy
our needs, is not stable and limited. It is plastic and relative. Tradition and convention are added to the forces com-
posing an animal's environment. These multiply the possibilities of behaviour indefinitely. In proportion as a man
frees himself from a blind adherence to custom, the more
personal his environment will be. To know such a man's environment is to become acquainted with a unique world. It
is to know not only his ancestry, his history, his habits, his
occupation, and his social milieu, but also his purposes, the
ends which he consciously seeks and which are the meaning
of his actions to him. It is to know his mind. But a mind,
being unique, can never be absolutely known. Even if it
were completely revealed in behaviour, conversation, and
writing, and if all the occasions that have served to form it
were discovered, one could never be certain to capture a man's
understanding of his words, or his interpretation of his attitude and actions.

Behaviourists are therefore right in excluding consciousness, purpose, and mind from psychology. These are in-
accessible to science: first, because they can never be precisely

seized; and second, because they introduce an indefinite number of objects which preclude a limited and stable environment. Mind can reflect upon all objects of experience, and these in turn can become objectives of action. So soon as this happens the exact control which experimental science demands is prevented and the progress of psychology is blocked. It thus seems impossible for psychology to deal with the most interesting aspect of human behaviour, those where action is guided and dominated by thought and is not blindly reflexive. To avoid this limitation of psychology certain behaviourists, in the name of what they conceive to be mechanism, have denied the efficacy of purpose and mind altogether. According to the argument, consciousness, purpose, and mind are waste products, attendant upon natural processes, like sparks from a locomotive. Or they are like the decorations on illuminated manuscripts, illustrating the text, and quite superfluous. Otherwise they would be forces, inexplicably interfering with natural processes. These arguments fail by misconstruing the notion of purpose, which is not a force but an end. Purpose does not direct action but *is* the direction which action takes. It is the rational explication of the objects of our desires and wishes. The end has no initial power, but, once thought has discerned it as the true object of our desires and they have attached themselves to it, as a lover to his mistress, so that satisfaction cannot be found elsewhere, then the end acquires a deputed power which it may never surrender. Since purpose defines the objects of desire which thereby become objectives of action, it is a determining factor of human behaviour, and the so-called mechanistic arguments against it are invalid. Yet, since science deals with material and efficient causes only, psychologists are compelled to disregard formal and final causes, purposes, and ends.

## II

The goal of ethics, on the other hand, is to discover the most organised system of ends, of goods, which a rational life can realise. This goal of ethics can never be fully achieved, for so long as man acts and reflects he may pursue and conceive novel ends. But though the most elaborate system of ethics is in origin an expression of personal preferences, it is not therefore arbitrary and unjustifiable by reason. My values have their roots in my nature. I can exhibit them, demonstrate that they are mutually consistent and do not defeat the interests which underlie them. Furthermore I can declare that if any one honestly questioned his heart he might find that my values represented it. It is not to psychology, then, that one must turn for knowledge of human goods. For psychology, although it may analyse the efficient causes of desire, cannot estimate the value of its objects, of the ideal form of a rational life. If psychologists talk of a normal organism, they mean one whose desires are adjusted to its environment, the one most likely to survive. If they speak of superior organisms and civilisation, they mean increased ability for adjustment to a more complex environment. Thus though psychologists speak of normal and civilised they are unable either to define or to evaluate them.

Knowledge of human goods is furnished by philosophers, when they are frank and speak for themselves; by the founders of religions, the saints, and the mystics; by the poets, and chiefly, as Socrates knew, by knowledge of oneself. Self-knowledge, though it may first look back upon the behaviour studied by psychology, moves in the opposite direction toward the objects sought. These it endeavours to comprehend, to purge of contradictions, to regard intently *sub specie mortalitatis*. From the vantage point of death one becomes a spectator of human life. Thought acquires the prestige of impersonality, without the sacrifice of its warm interest in life. The point of view of death differs from seeing things *sub specie æternitatis* both in essence and in purpose. It does not abolish time or elevate mind to the contemplation of a necessary order, which is the function of seeing things *sub specie æternitatis*, although consideration of death (as in the Phædo) may do this. It enables one to regard life in its totality and, without projecting it against the background of nature, to estimate each partial aim in the perspective of all others, and thus to distinguish the objects one truly desires.

The effort to detach oneself from the present and to incorporate it with the past and future in a satisfactory whole, which psychology does not attempt, is what makes action ethical. In the unique self the past exists in memory, which is one's personal tradition. Thus memory, besides being the mother of the muses, is the mother of ethics and of rational action. It enables us to confront our present condition, its projects, hopes, and fears, with the past, and by comparison to evaluate the present action. It enables us to utilise the whole of our experience in the active organisation of our life and thus to attain a continuity of being. Consequently a succession of full moments does not, as Pater thought, constitute a full life. For each of those separate selves which a past moment represented and which the subsequent one renounced lives in memory to advance its claim to existence against the present; and only similar circumstances are needed, a chance odour, or gesture, or phrase, to revive it, and make one feel the desolation of its loss. These intermittances of the heart, as Proust calls them, are dependent on the infinite passive occasions of sensation, and since they never represented an ideal actively striven for, no analysis is able to penetrate to an underlying unity. On the other hand the consequence of dispossessing oneself of the past in order to live in the moment is a reduction of the personality to indecision and apathy. Besides, the past preserved in memory and the future that we anticipate enrich the present and give it its fulness of being, as a musical phrase has more significance in a symphony than when played in isolation.

As one interrogates the present, with its What shall I do? What shall I be? it expands to absorb the relevant testimony that relates it to the past and to the future. Ordinarily the present includes a fairly definite content, some concrete situation and prospect, often trivial, as a dinner to be ordered. Choice when it is not automatic can easily review the relevant factors; one's favourite dishes, the season of the year; possible illness on the morrow. At other times the relevant relations are endless, particularly when an irrevocable choice forces us to discriminate among all the elements of our being: love, honour, country, and religion each claiming our allegiance. The infinite variety of situations that may arise and the impossibility of relating them to a definite past and a definite future are responsible for the differences of ethical systems. A philosopher's conception of the typical situation will define his problems and dictate the general terms of his solution. Buddha saw sorrow and suffering as the main portion of human existence. His endeavour, therefore, was to emancipate mankind from them. Aristotle started with man's desire for happiness. Therefore he analysed the actions of men, the pursuit of wealth, of honour, and of knowledge to see which conformed most with the essential nature of man. Amiel's situation was intensely personal, but he stated his problem in universal terms. Amiel recognised from his youth the necessity of an organising purpose and a continuous effort. His culture and sympathies, however, extended to all human actions; to limit his life to one of the manifold beings he felt contained within himself seemed a violation of the ideal.

Now what is the context, the appropriate situation and problem, from which ethics should start? Is it some general aspect of life common to all people, like sorrow or suffering, or the generic nature of man, or the attempt to discover an organising purpose? Or is it our immediate context, the world to which our traditions, conduct, desires, and ambitions have engaged us? It is this world that confronts us daily. Our actions in it are the theme of the novel, the drama, and the epic, which are an almost inexhaustible field for ethical study. Each work is a representation of an action, and in proportion as the writer concentrates his imagination on the situation before him, on his *donnée*, and reveals its possibilities, the action will illustrate some ideal. Literature always retains the concrete immediacy of life, the movement of an action never being from a situation to a principle. But all the comprehensiveness of a principle, the innumerable unsuspected relations which it opens when once intuition has leapt the gap between a formula and the fact it covers is implied by an action at its close. The characters are still flesh and blood, but as they finally define themselves their situation includes all their relevant past and all that is significant in their future, so that they become transparent, and the whole moral world which they represent shines clearly through them. Hence it is possible that a profound ethics and a great work of art may introduce us to the same moral world, so that the orientation of our being, emotional and intellectual, after reading the *Ethics* of Spinoza and *The Wings of the Dove* say, will be identical.

If ethics is to be persuasive and reasonable it must be founded on the most complete experience possible. The context from which it arises, as in life and literature, should be rich and concrete. The defect of most ethical systems is that they quit life too abruptly. Instead of studying the complex conditions which underlie any achieved good, as psychology is contented to do, philosophers ignore them, except in their generality, and so attain a factitious unity. Consequently rationalistic philosophers invert the proper procedure of thought. They start from the typical, the general, and the rational, whereas these are the ultimate fruits of reflection. When an ethics, however, repudiates the purpose of rationalism as well as its method, it severs itself from all connection with the good. If it speaks of goods and ideals, it speaks of them only provisionally and instrumentally. Its excessive preoccupation with the conditions marks the return of ethics to that immersion in the present from which it initially arose.

Humanism differs from other ethical systems by its data and by its method. Its data are each individual in his context; his inherited values, his body, his capabilities, and the relations formed by them. It is the task of each individual to preserve himself in the world, and to establish a continuity of being. The essence of humanism is the refusal to allow any sudden break of development, any shift of basis that arbitrarily repudiates one's past, such as breaking one's word. Its method is to survey life in the light of death. By this means one's personal situation can be enlarged by history, and by the contemplation of the ideals which men pursue. The more vivid the conception of an ideal society and a rational life within it, so long as it does not weaken one's personal reality, the more likely is life to yield happiness.

Psychology and ethics deal with the same subject matter, human behaviour, but they regard it from opposite points of view. Psychology regards it externally as a physical phenomenon having already taken place in time. Like any other science psychology tries to correlate its diverse data and to reduce them to the simplest elements possible. But since psychology requires that the organisms which it studies should be essentially the same and that the environment to which they react should be stable and limited, it cannot deal with the behaviour dominated by mind. For mind is unique and its possible objects are infinite. Its language is that of meaning, purpose, end. The effort of a moral individual is to know what he wants, to know his mind. Hence ethics regards human behaviour internally and as directed towards the future. The goal of ethics is the satisfactory synthesis of the unique perspectives of different minds. It approximates this synthesis by studying the dialectic of desire, the logical implications of each purpose in relation to all other objects. In this way ethics will describe ideally how an individual may harmonise with himself and with society, which psychology can never do, and thus point the way to happiness.

# The Well of Discipline

SHERLOCK BRONSON GASS

The lapidary precedes the historian, and the sound of the mallet is heard in the land chipping *Hic Jacet* on the monuments which humanism has erected, with an epitaph which runs blithely thus:

> "Humanism enjoyed four hundred years of prosperity in the later world and then gave way to Modernism. From Mid-Fifteenth to Mid-Nineteenth Century, Humanism traced the patterns of the Occident. Then, with a dramatic flourish comparable to that of the Renaissance, a new pattern was superimposed on the palimpsest of the West, based on the concepts and methods of Natural Science."

Meantime, while the historian waits for a deeper perspective, I am writing in the belief that there is more vitality in humanism than the lapidaries have given it credit for. Humanity, at all events, is perennial, and men are not likely to forget for long that science is not ineluctable nature itself, but only human knowledge, and that all knowledge, even knowledge of nature, is pursued at will for whatever it is worth to them in their own esteem—that behind the pursuit of natural science lies the authority of the evaluating mind.

The human worth of the sciences, I ardently echo, is beyond compare. They have, it is true, played a sardonic trick on their pursuers, and have seemed for the moment honestly to nullify any significant worth in human existence. But men may still recollect that it is they themselves who have made the nullifying discovery. They are worth at least what that discovery implies—an intelligence, a power to think and judge, and an impulse to act selectively on the basis of a sense of values—or why have they pursued the sciences at all? With these resources to start with, and science in their scrip, they may also have the humour to see that there remains to them, as of old, the eternal task of making the best of it—the very task to which science itself is a contribution. When this perception shall have grown lively enough, humanism will again come into its own.

Granted a will to return to humanism, however, the return itself will not be simple. Something, we shall find, has been lost in the meantime. Value and significance are not handed to us on a platter; they are themselves products of thought. If life, then, has seemed to be emptied of them by the findings of natural science, it is equally possible to suppose that this bathos is due to a diluted capacity for thought in precisely the field of thought where value and significance are conceived.

This is the possibility that I have set out to examine. The broad hint of it lies on the surface. If discipline of the mind has any virtue—and modernism itself with its austere regimen is its current champion—that virtue has been lifted from the field of thought where human values are explicitly involved, to a field of thought from which they are explicitly banned. By every calculation, therefore, the minds thus affected should have lost something of their capacity to think in the undisciplined area, and should have lost something of their powers to conceive or discover the values that, under happier auspices, give life its significance.

# I

In imagination we dramatise the Renaissance as a sweeping revolution. Whether humanists or modernists, we look upon it as a beginning, or a resumption, at all events as the turning-point from which we are the continuators in a straight line. Historians of philosophy, of letters, of politics, of science all concur. More impressively still the men of the Renaissance themselves were quite conscious of the change —Bessarion, Aldus, Erasmus, da Vinci, Galileo, Bruno, to take names at random. The shift of curiosity from the divine to the secular, and the responsive shift of discipline from scholasticism to humanism opened out new vistas to the voyaging mind. It would be hard to exaggerate the almost theatric reversals which the times witnessed and welcomed.

Sweeping as it was, however, the revolution of the Renaissance was less radical than that of the second half of the nineteenth century. In contrast to the latter the changes wrought by the Renaissance were on the level of explicit ideas. The essential stuff of thought was unchanged. New ideas were astir, but the elements of which they were built were the old elements. Theology gave way to humanism; God as the centre gave way to man as the centre. But after all, God had been conceived as a father and man as a child of God, and, God or man, their psychology was the same. The very literature which had laid the premisses of mediæval thought—the Bible—permeated the consciousness of the humanistic period yet more deeply.

The shift of discipline from sacred to profane letters, as a consequence, made no profound break in the consciousness itself. The major impulses of the two periods blended easily and naturally. The religious impulse of the Middle Ages lent itself triumphantly to literary expression; there was the *Divine Comedy*. The literary impulse of the Renaissance lent itself no less triumphantly to religious themes; there was *Paradise Lost*. Natural science, indeed, began its modern course under the impulse of the Renaissance. Still, from the fifteenth to the nineteenth century, while

270

the common discipline of the West was humanistic, natural science did not profoundly alter the minds of men. It was an incident, a special play of curiosity and thought on the part of men whose minds were formed and informed in the medium of humane letters. Even Doctor Johnson had his chemical apparatus.

Not until the latter half of the nineteenth century did the common discipline of letters begin to give way. Up to that time, therefore, there had been a basic continuity in the cultivated consciousness of the West, not only from the Middle Ages but from high antiquity itself. For the Renaissance was avowedly a resumption of the broken threads of ancient thought. And its humanism, however loosely it spliced the break, was evidence that here too the essential elements of its reason were the same. What so intoxicated the Renaissance mind was the very spontaneity of its grasp of ancient ideas. And this affinity has been the mark of humanism ever since.

Now continuity is not necessarily a virtue. Nothing, alas, is so persistent as error and evil. One aspect of the shift to modernism, however, seems to me itself an evil, promising persistence—a rupture at the basis of reason. Modernism, indeed, also had its dramatic confrontations, its moments of intense self-consciousness. New conceptions came into tragic conflict with old, yielding many a Robert Elsmere, and many a family cleavage like that between the elder and the younger Gosse. Such conflicts are disconcerting and painful, and for a generation or two terribly impressive. It is not to such overt changes, however, that I refer. They belong to the normal life of the mind. It is the very function of intellect to incur and mediate them. One is inclined to bid the intellect be a man and face the frank hazards of the life of reason. I refer rather to a change, not in ideas, but prior to ideas, among the ultimate premisses of thought, in the discipline by which the powers of the mind and the fortunes of ideas are themselves in a large measure disposed. And this change, it seems to me, has proved a scotching of the goose that lays the golden egg.

## II

Where is the bottom of the well into which discipline—vaunted so highly by both humanist and modernist—is poured? Discipline, as distinguished from any guise of propaganda, is a delicate affair. Its concern is not for the specific ideas with which perforce it must do its deed, and which it pours into the depths in an unremitting stream. Its subtle task is to enrich and enhance the powers of thought and yet leave them free—free to think, and free to judge even the ideas by which they are enriched.

The bottom lies deeper, therefore, than the level at which the Huxleys, the Spencers, the Eliots placed the controversy—the relative merits of two sorts of knowledge, of Homer and Sophocles, of Plato's Ideas and Cæsar's battles, of *Jerusalem Recovered* and *Paradise Lost,* as against the constitution of matter and the laws of nature. These relative merits are themselves matters of judgment, as the controversy witnesses. And it is precisely the quality of such judgment that is momentously at stake.

Of course the Hellenist must know his Greek and the astronomer his physics. They are specialists, and the question is not of them. It is a question of that common humanity of which Hellenist and astronomer, poet and chemist, man of leisure and man of affairs are alike responsible members. As between humanist and modernist a sort of official decision has already been rendered, and the common discipline, together with the faith that animates it, has gone over to the sciences. Is it ill-humoured to point out that

272

the decision itself has been arrived at and progressively confirmed in that field of judgment from which discipline has been progressively withdrawn? At all events, it is toward that deeper level that I am delving, to get at the roots of that common humanity.

The Darwinian hypothesis of the descent of man is a biological way of dealing with a reflection old in the tradition of humanism. From Plato down, curiosity has toyed with theories of the origin of language. Language is patently artificial, a device, a product of human ingenuity. That a child is born without speech might mean nothing, since there are instincts that emerge only in the course of development. But language differs from language; every term in every language is arbitrary; the child, whatever his blood, picks up the speech of his community; individuals differ in the extent and character of their deliberate acquisition. All these considerations point to its artificiality. One speaks, indeed, before one's mind is mature enough to reflect upon the accomplishment. But that is the very point, as will appear in a moment.

Whatever the theory, the origin of speech implies ancestors before speech. And those ancestors—is it fantastic to identify them, in a slightly modified version of our evolutionary history, with the prehuman race of the Darwinian rendering? We should not, I think, have called them men. For bound up with language is all that we think of as human —the power of communication, the fixation and tradition of thought, the comparison and criticism of ideas, co-operation on the basis of common principles, all history and philosophy, all literature and science, the very process of reason itself prior to its expression.

I say reason, not intelligence. Intelligence itself—a primary mystery—is scarcely the monopoly of men. The cat here on the hearth has a share of it, and the mouse of which she is apparently dreaming. It is not intelligence that distinguishes the human species sweepingly from the brute, but a particular deployment of it, a way of using it or managing it, that we call *reason*.

To linger in imagination over this moment of evolution is to linger over a transition from the dumb fluidity of animal consciousness to its articulation by the use of language. Sheer animal consciousness may alight, perhaps, upon any imaginable concept. Its rational defect is its inability to return after departure to the same spot. Who by taking pains could return again to precisely the number 91 but for the articulating, identifying, stabilising symbol? The rational use of the native intelligence thus hangs upon an ability to identify particles of consciousness arbitrarily shaped, to quit them, and then to return. And speech serves this end; so far as it is carried it precipitates fluid consciousness into stable, negotiable blocks for the architectural structures of thought.

Now it is true that what is original, what is new, what is invented or discovered by the thinking mind itself emerges, not in the articulate particles—they are perforce old stuff—but in the perception by the intelligence of relations between them. This spontaneous perception of relationships is the play of reason; thought is a sort of creative miracle.

On the other hand—and this is the point I am driving at —just because thought is the perception of relationships between particles of old stuff, the particles themselves condition these perceptions. I see only such relationships as hold between the particles I happen to possess; certainly I can see none between such as I do not possess. And those I have are none of my own creation. They are handed down to me. In this sense the power of thought the "faculty" of reason, is a *tradition*.

In fancy I may picture a Romulus—abandoned on a hillside and suckled by a wolf—inventing for himself a system

of symbols with which to articulate his own fluid consciousness, conning them into spontaneity, and building them into
thought. But in reality he would not—he could not. The
actual articulations with which one thinks are not native to
the consciousness. Who of us can count more than a stray
one or two of his own invention, even with the hint and
model of a whole armory of them already in possession?
They are, on the contrary, a heritage. And what one can
think is conditioned by that heritage—such items of it as
through hap or care one has previously acquired.

All that I, for instance, can think in the field of chemistry
is sharply limited to what I can construe with the articulate
particles in that area of my consciousness. In my actual experience that area has been poorly endowed. All that I can
think there I could say in a bad quarter of an hour. And
what I can think there is cabined and cribbed by the special
particles I happen to possess.

This analysis, so obviously valid in any special field of
thought in which one is aware of one's ignorance, holds no
less, it seems to me, for that universal ignorance in which
all of us are born. If it does hold there, it may stand as
one version of the hypothesis of human evolution—rational
mind out of animal consciousness, man out of brute. The
change that effected this evolution was not accomplished,
however, once for all in some remote past. The outer device was transmissible, and hence became a racial characteristic. But the change itself must still be re-enacted in every
growing child. Something of it is re-enacted in the emergence of every idea in the rational mind. How far it is carried and how complete the evolution depends upon deliberate cultivation.

Intelligence is pure gift, the prior condition and animat-
ing agent of all thought. Whether intelligence itself may
be increased by exercise is a matter of faith or doubt, as one

275

chooses. In face of a primary mystery one can only be humble and dumb. But of that ingenious artifice, the arbitrary articulation of the consciousness into stable particles, there can be no doubt. It is a human invention in human hands. What can be done with these particles by way of thought depends in a given mind upon their range, the richness of their substance, their stability, and their clarity. And they can, with care, be extended, enriched, stabilised, clarified.

That there are larger units, whole structures of thought, with which discipline may be occupied goes without saying. Not all the heritage of the civilised mind is deposited in these particles. But the larger units are themselves built of the smaller, and what any mind makes of them hangs on its prior possession of the elements of which they are built, and the quality of those elements. In childhood one may have read, say, *Gulliver*, or *Through the Looking Glass*, with delight, and in maturity may still read them with delight. The outer symbols are the same now as then, but the responsive thoughts are not. In response to each symbol now there rises richer substance than the mind then possessed, grounds for relationships which then escaped detection.

The two, indeed—particle and structure—are inseparable in practice. It is in use that the particles have accumulated their substance and quality; it is by finding them in use that the mind identifies and enriches and clarifies them for itself. But it is they, I think—the ultimate premisses of all thought and the basis of all understanding—that lie at the bottom of the well into which discipline is poured.

For in the first place they lie at the deepest level to which discipline can go. That is something. But by a happy fortuity there, at the very node between animal consciousness and rational thought, they occupy a strategic position. Through them the fluid streams of consciousness, rising from below, are articulated for thought—and one thinks what he can with the shapes thus formed. And through these same shapes come the chief enrichments of the consciousness from above. For in reality what I apprehend of the thoughts of others is not their thoughts but my own. It is what I build in my own mind with the particles of my own consciousness called up by the symbols they have used. They are the determinants, coming and going, and a discipline that thickens and deepens and clarifies them enhances at one stroke both the give and the take of the mind, its power to think and its power to learn.

They lie at a strategic point, moreover, in another and no less momentous transaction. They not only articulate the individual mind for thinking; coming from a common tradition they tend, in the measure in which that tradition is mastered, to articulate disparate minds alike. Only so can two minds think the same thought. It is here that mind comes together with mind—or forever fails to come together. And situated between two realms of freedom—the wild realm of animal consciousness and the cultivated realm of reason—they alone are amenable to coercion. Arbitrary agreements, sheer conventions, subsequent to all native idiosyncrasies and prior to all conflict of prejudice or opinion, they are open to utter community. And since in relation to all thinking they are the ultimate premises, they afford the unquestioned common grounds imperative for mutual understanding and community of idea.

Discipline can thus bring its pressures to bear upon them with a clear conscience, assured that here it can do its essential task without violating its own principles—cultivate the individual judgment without infringing upon its freedom, and bring mind into community with mind without the weakness of assumption or the affront of dogmatism. Assured, too, that in a sort of beneficent circle community itself breeds both mind and further community. For given a broad community in these particles, the common legacy comes the purer to its inheritors; recurrence of each particle confirms and enriches and clarifies it in the experience of each mind. In a community without community, on the other hand, occurrence and recurrence tend rather to lead it astray and confuse it; and though men talk in common symbols, they build them into tacit obliquities of mutual incomprehension.

Is it too much to suggest, in passing, that the phenomenon of the brilliant period, the curious clustering of great names in the bead-roll of history, may be explained as a moment when by a community of mind with mind, here at the basis of all thought, a fine individual clarity and a lively spontaneity of mutual understanding have lifted the current of ideas to a high level? At all events, by such community the capacity of the mind both to think and to learn is heightened and the ardour of thought is stimulated, expression meeting comprehension, and comprehension quickening the impulse to think.

### III

I have gone a long way about and brought up with a conclusion that on its own showing should be as valid for modernism as for humanism. That, indeed, is my own sense of it—that here is the organic economy of thought in whatever field. And in fact, as I have intimated, its application is likely to be most obvious in the sciences, which we come upon after the mind is in some measure formed. Each science has a special articulation and nomenclature outside our normal experience, without which we can think but meagrely and vaguely in that area. The part they play there is evident. To these articulate particles it gives precise definition, at once for the sake of accuracy of calculation and for the sake of mutual understanding and wide co-operation

278

among those who pursue it. Incidentally by its technology it escapes the loose corruptions with which lay usage always threatens a vernacular. The extraordinary results of the discipline which establishes these articulations, these precisions, and these communities need no bush.

It is perhaps less obvious that discipline is even more imperative in that other area which the casual, voluble experience of living begins to articulate before we are aware, laying the premises of that common mind which we tend to take for granted as a native gift. Though it is not a native gift, no man feels deficient in it, as Descartes pointed out. What it yields him is life as he knows it; it is his apprehension of reality. In one sense this trust is his intellectual virtue. It marks his faith in the judgments of reason—the best reason he knows. He may be aware of his ignorance in this or that field of knowledge—know that he knows nothing of astronomy, of Homer, of plumbing, of torts. But no one knows everything; these ignorances are comparable to those of other men; by turning his mind to them he could master them.

By turning his mind! This contrast between *mind*, on the one hand, and on the other hand specific knowledge to which a *mind* may be turned, is the very heart of the conflict between humanist and modernist. To the modernist, justifiably proud of his special methods, that mind which comes to him unaware is a casual and amateur affair. As a process of reason it is the way fools think, and asses, and the cohorts of stupidity. Well, it is.

To the humanist, however, this liability is precisely its momentous importance. Here is mind itself by which man becomes human out of brute, mind in symmetry as it develops by confronting life and carrying on the adventure. According to its competence it apprehends the scene, the play, and the players, conceives the significance of the plot, exercises its judgment, lays its guiding principles, and conducts its affairs in wisdom or unwisdom, justice or injustice, harmony or inharmony. That it may be the mind of a fool is always its tragic possibility.

In shifting the basic common discipline from humane letters to natural science, then, modernism has, in so far, *abandoned the mind*. I say this in conscious enjoyment of hyperbole. There remains just so much of mind as develops in casual experience—that corrupting casual experience which science so sedulously avoids in its technology. But the point at issue is one of discipline, the conscious extension of mental competence beyond the limits of casual experience. Plainly the discipline of natural science neglects much of the mind as irrelevant.

For natural science is an attempt to picture and understand the material universe as it still would be if the knower were not in it—things and their relations to each other. The virtue sought by the man of science is the ability to ignore what he, by the accident of his conscious existence, thrusts into the situation. Obviously this discipline will articulate the consciousness for thought only here within this field of knowledge—among things and their relations, to the rigid exclusion of the knower and his affairs.

Humane letters, on the other hand, make no such exclusion. They too deal with things and their relations. But they include what natural science ignores—the knower and his responsive evaluation of what he knows. Literature looks out from the common centre at which the experience of life itself places us. It is an imaginative, reflective extension of that experience. And it does directly what experience itself does only indirectly if at all, for being articulate or nothing—symbol and meaning forever hand in glove—it specifically articulates the reader's mind, enriching and clarifying the premisses of consciousness with which in turn that mind thinks in the field of common human responsibility. Here is the telling difference between the literate and the empiric mind—not in intelligence, not in specific knowledge, but in the substance and quality of the premises of thought.

Literature uses the unprecise vernacular, it is true; but that is its virtue. For the vernacular, in contrast with any and all technologies, is the idiom of the mind itself, its fundamental humanising tradition. It is the essential historic feat of any civilisation, not so much perhaps to have conceived its guiding ideas—ideas change—as, in conceiving them, to have slowly evolved the articulate elements by which its heritors may conceive their own. Nature cares nothing for them or for what is made of them. They are none of hers. We come by them only through familiar contact with the tradition which has shaped and accumulated them.

Here, then, is the great human task—now for the first time in the history of the West abandoned to the mercies of casual experience. Man is a social being in more than his habits and his institutions. His humanity itself hangs on his sociability. Deprive him of his social legacy of articulations and he is once again the sub-human animal. It was the essence of humanism as a discipline that it attempted, not to inculcate a doctrine, but to carry on and on this ultimate humanising process. And in this it served three ends, distinct but interdependent—mind, community, and the tradition on which both mind and community depend.

## IV

From Plato to Irving Babbitt humanists have been occupied with the idea of leadership, since men are social beings, unhappy and self-destructive in mutual hostility, happiest and greatest when co-operating in community in the

281

wisest available ideas. Whose ideas? Plato proposed the leadership of philosophers. But he himself did all that a philosopher can do. He was of the greatest; in one of the high masterpieces of human thought he proposed a scheme for the salvation of Greece—and while he wrote and Athens read, Greek civilisation declined. Something had departed that but an age before had made of Athens the supreme exemplar of what human existence may come to at its best, in zest of life and ardour of co-operation, in brilliance and profundity of thought, something that had created a society more lovely than any other in recorded history, and produced a literature and a full free current of ideas that are still the model and despair of all our aspirations.

May this loss have been loss of disciplined community at the basis of all thought? Each man thinks not what he will but what he can with the articulate particles of his consciousness. Only by community here can one mind think the same thoughts as another. In such community minds will hold their common ideas with heightened ardour, as in friendship a common thought rises to new vitality by being shared in utter comprehension. It was not an accident that friendship played so profound a part in Greek life, not an accident that thought and letters so flourished. For expression had met understanding, and understanding had enriched the common premisses of thought. One among them, at all events, made the association.

"Not long afterwards," says Thucydides, "nearly the whole Hellenic world was in commotion. When trouble had once begun in the cities, those who followed carried the revolutionary spirit further and further. . . . *The meanings of words had no longer the same relations to things.* . . ." And he goes on to detail wherein the confused meanings of terms unsettled the mutual comprehension upon which the harmony of civilised life depends.

As for us, we are in something of a like predicament. The most striking aspect of contemporary life is the contrast between the fruitfulness of the scientific world, its vitality, its harmony, its world-wide co-operation, and our frankly acknowledged moral bankruptcy—vigour and fecundity in the area to which discipline has been shifted, and futility and chaos in the area from which discipline has been withdrawn. It is not that men have ceased to be concerned with moral choice. So long as they pursue on reflection what seems to be good, so long are they exercising their moral nature. Never, I dare say, has there been a wilder play of reflection on what seems to be good.

If we are suffering a moral chaos it is not from the abandonment of morals but from a helpless discrepancy, an incapacity to think the same thoughts. Given another Plato, our only chance of accord under his leadership would be such community with him and with each other in the articulate elements of his utterance as would evoke the same living thoughts in our various minds.

The task of creating such community is a subtle one, immeasurably more difficult than the corresponding task of modernism. The particles of consciousness with which we think here are quick with feeling—with sentiment, impulse, passion, and desire, drawn in each individual from his own native depths. They are neither such sheer conventions as the units of measure that make up the syntax of scientific thought, nor objective and tangible like the data of nature with which science deals. They are the dynamic forces of life itself, spontaneous and imperious, and they impel us whether or no. Whether they are to drive us in anarchy or in harmony, however, depends upon our ability so to channelise them, so to articulate and identify them for thought, as to bring us into mutual understanding of those ideas in which they play a part. The first service of the hu-

manistic discipline was that it put the individual mind into
intimate contact with the tradition of humane letters in which
were embodied and shaped the articulate elements of such
ideas. It was the second and no less significant service of
this discipline that in clinging sedulously to the great tradition of that literature it tended to give to all minds thus
imbued *the same* elements filled with *the same* substance,
and so put mind into community with mind. In abandoning
the common discipline of this area of the consciousness modernism has not only done something to dilute our powers
of thought there, but has left us, mind and mind, out of
community and in a moral confusion that lies, not in the
open conflict of ideas, but in tacit disparities of idea that
never meet.

Modernism reaches its ultimate goal in a knowledge of
nature. But nature has no need of our knowledge. It is *we*
who need it, for our own ends. In the measure in which, for
the conception of those ends, we lose our powers of thought,
so precariously wrought in the long travail of the past, and
so dependent upon unremitting reconquest, we shall in fact
have killed the goose that lays the golden egg.

# Courage and Education [1]

### RICHARD LINDLEY BROWN

Diverse and variegated as the texture of our contemporary life and literature is, a great part of it may be shown to have a fundamental unity. That unity lies in a certain fear and hopelessness,—occasioned by a mechanistic philosophy and ultimately owing, I think, to the misapplied and ill-digested implications of a popular scientific education. One meets everywhere some attempt to analyse and explain the life and destiny of man solely on the basis of his physique or environment, or on some other basis equally uncoloured by human imagination and idealisation. This attitude is not universal with us, nor is it even general, but it contains almost all that is original with us, and if we consider what is original as also characteristic, we can only postulate that the characteristic feature in our contemporary literature is the interpretation of life as a phase of merely animalistic existence.

Now, this admission that man in no way transcends the limits of purely physical life is an act of cowardice to which no previous generation has ever so thoroughly committed itself. This admission is directly contrary to the general spirit of Ancient philosophy, impossible to the serenity of the Middle Ages, repugnant to the exuberance of the Renaissance, unnatural to the Romanticism, however defined, of the early nineteenth century. And even during the faltering generations just preceding our own, there were still eloquent humanists able to show that whatever man's circumstances may be, and whatever his origin may have been, man was yet

[1] A Senior paper read at Bowdoin College, Commencement, 1929.—Editor.

able to form for himself an intellectual and spiritual life and destiny independent of origin and circumstance.

This courage of the past—this self-confidence of the past by which it was enabled to broaden the scope of its life and pass on to us a social and imaginative heritage by which every situation and relationship of our lives is rendered more beautiful—was not the result of accident. It was the result of long and untiring efforts in self-cultivation, and the records of these efforts are to be found in the great literatures which not only recorded, but inspired and motivated them. In those times the staple of education was the study of literature; and, for my present purposes, the important features of this study were, that it was thorough and exact, that it neglected no labour which might aid in the central purpose, and that, in requiring a certain common background in all students, it was eminently a social and even international thing.

To attain the same degree of courage and self-confidence, it would be necessary to us to make the same effort of self-cultivation. The quality of contemporary literature suggests that we are not exerting that effort; manners and excesses and failures in contemporary life equally suggest that we are not. And if we examine the habitual methods of contemporary teachers of literature, we find so many differences between these methods and those of the past that it is plain that our educators have all but lost sight of their central objects.

As early as 1882, in *Literature and Science*, Matthew Arnold set forth a rather singular prophecy, describing with great exactness much of our present situation. "As with Greek," he said, "so with letters generally: they will some day come, we may hope, to be studied more rationally, but they will not lose their place. What will happen will rather be that there will be crowded into education other matters

286

besides, far too many; there will be, perhaps, a period of un-settlement and confusion and false tendency; but letters will not in the end lose their leading place."

It is essential to consider how far this prophecy has been realised, for it penetrates the very heart of our problem; it suggests the entire lack of a central emphasis which char-acterises even the literary education of our day. American education might very well be said to be passing through a period of unsettlement and confusion and false tendency, but by no manner of means might it be said that in American education letters had obtained or regained their leading place. Although the colleges swarm with students of literature, the greater part of these students have a more accurate knowl-edge of the problems of the natural sciences or of economics than they have of the problems and methods of literary study. As a plain matter of fact, a great many undergrad-uates choose to specialise in literature, and particularly in English literature, because they believe it a study easier than any other. And through a smattering of all the ologies which has been their education from early childhood, they interpret and condemn great masterpieces of which they have never learned the true significance, since they have never confronted soberly the old traditions that illuminate and sustain those masterpieces. It is largely because our educa-tion deals seriously with almost every subject except litera-ture, that literature has lost its leading place; and it is be-cause literature has lost its leading place that education has lost much of its inspiring power, and our contemporary literary innovators are characterised to such a degree by fear and hopelessness.

It is not unnatural, however, that popular opinion, which to-day influences even the teaching of literature, should con-sider scientific education so important, for the public sees its leaders in every field profoundly influenced by science. The leader of our political organisation, like most of our leaders, happens to be a scientist; most of our philosophers are scientists, and our magazines deal monthly with the concessions that our religious leaders are making to the new implications of science. It is not unnatural that science should be popularly considered an important study and the study of literature the recreation of an idle day. And it follows just as naturally that swarms of undergraduate students should have imposed upon the teaching of literature much of the dilettantism which this popular view suggests is inherent in it. The typical student of literature—of English literature, for example—may be known by four characteristics,—a fear of Spenser, a dislike of Milton, a hatred of Wordsworth, and a suppressed desire to write a musical comedy. This is the type of student that must be taught, and it easily follows that the teaching of him should come to lack the thoroughness and exactness, the desire to master ancillary subjects, and the common background, which I have enumerated above as having once been the ideals of literary study.

The place of these ideals is taken by a dilettantism which displays itself in two forms,—in individualism and in sciolism. The first, a shallow type of individualism, is directed by the theory that a student's peculiar tastes are the ultimate criteria by which he should make his judgments, and that he must be seduced into a liking for literature by the application of whatever literary candy pleases his palate. The thought that a man should be somewhat adapted to his reading, and not his reading to him, is altogether alien to this theory, and the existence of common social ideals, which, if they are not present in the student, should be developed, is not suspected by its propounders.

It is to the adoption of this principle by many secondary-school teachers that we owe the presence in our colleges of the campus radicals who curse their fates and the restraints prohibiting them from living their own lives. The ordinary progress of students guided by such principles is to begin easily with something on the level, say, of Kipling, and gradually to work up to the high seriousness of the poetry of Oscar Wilde. The popularity and influence of the sort of contemporary literature which I have mentioned may be very well explained, I think, by the existence of this view in the minds of many of our educators.

The sciolism which is the second form of our literary dilettantism,—a shallowness which investigates only the superficialities of things, which delights in accepted definitions and phrases,—is largely involved in the manner in which our times have forsaken the study of the classics, as well as of the other literatures and other subjects without which the study of no one literature can be complete. No teacher of science would admit to his classes students unversed in mathematics; he would say that science without some mathematical knowledge was an impossibility. Now, a knowledge of the literature and customs of classical antiquity is just as necessary to the student of a modern literature as a mathematical knowledge is to the student of science. The teacher of literature, however, who demanded from his students this indispensable knowledge, would soon lecture to empty halls. Popular opinion, as reflected by those who are to be taught, is altogether on the side of those "other matters, far too many," which have been crowded into education.

The teacher of literature may well turn out, in the end, to be the sole means by which society and literature can be raised from their present depression, and then only provided his influence be stricter and more humane. For a materialistic epoch such as ours, the only refuge and the only basis for further progress is in the idealistic humanity of the past; but the search of the past must not be such a frail and self-

289

indulgent one as condemns before it understands. Whether we have outworn the ideals of history or whether they were projected into a realm of life beyond our present power of realisation, in either case they reflect the tendency directing all human achievement,—a tendency to rise to a plane uncircumscribed by the limits of physical existence. Accordingly, the teacher of any branch of our cultural heritage has within his hands the reins of destiny; slackly and half-heartedly he may lose them from his grasp, or by firmly holding them he may guide the future toward a new triumph of the human spirit. There is no sound where there are no ears, nor without the development of the inner mind and segregated human life, of which our literature has been both the motivation and the record, could there again be true community or beauty in the world.

# A List of Books
## Published Since 1900

NOTE—The following list contains most of the recent books that are humanistic in a strict sense, together with a few books humanistic in a sense more general and indefinite. Magazine articles have been excluded; but illuminating articles dealing with various aspects of humanism may be found in the 1928 and 1929 volumes of *The Forum, The Bookman, The Hound and Horn, The Criterion,* and *The Nineteenth Century and After.* Helpful recent critiques of the work of Irving Babbitt and Paul Elmer More are those by a young English critic, Philip S. Richards, in *The Nineteenth Century and After* for April, 1928, May, 1928, and April, 1929, and an article on "Mr. More and the Gentle Reader" by G. R. Elliott in *The Bookman* for April, 1929.

SANTAYANA, GEORGE. Interpretations of Poetry and Religion. 1900.

BROWNELL, W. C. French Art, Revised ed. 1901.

—— Victorian Prose Masters. 1901.

MORE, PAUL ELMER. Shelburne Essays, First Series. 1904.

CHESTERTON, G. K. Heretics. 1905.

COX, KENYON. Old Masters and New. 1905.

MORE, PAUL ELMER. Shelburne Essays, Second Series. 1905.

—— Shelburne Essays, Third Series. 1905.

WOODBERRY, GEORGE EDWARD. The Torch: Eight Lectures on Race Power in Literature. 1905.

MORE, PAUL ELMER. Shelburne Essays, Fourth Series. 1906.

COX, KENYON. Painters and Sculptors. 1907.

LASSERRE, PIERRE. Le Romantisme français. 1907.

BABBITT, IRVING. Literature and the American College: Essays in Defence of the Humanities. 1908.

FRYE, P. H. Literary Reviews and Criticisms. 1908.

MORE, PAUL ELMER. Shelburne Essays, Fifth Series. 1908.

SEILLIÈRE, E. Le Mal romantique. 1908.

BROWNELL, W. C. American Prose Masters. 1909.

CHESTERTON, G. K. Orthodoxy. 1909.

MORE, PAUL ELMER. Shelburne Essays, Sixth Series. 1909.

BABBITT, IRVING. The New Laokoon: An Essay on the Confusion of the Arts. 1910.

MORE, PAUL ELMER. Shelburne Essays, Seventh Series. 1910.

COX, KENYON. The Classic Point of View: Six Lectures on Painting. 1911.

BABBITT, IRVING. The Masters of Modern French Criticism. 1912.

MORE, PAUL ELMER. The Drift of Romanticism (Shelburne Essays, Eighth Series). 1913.

BROWNELL, W. C. Criticism. 1914.

COX, KENYON. Artist and Public. 1914.

MORE, LOUIS TRENCHARD. The Limitations of Science. 1915.

MORE, PAUL ELMER. Aristocracy and Justice (Shelburne Essays, Ninth Series). 1915.

MATHER, FRANK JEWETT, JR. Estimates in Art. 1916.

BROWNELL, W. C. Standards. 1917.

MORE, PAUL ELMER. Platonism (The Greek Tradition, Introduction). 1917, 1927.

SHERMAN, STUART P. Matthew Arnold: How to Know Him. 1917.

—— On Contemporary Literature. 1917.

SHOREY, PAUL. The Assault on Humanism. 1917.

ADAMS, GEORGE PLIMPTON. Idealism and the Modern Age. 1919.

BABBITT, IRVING. Rousseau and Romanticism. 1919.

GASS, SHERLOCK BRONSON. A Lover of the Chair. 1919.

MORE, PAUL ELMER. With the Wits (Shelburne Essays, Tenth Series). 1919.

ELIOT, T. S. The Sacred Wood: Essays on Poetry and Criticism. 1920, 1928.

INGE, W. R. The Idea of Progress. 1920.

PATRICK, G. T. W. The Psychology of Social Reconstruction. 1920.

LASSERRE, PIERRE. Cinquante Ans de Pensée française. 1921.

MORE, PAUL ELMER. A New England Group and Others (Shelburne Essays, Eleventh Series). 1921.

—— The Religion of Plato (The Greek Tradition, Vol. I). 1921.

CANBY, HENRY S. Definitions. 1922.

FRYE, P. H. Romance and Tragedy. 1922.

SHAFER, ROBERT. Progress and Science: Essays in Criticism. 1922.

FOERSTER, NORMAN. Nature in American Literature: Studies in the Modern View of Nature. 1923.

HOUSTON, PERCY H. Doctor Johnson: A Study in Eighteenth Century Humanism. 1923.

MASSIS, HENRI. Jugements I. 1923.

MATHER, FRANK JEWETT, JR. A History of Italian Painting. 1923.

MORE, PAUL ELMER. Hellenistic Philosophies (The Greek Tradition, Vol. II). 1923.

WATERHOUSE, FRANCIS A. Random Studies in the Romantic Chaos. 1923.

BABBITT, IRVING. Democracy and Leadership. 1924.

BROWNELL, W. C. The Genius of Style. 1924.

CANBY, HENRY S. Definitions, Second Series. 1924.

CRITICISM IN AMERICA. (Essays by Irving Babbitt and others, ed. by J. E. Spingarn.) 1924.

ELIOT, T. S. Homage to John Dryden. 1924.

HULME, T. E. Speculations (ed. by Herbert Read). 1924.

MASSIS, HENRI. Jugements II. 1924.

MORE, PAUL ELMER. The Christ of the New Testament (The Greek Tradition, Vol. III). 1924.

SEILLIÈRE, E. J.-J. Rousseau. 1924.

GASS, SHERLOCK BRONSON. Criers of the Shops. 1925.

MORE, LOUIS TRENCHARD. The Dogma of Evolution. 1925.

CERF, BARRY. Anatole France: The Degeneration of a Great Artist. 1926.

FERRERO, GUGLIELMO. Words to the Deaf. 1926.

GIESE, W. F. Victor Hugo, The Man and the Poet. 1926.

SHAFER, ROBERT. Christianity and Naturalism: Essays in Criticism, Second Series. 1926.

BROWNELL, W. C. Democratic Distinction in America. 1927.

MATHER, FRANK JEWETT, JR. The American Spirit in Art (The Pageant of America, Vol. XII). 1927.

—— Modern Painting. 1927.

MORE, PAUL ELMER. Christ the Word (The Greek Tradition, Vol. IV). 1927.

MUNSON, GORHAM B. Robert Frost: A Study in Sensibility and Good Sense. 1927.

Von Hügel, Baron Friedrich. Selected Letters, 1896-1924. 1927.

Babbitt, Irving. French Literature (A. L. A. booklet). 1928.

Benda, Julien. La Trahison des Clercs. 1928. (Trans., The Treason of the Intellectuals. 1928.)

Eliot, T. S. For Lancelot Andrewes: Essays on Style and Order. 1928.

Elliott, W. Y. The Pragmatic Revolt in Politics. 1928.

Foerster, Norman. American Criticism: A Study in Literary Theory from Poe to the Present. 1928.

Maritain, Jacques. Three Reformers: Luther—Descartes—Rousseau. 1928.

Mercier, Louis J. A. Le Mouvement humaniste aux États-Unis. 1928.

More, Paul Elmer. The Demon of the Absolute (New Shelburne Essays, Vol. I). 1928.

Munson, Gorham B. Destinations: A Canvass of American Literature Since 1900. 1928.

Rand, E. K. Founders of the Middle Ages. 1928.

Sherman, Stuart P. Shaping Men and Women: Essays on Literature and Life. 1928.

Benda, Julien. Belphégor (Trans., Introduction by Irving Babbitt). 1929.

Canby, Henry S. American Estimates. 1929.

Chesterton, G. K. Generally Speaking. 1929.

—— The Thing. 1929.

Elliott, G. R. The Cycle of Modern Poetry: A Series of Essays toward Clearing our Present Poetic Dilemma. 1929.

Foerster, Norman. The American Scholar: A Study in Litteræ Inhumaniores. 1929.

Frye, P. H. Visions and Chimeras. 1929.

Munson, Gorham B. Style and Form in American Prose. 1929.

Warren, Austin. Alexander Pope as Critic and Humanist. 1929.

Wickham, Harvey. The Impuritans. 1929.

Zeitlin, Jacob, and Woodbridge, Homer. Life and Letters of Stuart P. Sherman. 2 vols. 1929.